Key Concepts in
Public Relations

Recent volumes include:

Fifty Key Concepts in Gender Studies
Jane Pilcher and Imelda Whelehan

Key Concepts in Medical Sociology
Jonathan Gabe, Mike Bury and Mary Ann Elston

Key Concepts in Leisure Studies
David Harris

Key Concepts in Critical Social Theory
Nick Crossley

Key Concepts in Urban Studies
Mark Gottdiener and Leslie Budd

Key Concepts in Mental Health
David Pilgrim

Key Concepts in Work
Paul Blyton and Jean Jenkins

Key Concepts in Journalism Studies
Bob Franklin, Martin Hamer, Mark Hanna, Marie Kinsey and John Richardson

Key Concepts in Political Communication
Darren G. Lilleker

Key Concepts in Teaching Primary Mathematics
Derek Haylock

Key Concepts in Nursing
Edited by Elizabeth Mason-Whitehead, Annette McIntosh, Ann Bryan, Tom Mason

Key Concepts in Childhood Studies
Allison James and Adrian James

Key Concepts in Radio Studies
Hugh Chignell

The SAGE Key Concepts series provides students with accessible and authoritative knowledge of the essential topics in a variety of disciplines. Cross-referenced throughout, the format encourages critical evaluation through understanding. Written by experienced and respected academics, the books are indispensable study aids and guides to comprehension.

BOB FRANKLIN, MIKE HOGAN,
QUENTIN LANGLEY, NICK MOSDELL AND
ELLIOT PILL

Key Concepts in
Public Relations

Los Angeles • London • New Delhi • Singapore • Washington DC

First published 2009

SAGE Publications Ltd
1 Oliver's Yard
55 City Road
London EC1Y 1SP

SAGE Publications Inc.
2455 Teller Road
Thousand Oaks, California 91320

SAGE Publications India Pvt Ltd
B 1/I 1 Mohan Cooperative Industrial Area
Mathura Road
New Delhi 110 044

SAGE Publications Asia-Pacific Pte Ltd
33 Pekin Street #02-01
Far East Square
Singapore 048763

Library of Congress Control Number: 2008928944

British Library Cataloguing in Publication data

A catalogue record for this book is available from the British Library

ISBN 978-1-4129-2318-7
ISBN 978-1-4129-2319-4 (pbk)

Typeset by C&M Digitals (P) Ltd, Chennai, India
Printed in India at Replika Press Pvt Ltd
Printed on paper from sustainable resources

contents

contents

v

contents

contents

notes on the text

At the end of each entry, the initials of the author are shown:

Bob Franklin	BF
Mike Hogan	MH
Quentin Langley	QL
Nick Mosdell	NM
Elliot Pill	EP

Each concept contains cross references in **bold** guiding readers to related concepts.

notes on authors

Bob Franklin (BA PhD) is Professor of Journalism Studies at the Cardiff School of Journalism, Media and Cultural Studies. He is the Editor of *Journalism Studies* and *Journalism Practice* and co-editor of a new series of books to be published by Sage, entitled *Journalism Studies: Key Texts*. He is a member of various journal editorial boards including *Brazilian Journalism Review, Communication Issues, Fifth Estate Online, The Journal of Political Marketing* and *Social Semiotics*. Recent books include *Pulling Newspapers Apart: Analysing Print Journalism* (2008); *The Future of Newspapers* (2008); *Local Journalism, Local Media: The Local News in Context* (2006); *Television Policy: The MacTaggart Lectures* (2005); *Key Concepts in Journalism Studies* (2005) with Hamer, M. Hanna, M. Kinsey, M. and Richardson, J.E. *Packaging Politics: Political Communication in Britain's Media Democracy* (2004). He has published more than 200 chapters, articles, government reports and pamphlets with contributions to journals such as *British Journalism Review, Journal of Educational Policy, Journal of Political Marketing, Journal of Public Affairs, Journalism Practice, Journalism Studies, Parliamentary Affairs, Political Communication, Political Quarterly* and *Public Relations Review.* He is a Trustee of the George Viner Trust (for journalism trainees from ethnic minorities) and was Visiting Professor at the Reilly Centre for Media and Public Affairs in the Manship School of Mass Communications, Louisiana State University, in spring 2008.

Mike Hogan lectures on the masters course in International Public Relations at Cardiff University. He graduated with a BSc in Economics from University College, London, then trained as a journalist on a number of newspapers including the *Financial Times* and the *Daily Mirror*. He joined the BBC in 1973 and worked variously as a reporter, producer and director across a wide range of news and documentary output. He edited *The Money Programme* and was Deputy Editor of *Panorama*. After the BBC, he joined Channel 4 where he edited *The Business Programme*, winning a BAFTA award for television journalism. Following a career in journalism, he moved into public relations where he was Head of European Media Relations for Price Waterhouse Coopers and then Head of Global Communications and Crisis Management for the Royal Dutch Shell Group. His research interests centre on reputation management and corporate social responsibility.

Quentin Langley is an elected Council Member of the Chartered Institute of Public Relations (CIPR) and a former Chair of CIPR International. He serves on the Institute's Education and Professional Standards Committee. Before joining the University of Cardiff in 2003 Quentin had more than 15 years PR practice experience. He was Head of Global Public Relations for chartered surveying firm Knight Frank, and worked (with Mike Hogan) in the Global Media Relations Office of Shell International. He is an international journalist in print, online and broadcast media and the editor of his own website, quentinlangley.net.

Nick Mosdell is a lecturer and researcher at the Cardiff School of Journalism, Media and Cultural Studies. He teaches research methods on a number of international masters' and undergraduate courses, including teaching and co-ordinating research methods modules on the Institute of Public Relations-accredited masters programme in International Public Relations. He has published books, journal articles, and reports in the areas of media and military relations and children and television. He is co-author of *Shoot First And Ask Questions Later: Media Coverage of the War in Iraq* (2006) and *Practical Research Methods for Media and Cultural Studies: Making People Count* (2006).

Elliot Pill is lecturer and course leader for the MA in International Public Relations at Cardiff University. He trained and qualified as a newspaper journalist before moving into public relations consultancy where he worked at leading US consultancies, including Hill and Knowlton where he was a main board director of the youth and consumer division. He has designed and delivered global communication campaigns for clients such as Adidas®, Billabong®, Motorola®, Reebok®, Gillette® and Pioneer®. He has an MBA from Cardiff Business School and is completing his PhD entitled. Diversity: a ticking time bomb for the UK PR industry. His research interests also include: the cult of celebrity and the role of PR; Global corporate message translation; relations between journalists and public relations practitioners.

Introduction

Public relations (PR), having enjoyed steady growth in the UK since 1945, has experienced a rapid expansion since the 1980s. This growth has been evident across the corporate private sector, the communications activities of central and local government and other public organisations, as well as the many and distinctive organisations that constitute the voluntary sector (Deacon, 1996). PR has expanded in terms of the number and size of consultancies, their revenues and profitability (Miller and Dinan, 2000), the burgeoning numbers of practitioners employed in public relations activities (Davis, 2002; Franklin, 1988, 2004), the growth in university provision for their education and training, alongside their professional organisation in bodies such as the Chartered Institute of Public Relations (CIPR), initially formed as the Institute of Public Relations in 1948 (Fedorcio et al., 1991; Michie, 1998).

This rapid expansion has generated both advocates and detractors, with PR receiving a bad press from at least three quarters. Journalists, for example, have typically harboured a dislike of PR practitioners (Baskin and Aronoff, 1992; L'Etang, 2004). This may reflect little more than the superior salaries and working conditions that PR practitioners have increasingly come to enjoy compared to their journalistic colleagues. But journalists' antipathy more likely reflects their grudging acknowledgement of the growing reliance of news media on PR copy which increasingly helps to shape and inform journalists' editorial (Davis, 2008; Lewis et al., 2008a, 2008b). A decade ago, the Editor of *PR Week* estimated that a minimum 50 per cent of broadsheet newspapers' copy and 'more for tabloids' is now written and provided by PR practitioners who now 'do a lot of journalists' thinking for them' (Franklin, 1997: 20). Many journalists, PR practitioners and academic researchers claim that this reliance on PR materials has grown (Fletcher, 2006; White and Hobsbawm, 2007; Williams and Franklin, 2007). Distinguished scholar Jurgen Habermas has even suggested that 'public relations ... techniques have come to dominate the public sphere' (1989: 193), while McNair (1996), Schlesinger (1990) and Miller (1998) have also criticised the implications of PR for citizen access to the public sphere.

Public as well as academic discourses have similarly been critical of PR, most notably because of the increasing public association of PR with propaganda, spin and spin doctors; and to a degree which involves more than the cynical and ill informed tendency, noted by Harrison, of believing PR to be merely 'putting a gloss on things' (1995: 1). As well as being ill informed, such criticisms are poorly targeted since 'media relations is only a small part of the public relations brief' (Fawkes, 2001: 6). However, since the mid 1980s, and especially during Alastair Campbell's tenure of the post of Director of Communications for New Labour, public scepticism about spin and a distrust of spin doctors has developed apace. Campbell's dispute with the BBC over coverage of the Iraq war, public and media discussions of the so called 'dodgy dossier' and ultimately the tragic death of Dr David Kelly, were considered by the Phillis inquiry which reported a 'three-way breakdown in trust' between the government and its spin doctors, the news media and the public (Phillis, 2004; Barnett, 2005).

There is a discernible irony about these criticisms since a key element in the many and sometimes conflicting understandings of PR is stressed by the Institute of Public Relations' (IPR) definition, framed in 1987, which suggested that 'public relations practice is the planned and sustained effort to establish and maintain goodwill and understanding between an organisation and its publics' (Fawkes, 2001: 7).

A consideration of the plethora of definitions of PR is the focus for the following section of this Introduction to *Key Concepts in Public Relations*. Subsequent sections deal in turn with the growth and development of the PR industry and PR practice, along with developments within PR education and training. Taken together, these provide a context for the final section which sets out the aims and objectives of *Key Concepts in Public Relations*.

WHAT IS PUBLIC RELATIONS?

Attempts at reaching a precise definition typically prove frustrating. What seems self-evident and simple can confound. As if to illustrate the point, definitions of PR abound and vary between those which are so general as to potentially embrace almost anything, to more proscriptive definitions that fail to capture the range and complexity of PR practices and ambitions. Somewhere near the 'general' end of this spectrum, PR is understood as 'a complex and hybrid subject' which 'draws on theories and practices from many different fields' including 'management, media, communication and psychology' (Fawkes, 2001: 3). With a sharper definitional focus, some genealogists of the professions claim 'public relations is the child of journalism' (White and Hobsbawm, 2007: 283), while others identify different familial connections suggesting PR 'is the younger sibling of its competitor promotional industries of advertising and marketing' (Miller and Dinan,

2000: 5); Harrison (1995: 4–7) and Fawkes (2001: 5–8) however are at pains to distinguished PR from both marketing and advertising.

The definition agreed by the World Assembly of Public Relations at its convention in Mexico in 1978 underlined the multidisciplinary character of PR practice and education. On this account, PR is 'the art and social science of analysing trends, predicting their consequences, counselling organisation leaders and implementing planned programmes of action which will serve both the organisation's and the public interest' (cited in Harrison, 1995: 2). The reference to both 'arts' and 'social sciences' highlights the distinction between understandings of PR as a rigorous, positivistic, quantitative, science-based discipline, which deploys specific communication tools and models for the analysis of communication situations, and the 'affection' which some practitioners retain for 'the looser more creative aspects of the work' (Fawkes, 2001: 4). The USA leans more than the UK to the social science based view of PR. This definition by PR practitioners highlights another key feature of PR, namely that successful outcomes serve both the interests of the 'organisation' and the 'public' with no necessary antipathy between the two.

Rex Harlow, in his classic article in *Public Relations Review* (1976: 36), identified 472 definitions of PR before formulating his own composite version based on these various accounts. PR, he suggests:

Is the distinctive management function which helps establish and maintain mutual lines of communication, acceptance and cooperation between an organisation and its publics; involves the management of problems or issues; helps management to keep informed on and responsive to public opinion; defines and emphasises the responsibility of management to serve the public interest; helps management keep abreast of and effectively utilise change, serving as an early warning system to help anticipate trends; and uses research and sound and ethical communication techniques as its principal tools.

While Harlow's formulation lacks the merit of brevity, it does describe 'what public relations is and what public relations people do' (Harrison, 1995: 3). It also affirms unequivocally that a key purpose of public relations is to serve the public interest. Additionally, the definition introduces the notion of ethical practice which is central to contemporary PR.

A more recent account by PR academic Jacquie L'Etang stresses the representational role of public relations. Hence PR is 'the practice of presenting the public face of an organisation [be it a company, educational institutions, hospital or government] or individual, the articulation of its aims and objectives and the official organisational view on issues of relevance to it'. To fulfil this role successfully, PR must 'target publics to engage sympathetically at emotional and intellectual levels with the organisation to encourage publics to take on board the organisation's point of view' (L'Etang, 2004: 2). It is interesting to note that L'Etang, like Harlow, discusses 'publics' rather than a single 'public' signifying the reality of a plurality of communities rather than a single uniform public, as well as the potentially fissured and competing interests and objectives which these communities might pursue.

If you turn to page 175, you will find that in this respect L'Etang's account is in concordance with the understanding of PR offered here. Again there is an emphasis on 'publics'. According to the Chartered Institute of Public Relations (CIPR), we suggest that:

> Public relations is about reputation the result of what you do, what you say and what others say about you. It is also 'the planned and sustained effort to establish and maintain goodwill and mutual understanding between an organisation and its publics'. (http://www.cipr.co.uk)

Key to understanding this definition is that the word 'publics' is plural. All organisations have a series of publics, or stakeholders, on whom their success depends. These publics are divided in many different ways, but Haywood's division into six categories is widely accepted. These are: (1) customers (past, present and future); (2) staff (past, present and future); (3) investors (past, present and future); (4) politicians and regulators; (5) neighbours and (6) business partners (distributors, suppliers, etc.).

THE DEVELOPMENT OF PUBLIC RELATIONS

In the USA, PR began to emerge as a distinctive professional practice towards the end of the 19th century. Harrison suggests that 'public relations' was first used in 1882 by Dorman Eaton in a lecture, delivered at Yale University, titled 'The Public Relations and Duties of the Legal Profession', to signify 'looking out for the welfare of the public' (1995: 14). But in these early days, PR has largely been interpreted as a defensive response to the emerging investigative ('muckraker') journalism that generated a good deal of hostile and critical probing and reporting of contemporary business practices, a series of corporate scandals and industry responses to a succession of industrial disputes and strikes (White and

Hobsbawm, 2007: 283). According to PR scholar Scott Cutlip, 'these attacks created the need for institutions and industries under attack to defend themselves in the court of public opinion' (1994: 3). Historians critical of PR interpreted its emergence as 'the growth of corporate propaganda as a means of protecting corporate power against democracy' (Carey, 1995: 18; Stauber and Rampton 1995).

Early PR pioneer Ivy Ledbetter Lee was initially a business journalist who came to realise that the best way for business to defend itself against these press attacks alleging dishonesty and corruption was a more open, less furtive, approach to public information and the news media. Goldman suggests that the activities of muckraking journalists gave Lee an 'exciting idea'. He began to question whether the 'business policy of secrecy was really a wise one? If publicity was being used so effectively to smear business, could it not be used with equal effectiveness to explain and defend business?' (1948; 6, cited in Harrison, 1995: 17). Lee opened a PR agency in 1904 and two years later set out the principles guiding his new project; the principles capture neatly much of the media relations aspects of PR. 'In brief', Lee claimed:

> our plan is frankly and openly, on behalf of the business concerns and public institutions, to supply the press and the public of the United States prompt and accurate information concerning subjects which it is of value and interest to the public to know about. Corporations and public institutions give out much information which the news point is lost to view. Nevertheless, it is quite important to the public to have this news as it is to the establishments themselves to give it currency. I send out only matter every detail of which I am willing to assist any editor in verifying for himself. (Cited in Heibert, 1966: 48)

In the UK a different impetus stimulated the growth of PR. It was the need for government and other public bodies, locally and centrally, to promote and explain policy, especially during and immediately after the Second World War, which triggered the development of PR (Franklin, 1988: 1–14, 2004: 96–118; Miller and Dinan, 2000: 8; White and Hobsbawm, 2007: 283).

The growth in local government PR formally began when Kingsley Wood used the term 'public relations' to describe the job he had offered to Stephen Tallents at the GPO (West, 1963: 6). The publication of the 1945 *Report on Relations Between Local Government and the Community*, the establishment of a Consultative Committee on Publicity for Local

Government, and the 1962 report of the Association of Municipal Authorities (AMA) titled *Local Government Publicity* which recommended the establishment of a local government publicity officer, were each landmarks in the early development of UK public sector public relations (Franklin, 1988: 1–8). But it was the reorganisation of local government in 1974 and the creation of the larger Metropolitan County Councils and their need to create an identity, communicate with their respective publics and improve the image of local government, which was too frequently perceived as boring, expensive, remote and bureaucratic, that triggered a change in the pace of growth for local government PR (Society of County and Regional Public Relations Officers, 1985: 310). Significantly, PR was also to be better resourced than previously. The West Yorkshire Metropolitan County Council in its first year of operation appointed five specialist staff and allocated a budget of £106,440 for PR. Sheffield City Council had a full-time staff of 10 PR specialists and one of the largest PR budgets amounting to £161,000 (*Yorkshire Post*, 2 February 1974). Perhaps ironically, it was the campaign to prevent the abolition of the new Metropolitan Counties a decade later which witnessed another spurt in local government PR staffs (Franklin, 1987a, 1987b).

Sustained growth across the 1980s enabled the IPR Local Government Group's report *Beyond The Horizons* to claim that 'a thousand public relations professionals work in local government, producing 60,000 items of publicity a year and spending £250 millions; they generate over a 100,000 news releases annually with coverage running into miles of print' (Harrison, 1995: 151). By the new millennium, a survey by the Local Government Association of all 410 authorities in England and Wales revealed that 85 per cent of all authorities employ one or more PR practitioners while 25 per cent employ five or more PR staff; in the larger authorities the average staff size is 13 PR practitioners. Budgets for PR vary considerably reflecting the size of the authority as well as its commitment to PR, but in 2001/2 across 142 local authorities, the budgets for PR varied between £17,000 to £3,945,500 in a large London borough; the average budget for a London borough was £713, 250, for a county council £400,000, for a metropolitan borough £467,750 and £229,000 for a unitary authority (Vasterman and Sykes, 2001, cited in Franklin, 2004: 103–5).

In UK central government, developments in PR similarly post-date the Second World War. The Central Office of Information (COI) was established on 1 April 1946 as successor to the overtly propagandist wartime Ministry of Information. For broadcaster Michael Cockerell, the COI constitutes the 'heart of the government information machine' (Cockerell et al., 1984: 57). It is home to 'the technicians of the machine' – the journalists, press officers, PR advisers, producers, editors, film-makers and web designers who assist the government in communicating information to the public. Establishing the COI in 1946, Attlee claimed that 'it is essential to a good administration under a democratic system that the public shall be adequately informed about the many matters in which government's action directly impinges on their daily lives' (HC Debates, 17 December 1945, col. 916). During Attlee's post-war administration, the nationalisation of major industries such as coal, electricity and gas, as well as the establishment of national health and social welfare systems, required much explanation to citizens and voters and consequently PR staffing and budgets grew accordingly (Wildy, 1985). Nationalisation of industries and services also triggered an early spurt of growth in private sector PR to respond to this political pressure towards nationalisation (Miller and Dinan, 2000: 8). Paradoxically, the flurry of privatisation legislation during the Thatcher administrations of 1979 to 1990, which returned many of these nationalised industries to private ownership, provided the engine for further substantial growth in public and private sector PR (Franklin, 2004: 77–80; Miller and Dinan, 2000: 10–23). The election of New Labour with its emphasis on image, presentation, spin and news management encouraged notable increases in COI budgets from £110.7m in 1997 to £173.4m in 1998, £199.9m in1999 to reach an unprecedented £295.4m in 2000/1 (COI Annual Report and Accounts, cited in Franklin, 2004: 79).

PR growth was also evident in the increasing numbers of press and PR officers employed by the government information service, which grew from approximately 1200 in the mid 1990s to 2300 a decade later (Franklin, 2004; Jones, 2006). In specific departments the growth was striking. Between 1979 and 1999, for example, the Department of Health and Social Security (DHSS) increased the number of information officers it employed by 488 per cent (from 24 to 141). At the Ministry of Agriculture, Fisheries and Food (MAFF) the growth was 77 per cent (22 to 39), at the Department of Transport (DoT) 185 per cent (13 to 37) (Davis, 2002: 21). However, the decade between 1997 and 2006 has witnessed even more rapid expansion with growth in press and PR at the Ministry of Defence (MoD), rising by 389 per cent (from 47 in 1997 to 230 in 2006), 36 per cent at the Foreign and Commenwealth Office (FCO) (30 to 41), 100 per cent at the Prime Minister's office (12 to 24) and 106 per cent at the Treasury (16–31) (Davis, 2008). In summary, the development of a mediatised politics, where perception management, presentation, political marketing and advertising have become more prominent, has provided a congenial environment for the growth and development of public sector PR.

The private sector of UK PR has also flourished and expanded. Globally, the PR industry is characterised by the prominence of a few large companies such as Hill and Knowlton, Weber Shandwick and Burson-Marsteller, mostly based in the USA or the UK. The UK hosts the second largest PR industry measured by the twin indicators of income for the industry as a whole and the fee income of the 10 largest companies. Perhaps unsurprisingly, America stands in pole position with Japan in third place.

To suggest that in the UK, 'public relations is a growth industry', risks challenge for understatement, since during 'the 1980s and again in the mid 1990s, growth rates for medium and large British consultancies typically reached 20–40 per cent per annum' (Miller and Dinan, 2000: 5). Growth has developed apace, especially during the 1980s. Almost half the members of the Public Relations Consultants Association came into existence in the 1980s with as many PR consultancies formed in the decade as in the previous two decades combined. The 46 PR firms listed in the *Hollis* trade directory in 1967 had become 2230 by 1994, while the growth in practitioners was similarly striking. By the late 1990s, the 3318 practitioners employed in the top 114 PR consultancies had grown to 6578 in the top 150 consultancies. Income and revenues have grown to reflect this expansion in PR activity. The fee income of the 150 largest consultancies rose from £15m in 1979 to a remarkable £383m by 1998. Miller and Dinan conclude that 'the biggest consultancies show that the sector seems to have expanded by a factor of 31 between 1979 and 1998; this represents an 11-fold real terms increase and illustrates the very marked increase in the size of the consultancy sector in Britain since the end of the 1970s' (2000: 11–12).

Growth has been sustained into the new millennium, with Key Note's (2007) Review of the Public Relations Industry commenting that 'the PR industry is certainly very vibrant and 2006 saw growth in practically all sectors and all global markets'. Summarising the striking growth in numbers of agencies, practitioners employed and income and profits in UK PR across sectors up to 2005, Davis concludes 'that there are 2,500 agencies and 47,800 people working in the public relations profession in the UK. This figure excludes the 125,000 people working in the associated advertising and marketing industries, those working in PR support industries (e.g., press cutting, media evaluation, news distribution services), and the many professionals who have had media training. The estimated total turnover of the industry in 2005, consultancy and in-house, was £6.6 billions' (Davis, 2008: 76). PR, moreover, is spreading beyond the public and private sectors into the voluntary sector where a host of disparate organisations ranging from universities, trade unions, media organisations and charities from Save the Children and NSPCC to Stonewall and Greenpeace all employ substantive and growing numbers of PR practitioners to handle their media relations. Deacon's survey, for example, concluded that 31 per cent (57 per cent of the largest) of voluntary organisations employed press/publicity officers while 43 per cent (81 per cent of the largest organisations) employed external agencies to top up in house PR expertise (Deacon, 1996).

PUBLIC RELATIONS: EDUCATION AND TRAINING

Twenty years ago no university in the UK offered a degree-level course in PR – now 25 universities offer courses approved by the Chartered Institute of Public Relations (CIPR). Several offer more than one pathway, and there are degrees in political communications, financial PR and other specialist disciplines. Like journalism, however, PR has made only minor inroads into the older universities. Of the pre-1992 universities only two – Cardiff and Stirling – teach PR and only a handful such as Cardiff, City, Newcastle, Sheffield and Stirling teach journalism. Cardiff remains the only university in the elite Russell Group which offers PR degrees. PR, moreover, is making only limited gains in being accepted as part of curricula offered by business schools. This remains a core objective of the CIPR and for the PRSA – the situation is similar in the USA. MBAs and other business courses continue to take the outdated view that PR is somehow 'part of marketing'. This is despite evidence from the Burson Marstellar/*PR Week* survey that CEOs spend more time dealing with reputation than with any other issue – finance included.

More people now enter the profession with PR qualifications, but also more PR practitioners than ever before are studying for qualifications to enhance their career. CIPR offers a successful proprietary diploma – a one-year, part-time course. Within the past two years this has been rolled out for study at a number of overseas centres as well as dozens in the UK. The course is ranked at master's level and is open to students with practical PR experience seeking to underpin it with a solid grounding in theory. The CIPR also offers a range of short training courses in practical skills – usually between half a day and two days in length. This is another growing market and was a major consideration informing the Institute's move to larger and more prestigious premises in 2006. A large number of commercial suppliers offer similar courses and the number seems to grow every year.

Why have education and training grown so strongly? An obvious reason is that the employment market is growing. When PR traditionally recruited journalists in mid-career it was clear that they would enter the profession with a number of key skills already honed in a related field. But such a recruitment path is nowhere near sufficient for the needs of the profession today. It offers neither the numbers that business demands nor the full range of skills. As PR is increasingly accepted at boardroom level, a talent for writing and a nose for a story are no longer sufficient. Clients and employers expect business skills. Increasingly they seek them in people for whom PR was a first choice of career and not a mid-career switch.

PR education will undoubtedly keep growing. In particular, UK universities will attract increasing numbers of overseas students as the premium on PR continues to grow – along with a premium on English as the international business language. Roger Haywood, best selling author and the only person to serve as Chairman of the Chartered Institute of Marketing and President of the (now Chartered) Institute of Public Relations, believes that:

> Britain, as much as any country in the world, is setting the standard in PR at the moment. The British 'brand' is respected worldwide. It is no surprise that top British universities are attracting increasing numbers of overseas students. I see that as a trend which will grow. (Haywood, pers. comm.)

These developments in the PR industry and PR education and training during the 20th century, explain the need for a book such as *Key Concepts in Public Relations*.

KEY CONCEPTS IN PUBLIC RELATIONS: THE BOOK IN OUTLINE

Key Concepts in Public Relations offers students of PR, media and communication studies a unique, accessible and authoritative guide to the central concepts informing the expansive field of PR. Written by distinguished PR practitioners and academics working at Cardiff University, a key ambition for the book has been to bring together a rich experience of professional practice and scholarly work to develop and inform a balanced and complementary account of PR theory and practice.

More specifically, *Key Concepts in Public Relations* provides an extensive and detailed 'reference' or 'source' text for students and others with interests in PR. The book contains an alphabetical listing of the identified key concepts in PR. Each entry is approximately 300–500 words in length, makes use of extensive **cross-references** to related entries and concludes by suggesting further reading to allow readers opportunities to follow up subjects of interest in greater detail.

The book provides students with multi-disciplinary accounts of the wide range of concepts and terms that are central to an understanding of PR, both as a field of academic inquiry and an arena of professional practice. Additionally, we hope that *Key Concepts in Public Relations* might prove helpful to PR practitioners wishing to 'brush up' on the latest developments within their field and provide them with opportunities for reflection on their practice. We are also eager that a more general and lay readership will find something of interest to engage them in the discussions of advertising, celebrity PR, ethics, excellence theory, military PR, news values, propaganda, reputation management, soundbites and spin, which unravel across the pages of the book.

In addition to providing a thoroughgoing understanding of concepts central to PR, the book has a number of other objectives, including the ambition to:

- explore the overlapping concerns of PR and the cognate intellectual disciplines of media, communication, cultural and journalism studies;
- highlight the number and range of theoretical approaches to public relations;
- identify the wide range of methodological tools and approaches appropriate to investigations of PR;
- illustrate the multidisciplinary character of PR and trace its intellectual roots not only in media, communication and journalism studies, but in the social science and humanities disciplines of sociology, politics, economics, history, psychology, as well as business and management studies;
- provide extensive and explicit bibliographical guidance to a wide range of primary and secondary literature to facilitate further study;

- highlight and summarise academics' and journalists' critical assessments of recent developments in PR;
- alert readers to recent debates within PR.

It is perhaps equally important to state what has not been an ambition for this book. *Key Concepts in Public Relations* is *not* intended to deliver definitive or final accounts of particular concepts in PR, but to offer a preliminary overview, informed by up-to-date research and relevant reading, which will hopefully stimulate readers' thinking, prompting them to deliberate further on issues and to pursue additional study. Similar to all books it must be judged as 'work in progress' in a dynamic and changing scholarly and PR environment. We hope that *Key Concepts in Public Relations* will serve as a valuable, informative and engaging starting point for your studies of PR. That was undoubtedly our substantive ambition in writing this book.

Bob Franklin, Mike Hogan, Quentin Langley,
Nick Mosdell and Elliot Pill
Cardiff University, 2008

Account Management

Account management is the process of managing individual accounts within a **public relations** consultancy. Usually the account team comprises a director, account director, account manager and account executive with administrative support. The director is the most experienced member of the team and generally manages the senior **client** relationship and matters of strategy, budget and planning. They tend to have an overview role on the team and oversee teamwork.

The account director is the hands on, day-to-day driver of the programme and works closely with the rest of the team to meet communications objectives, manage budgets and plan teamwork. The account manager reports into the account director and also has a hands on role similar to that of the director, though is more focused on achieving programme goals, such as media coverage and managing events.

The account executive is the most junior member of the core practitioner team and works closely with the account manager to deliver programme objectives. They also carry out research, compile media lists and media coverage in addition to the many other responsibilities they have.

Good account management is the bedrock of a good client relationship and strong administrative support for the team is essential. They may manage time sheets, office supplies, contact reports, postage, team diaries and work closely with the director to ensure the smooth running of the programme.

Members in each account team may have a range of clients to support. For example, an account manager may be responsible for five different clients in a particular sector. Account management therefore is the process of juggling those responsibilities and programmes to deliver agreed communications campaigns for clients.

In production terms, account management is the delivery of public relations programmes to specific stakeholder groups. Account management tasks include: **research**, identifying key **audiences**, building relationships with the media, building relationships with clients, working in a team, preparing budgets, preparing status reports of activity, reconciling the actual hours spent on a project against the time quoted at the start of the project, event management, press release writing, media planning, presenting programmes and updates of activity on a weekly and monthly basis.

account management

Glen Broom and David Dozier in Grunig and Hunt's (1984) *Managing Public Relations* outline two dominant public relations roles. The **communication** technician carries out public relations programmes but is not involved in making organisational decisions and is removed from the strategic process. They are focused on delivery and implementation of agreed communications programmes. The communication manager plans and manages the programme, advises senior management and adds value to business strategy formulation and implementation.

Broom and Dozier outline three main types of manager role. The expert prescriber defines problems and builds programmes to shape stakeholder perception. The communication facilitator is a mediator between the organisation and key stakeholder groups. A **boundary spanner** role as suggested by Moss and Warnaby (Kitchen and Schultz, 2001). The problem-solving process facilitator takes a subjective view of the communications problem and helps act as a counsellor within organisations. A consultant often fills this role.

The role of the account manager is therefore a complex one. It requires a variety of communication and management skills as well as the ability to assume a range of different roles to different situations.

FURTHER READING

Cutlip, S.M., Allen, H. and Broom, G. (2000) *Effective Public Relations*, 8th edn. London: Prentice Hall International.

Gregory, A. (2000) Planning and Managing Public Relations Campaigns. London: Kogan Page.

Grunig, J.E. and Hunt, T. (1984) Managing Public Relations. New York: Holt Reinhart and Winston.

EP

key concepts in public relations

Advertising

Advertising is the paid for promotion of goods, services, companies and ideas, usually by an identified sponsor. Advertising is part of the overall promotional strategy of an organisation and forms a lead element in the **marketing mix**. Other elements include publicity, **public relations**, personal selling, sales promotion, direct marketing and web marketing.

Commercial messages and election campaign displays were found in the ruins of Pompeii and the Egyptians created sales messages and wall posters. 'Lost and found' message advertising was common in Ancient Greece and Rome. As the printing process developed in the 16th and 17th centuries, advertising expanded along with the development of mass media newspapers. In the 17th century, advertisements started to appear in weekly newspapers in England. Regulation to control the content of misleading adverts was also adopted in the 17th century to target 'Quack ads', promoting medical and health cures in disease ravaged Europe.

As economies expanded in the 19th century, so did the advertising industry. In America, classified ads became popular, filling pages with small print messages promoting all kinds of goods. This successful format led to the growth of mail-order advertising. In 1843, the first advertising agency was established by Volney Palmer in Philadelphia. At first these agencies were brokers for buying advertising space in newspapers, but by the 20th century, these agencies started to take over the responsibility for the content as well.

The 1960s saw advertising adopt scientific and social science approaches to target new customers as technology provided broader platforms for targeting specific messages at mass **audiences** through radio, television and outdoor poster advertising.

Using creative techniques, images and words were used to position their product in the mind of the target consumer with a unique selling proposition. These campaigns were designed to form strong and positive associations between each **brand** and the reader or viewer. If the positive link could be made between the product, service, goods or association, then it was more likely that target consumers would adopt a positive approach and attitude to that product, service, good or association.

Today, advertising continues to evolve. Guerrilla promotions that involve unusual approaches such as product giveaways in public places, cars that are covered with brand messages and interactive advertising where the viewer can respond to become part of the advertising message, are all part of this evolution. Companies are even paying students to wear their corporate messages on parts of their body in return for money!

The industry has been criticised by AdBusters as being one of the engines powering a mass production system that promotes consumption and forms stereotypical views of sexism, racism and ageism. Indeed, critics question whether the medium is creating or reflecting cultural trends. Media Watch is one group that works to educate consumers about the effects of advertising.

FURTHER READING

Austin, E.W. and Pinkleton, B.E. (2001) Strategic Public Relations Management: Planning and Effective Communication Programs. Mahwah, NJ: Lawrence Erlbaum.

Ewen, S. (1996) PR! A Social History of Spin. New York: Basic Books.

Graydon, S. (2003) Made You Look – How Advertising Works and Why You Should Know. Toronto: Annick Press.

Sivulka, J. (1998) Soap, Sex and Cigarettes: A Cultural History of American Advertising. Belmont, CA: Wadsworth.

EP

Advertising (Codes)

Most countries around the world have either statutory legislation or industry bodies, and often both, to regulate the conduct and content of **advertising**. These bodies draw up codes of practice on everything from the kinds of products that may be advertised in various outlets, to the promises made in those adverts (most commonly, that there are no misleading or false claims made about a product or service), to the kinds of language and images that are deemed acceptable. In the UK, the regulatory body is an independent organisation established from within the industry, known as the Advertising Standards Authority (ASA). The advertising industry is expected to take responsibility for, and to adhere to, the codes of conduct which govern all kinds of advertising from broadcast media to direct sales promotion, in respect of misleading claims, offensive content and the use of personal information or unacceptable direct marketing techniques. The industry draws up these codes through the Committees for Advertising Practice (CAP).

The ASA also works in conjunction with the European Advertising Standards Alliance (EASA), based in Brussels, which is a self-regulatory industry framework that operates according to the 'blue book' that provides all relevant information about self-regulatory and statutory codes throughout Europe.

Similar arrangements exist in the USA through the Association of National Advertisers (ANA), which works in conjunction with the American Advertising Federation (AAF), and the Council of Better Business Bureaus (BBB).

These self-regulatory bodies not only draw up the codes but also adjudicate on complaints from individuals or organisations about the conduct or content of all forms of advertising. It is in the interests of all advertisers to comply with the spirit of this self-regulation to avoid the imposition of restrictive legislation. However, any industry code will always be subject to close scrutiny, and require regular revision as advertisers and marketers become increasingly sophisticated in their techniques.

FURTHER READING

Association of National Advertisers (ANA): http://www.ana.net/
Advertising Standards Authority (ASA): http://www.asa.org.uk/
European Advertising Standards Alliance (EASA): http://www.easa-alliance.org

NM

Advertising (Online)

The online forum has distinct features that work to its advantage as an advertising medium, nonetheless the arena contains many offerings of dubious worth. Most free branded content online – including the websites of major international newspapers such as *The Times*, the *Daily Telegraph* and the *Washington Post* – require readers to register, often giving considerable detail about employment, household income, interests and purchasing habits. This information allows advertising to become extremely targeted. Two readers of the same content will not be exposed to the same advertising. The web is also home to a plethora of highly specific niche publications with small but, in some cases, highly relevant audiences. Online advertising can be charged either on exposure or click through models. The former is charged on the number of relevant people to whom an advert is exposed: in the latter only for those who click through the advert to the supporting material behind. This distinction is valuable because consumers can be extremely selective about the advertising they read, either deleting or blocking pop-ups immediately or setting their browsers to do this automatically.

Many niche media are not big enough to sell advertising space on an organised basis but can run adverts supplied by major web brands such as **Google**. Well into 2005, Google – which both charges and pays out on a click through basis – was only paying out when a site had earned US$100. This meant that many smaller sites were not being paid at all. Since December 2005 Google has been paying electronically and can pay out much smaller amounts. According to PricewaterhouseCoopers (PwC) the value of online advertising in the USA reached US$9.63b in 2004, up 33 per cent on 2003 (http://www.infoworld.com/article/05/12/16/HNyahoo measureads_1.html [date accessed 9 January 2006]). Though these figures may have been inflated by quadrennial events (the Presidential election and the Olympics) PwC continued to detect growth through 2005. One of the strongest areas of online advertising is sponsored links on search engines. According to Jaffray the cost of customer acquisition via this channel is just US$8, compared with US$20 for the Yellow Pages, US$50 for online display adverts, US$60 for email and US$70 for direct (snail) mail (cited in Battelle, 2006: 35).

FURTHER READING

Battelle, J. (2006) *The Search: How Google and Its Rivals Rewrote the Rules of Business and Transformed Our Culture*. Boston, MA: Nicholas Brealey Publishing.
http://battellemedia.com/
http://searchenginewatch.com/

QL

Advertorials

Advertorials are paid-for feature articles; in truth they are a hybrid of an advert and editorial that appear in newspapers and magazines alongside normal editorial copy (Franklin and Murphy, 1998). Advertorials are a popular technique, particularly for promoting consumer brands (Cameron et al., 1996). Frequently, advertorials will be written using by-lined staff writers from the host publication and will employ typography and layout close to, or identical with, standard editorial. Clients like them because they so closely resemble editorial content that they are believed to be more credible than straightforward advertising. To differentiate paid-for features from editorial matter, publications are supposed to label advertorials as 'Advertising Promotion' or 'Advertising Feature'. Critics of the advertorial claim this labelling is often not included to the deliberate confusion of the readers (Smallman, 1996).

FURTHER READING

Cameron, G., Ju-Pak, K. and Kim, B.H. (1996) 'Advertorials in magazines', *Journalism and Mass Communication*, 73: 722–33.
Franklin, B. and Murphy, D. (1998) 'Changing times: local newspapers, technology and markets', in B. Franklin and D. Murphy (eds), *Making the Local News: Local Journalism in Context*. London: Routledge. pp. 7–23.
Smallman, A. (1996) 'Telling the editorial from the Adverts', *Press Gazette*, 10 May: 11.

MH

Agenda Setting

Agenda setting remains one of the most influential and significant concepts in the study of **public relations**, media and communication studies. The basic premise of agenda-setting theory is that the way in which news media report particular issues influences and helps to shape public awareness and debate about the subject (McCombs and Shaw, 1972). In a recent essay reviewing the development of the concept across more than three decades, communications scholar Maxwell McCombs claims that agenda setting has been the subject of 'hundreds of studies world-wide' (2005: 543). Moreover, as the news media have expanded to include Internet-based editions of newspapers, email **communication** and online chat rooms, the potential for articulating diverse agendas has grown markedly with research studies illustrating that 'agenda setting effects have been documented for these new media' (2005: 543).

Beyond McCombs' central argument that 'those aspects of public affairs that are prominent in the news become prominent among the public' (2005: 543), he suggests that media agendas are constructed by a process of selection and prioritising which bestows a certain prominence for particular issues guaranteeing them sustained coverage in news reports, while others are relatively marginalised or ignored. The analogy with a committee agenda is close at hand – and obvious. Committees rank agenda items to reflect their significance, with the least consequential matters receiving only scant attention or not being discussed at all (Weaver et al., 1981; McCombs et al., 1997). Consequently, agenda-setting theory has clear affinities with the theory of news framing (the suggestion that people who lack direct knowledge of events become reliant on media for their information, understanding and interpretation of those events, so that news media 'frame' reality for their audiences and 'how people think about an issue … is dependent on how the issue is framed by the media' [Semetko and Valkenburg, 2000: 94]). A similar affinity is evident with the theoretical tradition of media effects (the highly contested claim that media messages have a direct and significant effect on the knowl-edge, attitudes and even behaviour of members of the audience [Barker and Petley, 1997: 1–12; Philo and Miller, 1999: 21]). However, in agenda setting, the influence claimed for the media is less certain than in much theorising of media effects and rejects any suggestion of **propaganda**. In a classic formulation of agenda setting, the suggestion is that media *do not tell us what to think, but they do tell us what to think about*.

Agenda setting, however, does not posit a simple one-way **model** in which news media set the priorities for public debate, but suggests that a number of contesting agendas vie for prominence. A study of local press coverage of the 2005 general election in West Yorkshire, for example, highlighted the dissonance between the news agendas of local **journalists** and party press officers with the former concerned to report issues of local electoral salience (schools, hospitals, local traffic schemes), while the latter promoted a national news agenda by organising visits by national 'celebrity' politicians (electoral 'horse race' concerns, Europe, taxation and **spin** concerning the Gulf War) (Franklin et al., 2006: 260).

FURTHER READING

Franklin, B., Court, G. and Cushion, S. (2006) 'Downgrading the "local" in local reporting of the 2005 UK General Election', in B. Franklin (ed.), *Local Journalism, Local Media Making the Local News.* London: Routledge. pp. 256–70.

McCombs, M. (2005) 'A look at agenda setting: past, present and future', *Journalism Studies*, 6 (4): 543–58.

McCombs, M. and Shaw, D. (1972) 'The agenda setting function of mass media', *Public Opinion Quarterly*, 36: 176–87.

Philo, G. and Miller, D. (1999) 'The Effective Media', in G. Philo (ed.), *Message Received.* London: Longman. pp. 21–33.

Semetko, H. and Valkenburg, P. (2000) 'Framing European Politics: content analysis of press and television news', *Journal of Communication*, 50 (2): 93–109.

BF

Alternative Media

Alternative media defy simplistic definition and description. They embrace a wide range of publications including radical, community-based weekly newspapers (*Leeds Other Paper* and *Manchester Free Press*) that feature investigative **journalism** (Franklin and Murphy, 1991: 106–30; see also Harcup, 1994), soccer fanzines (Atton, 2006), 'What's On' guides, poetry magazines, newspapers or magazines articulating gay, ecological or feminist lifestyles, as well as explicitly political papers such as *An Phoblacht*, the loyalist *Belfast Telegraph* (Baker, 2005: 377) and in Israel, the legendary *Haolam Hazeh* (Meyer, 2008). Alternative media also occupy a range of media platforms including the 'alternative internet' (Atton, 2004). It is not only their contents that are alternative, moreover, but their editorial organisation, business plans, revenue sources, journalistic roles, **news values** and readerships (Harcup, 1994). A conference held in the mid-1980s, when the alternative press was expanding rapidly in number, offered the following description of alternative newspapers:

Local, anti-racist, anti-sexist, politically on the left, overtly rather than covertly political, not produced for profit, editorially free of the influence of advertisers, run on broadly collective principles ... Most alternative newspapers are small, their existence precarious. With one or two notable exceptions their circulations are in the hundreds rather than the thousands. But this tells us nothing about their influence nor their value. As virtually all the mass media are in the political centre or on the right, the voice of the local alternative newspaper is an important counterweight. Small need not mean insignificant. (National Conference of Alternative Papers, 1984: 1)

More recently Atton regretted this understanding of 'alternative' to imply little more than 'non-mainstream' (2002: 9–10). He supports Downing's (2001) suggestion that alternative media should be conceptualised within a framework of 'hybridity' in which the radical elements of alternative journalism mix readily with more conventional mainstream journalistic attributes. Downing concedes that 'if radical media have one thing in common, it is that they break somebody's rules', although he adds, 'rarely all of them in every respect' (2001: xi). Harcup underscores this commitment to hybridity by noting how frequently journalists who begin their working lives in the alternative media migrate to mainstream print and broadcast journalism later in their careers, transferring with them many valuable lessons, skills and experiences learned within alternative media (2005: 361–74).

Atton constructs a typology of alternative media which acknowledges and includes their probable radical content, but also stresses their potential to change roles and relations of production and distribution in the **communication** process. Consequently, alternative media may be committed to 'de-professionalising' the journalistic role by using volunteer labour and, ahead of the citizen journalists scribbling online, encouraging readers to become writers and accepting contributions from local amateur stringers (Atton, 2002: 27). A recent case study of the use of sources by the alternative newspaper SchNEWS (see http://www.schnews.co.uk) revealed that it seemed to offer 'an inversion of Hall et al.'s theory of primary definition' by offering 'ordinary people' privileged access to news media, but the authors acknowledge that these alternative sources are 'a counter elite that dominates an alternative hierarchy of sources' which seems to operate 'similarly to mainstream media sourcing practices' (Atton and Wickenden, 2005: 347–60) again signalling hybridity.

Alternative newspapers enjoyed a brief popularity and expanded greatly in numbers from the mid-1970s to the mid-1980s, but the iron rations of Thatcherism led to the collapse of alternative newspapers during the 1990s in the UK: only a handful of publications exist today. Undercapitalised, dependent on enthusiastic amateur journalists and distributed largely through informal networks, the great majority of alternative newspapers have been short lived: Internet-based publications may prove more resilient to such cost and labour pressures. But as Harcup's study of alternative journalists who migrate into mainstream media reveals, the influence of alternative media, its alternative news values and news agendas will continue to be a presence in mainstream news media.

FURTHER READING

Atton, C. (2002) *Alternative Media*. London: Sage.
Atton, C. (2006) 'Football fanzines and local news', in B. Franklin (ed.), *Local Journalism and Local Media; Making the local news*. London: Routledge. pp. 280–9.
Atton, C. and Wickenden, E. (2005) 'Sourcing routines and representation in alternative journalism: a case study approach', *Journalism Studies*, 6 (3): 347–60.
Downing, J. (2001) *Radical media; Rebellious Communication and Social Movements*. Thousand Oaks, CA: Sage.
Harcup, T. (1994) *A Northern Star: Leeds Other Paper and the Alternative Press 1974–1994*. Upton: The Campaign for Press and Broadcasting Freedom (North).
Harcup, T. (2005) '"I'm doing this to change the world": journalism in alternative and mainstream media', *Journalism Studies*, 6 (3): 361–74.
Meyer, O. (2008) 'Contextualising alternative journalism: *Haolem Hazeh* and the birth of critical Israeli Newsmaking', *Journalism Studies*, 9 (3): 374–91.

BF

Annual General Meeting

An annual general meeting, commonly abbreviated as AGM, is a meeting that official bodies and associations involving the **public,** including companies and shareholders, are typically required to hold by law.

An AGM is generally held every year to inform members of previous and future business activities. These past and future activities are documented in an annual report that outlines every aspect of company performance for the previous 12 months. In organisations run by volunteers or a paid committee, the AGM is generally the forum for the election of officers or representatives for the organisation. Where an issue arises at an irregular interval and cannot wait until the next AGM, an extraordinary general meeting can be called (commonly abbreviated as EGM). It is a meeting of members of an organisation, shareholders of a company or employees of an official body.

FURTHER READING

Mintzberg H. and Quinn J.B. (1991) *The Strategy Process, Concepts, Contexts, Cases*, 2nd edn. Upper Saddle River, NJ: Prentice-Hall.

EP

Audience

See **Publics**.

Audiences (Radio)

Information detailing (1) the numbers of people listening to a particular radio station (reach) and (2) how long they listen for (average hours per listener) has been gathered by Radio Joint Audience Research (RAJAR) for the 350 individual radio stations (BBC and commercial) which broadcast regularly in the UK (http://www.rajar.co.uk). RAJAR was formed in 1992, is owned by the BBC and the Association of Independent Radio Companies and produces quarterly reviews of audience figures which plot the shifting fortunes of individual radio stations as well as the all important relative success of the BBC and commercial radio sectors. It provides an informational service equivalent to that delivered by the Audit Bureau of Circulation (ABC) for newspaper **circulations** and the Broadcasters Audience Research Board (BARB) for **television audiences**.

RAJAR data for the final quarter of 2007 reveal that the BBC enjoyed a 55.4 per cent radio audience share (up 1 per cent on the previous quarter) while aggregate commercial audiences fell to 42.4 per cent (11.3 per cent of audiences achieved by *national* commercial with *local* commercial stations winning a 31.1 per cent audience share) (Plunkett, 2008a). The BBCs lead of 13 per cent over its commercial rival was its second highest ever recorded (up from 11.1 per cent in the previous quarter). BBC Radio 2 remains the nation's most popular station (12.82m listeners) with BBC Radio 1 (10.693m), BBC Radio 4 (9.289m) and BBC Radio 5 Live (6.174m) close behind. Two BBC stations lost audience in the final quarter of 2007; BBC Asian network lost 35,000 listeners over the quarter (from 476,000 to 441,000) while the prestigious news and current affairs station The World Service was down from 1.3m listeners to 1.18m. The major commercial radio services in terms of audiences and advertising revenues remain the national stations Classic FM (5.59m) and Virgin Radio, which rose slightly to 2.49m.

There are three key points about the radio industry and its audiences. First, funding has been relatively static for the past five years and was valued at £1.15b in 2006 (Ofcom, 2007), with the BBC radio spending (funded by licence fee) achieving £637m (55 per cent), followed by the national commercial radio spend of £270m (funded through advertising), with local commercial radio expenditure of £153m (13 per cent) and commercial sponsorship adding a further £91m (7.9 per cent).

Second, total listening hours for radio have fallen by approximately 4 per cent during the last five years, with the most substantive fall in listening among 25–34-year-olds (−17.3 per cent) and among children (−8–7 per cent); by contrast, listening by the over 55 age group has increased by 5.5 per cent (Ofcom, 2007: 9). The fall in listening hours also mainly reflects a decline in audiences for local radio with BBC local stations down by 6.7 per cent and local commercial stations losing 4.1 per cent of audience.

Third, in an age of media convergence, audiences are increasingly listening to 'radio programmes' on non-radio/broadcast platforms such as podcasts and downloads from online sources, which also include time-shifted listening. In the last quarter of 2007, for example, 12m people listened to a programme via the Internet, 8.1m people listened to radio on the web at least once a week, a further 7.6m have used the web for 'listen again' services while 4.3m have downloaded a podcast and 1.9m have listened to a podcast every week (Plunkett, 2008b). Such new ways to listen create considerable measurement problems for RAJAR which still uses 130,000 people who record their listening habits in a diary to assess the extent and character of audiences.

Ofcom (2007) The UK Communications Market 2007. London: Ofcom.

Plunkett, J. (2008a) 'Record audience figures for Moyles', Guardian, 31 January: G2.

Plunkett, J (2008b) 'Pagers have been ditched and it's back to radio diaries to measure listening', Guardian, 28 April: Media 8.

Radio Joint Audience Research: http://www.rajar.co.uk (accessed 23 April 2008)

BF

Audiences (Television)

The number of television channels broadcasting to UK audiences has grown very substantially since the arrival of Channel 4 in 1982 (at the time only the fourth UK television channel). Satellite television arrived in the late 1980s with Sky Television and British Satellite Broadcasting (later to merge to form BSkyB in 1989), while the fifth terrestrial channel (unimaginatively titled Channel 5 initially, now just Five) launched with muted enthusiasm in 1997. But by a decade or so later (in 2006), there were approximately 433 television channels broadcasting in the UK; a rise from 236 channels in 2002 (Ofcom, 2007: 101). These channels are funded variously by the licence fee (23 per cent of total television revenues in 2006, but down 2 per cent since 2002), advertising (32 per cent from 35 per cent in 2002) and significantly by sponsorship which overtook advertising in 2003 and now constitutes 37 per cent (up from 32 per cent in 2002) of all television revenues (Ofcom, 2007: 101). In 2006, total television revenues had grown to £10.8b from a 2002 figure of £8.9b.

This growth in channels and revenues has been matched by an expansion of delivery systems including cable, satellite and online/Internet delivery ('streaming') of television services in an age of convergence. By early 2007, 20.4m households (80.5 per cent) had multichannel digital television; the success of digital Freeview 'set top' boxes saw them installed in 8.4m households – a growth of 33 per cent in a single year.

In this newly established converged, multichannel, television ecology, the audience share of the five main channels has necessarily declined from 77.7 per cent in 2002 to 66.8 per cent in 2006, although these

key concepts in
public relations

losses have been constrained to some degree by unrolling 'spin off' channels such as E4, More 4 and FilmFour (of Channel 4), ITVs 2, 3 and 4, Five's Fiver and Five US. The audience share of the two largest and earliest channels ITV and BBC has declined significantly during the last 25 years. In 1982, for example, ITV enjoyed 50 per cent of all audience share while BBC1 captured 38 per cent of total television audience. By 2007, these percentages were reduced to 19.2 per cent (ITV) and 22 per cent (BBC1) (BARB, 2008).

Significantly, the massive increase in the availability and range of television services has impacted only minimally on the number of television 'viewing hours' per viewer which grew modestly from 3 hours 34 minutes each day in 2002, to 3 hours 44 minutes in the following year but which fell subsequently to 3 hours 36 minutes in 2006 (Ofcom, 2007: 101).

Audience viewing figures vary markedly across the viewing day. During weekdays there are modest peaks in viewing at breakfast (5.2m) and lunchtime (6.9m), with a steady rise in viewers from approximately 3.30 p.m. to a peak of 23.3m at 9.15 p.m. before rapidly falling away to effectively zero between 10 p.m. and midnight. Different patterns of viewing occur at the weekend. There is no breakfast or lunchtime peak although afternoon audiences are broadly 50 per cent up on weekdays and the evening peak is slightly greater at 23.7m. Age also affects audience reach across the viewing day. Viewers aged 65 and above watch more television than younger audiences across most of the viewing day, except for breakfast time when children predominate – especially between 7.30 and 8.30 a.m. In the afternoon the audience is older since children are at school, during peak time (6–10 p.m.) audience age exhibits little difference while average audience age toward the end of the evening rises as children retire to bed (Ofcom, 2007: 160–1). The changing character of audiences, reflecting shifting patterns of viewing representing age and other demographics is important for advertisers, marketing companies and PR agencies who will wish to tailor their messages to niche audiences, which can be identified as watching at different time slots across the viewing day.

FURTHER READING

BARB (2008) Broadcasters' Audience Research Board: http://www.BARB.co.uk (accessed 1 May 2008).
Ofcom (2007) *The UK Communications Market 2007*. London: Ofcom.

Blog (Blogger, Blogging, Blogosphere)

A blog is a weBLOG, often in diary form and usually updated daily or more frequently. Many are purely personal accounts but some are written as genuine contributions to the media or politics. As with all online publishing, blogging is freed from the constraints of filling a physical space on a page, so the length of articles in the same series may vary widely.

Journalistically, blogs passed several key milestones in 2004, when bloggers were accredited for the first time as journalists at the US presidential nominating conventions. The same year also saw the exposure by bloggers on http://www.freerepublic.com of CBS in an embarrassing forgery scandal that led to the retirement of Dan Rather. The contributions of blogging to journalism are varied, and hotly debated. For example, Matt Drudge (http://www.drudgereport.com) was the first journalist to break the Monica Lewinsky story, though journalists in the mainstream media (MSM in blogspeak) had been aware of the story for some time.

Bloggers are not necessarily professional **journalists** (though many journalists are bloggers) and are therefore not constrained either by codes of ethics or (in many cases) by the need to protect a valuable media brand from ridicule if a story turns out to be inaccurate. Bloggers were famously derided by Jonathan Klein of CBS as 'a guy sitting in his living room in his pyjamas' (Fox News, 10 September 2004). However, this was during the debate about forged documents used by *60 Minutes II*, which ultimately vindicated the bloggers.

Politics within the blogosphere is widely varied and includes representation of fringe and minority viewpoints, which find few outlets in the MSM. In the run up to the 2004 US Presidential election Lada Adamic and Natalie Glance (http://blog.blogpulse.com/archives/000156.html) studied almost 1500 influential blogs, defining 759 as liberal and 735 as conservative. This contrasts with daily newspapers, around two-thirds of which endorsed John Kerry in that election, and would thus probably be described as liberal. Conservative blogs were more frequently cited than liberal blogs. According to Adamic and Glance, blogs frequently cite each other across the political divide, thus minimising any tendencies to cyber-balkanisation. Some 59 per cent of mentions of John Kerry were in conservative blogs, while 53 per cent of mentions of George Bush were in liberal blogs, thus suggesting a negative tone to blog commentary.

Salam Pax (a pseudonym), an Iraqi architect who wrote a blog recording his accounts of the bombing of Baghdad during the Second Gulf War and their dissonance from mainstream journalistic reports, is undoubtedly one of the most well known bloggers. His blog 'Where Is Raed?' offered an alternative account of the war, experienced from the position of the ordinary citizen and unmediated by journalists. Pax symbolises some of the virtues claimed for bloggers. Haas identifies three significant claims made for blogs. First, they shape or 'steer' mainstream reporting and set an **agenda** for conventional media reporting (2005: 389). Second, blogs deliver reporting which is independent and alternative to the mainstream. Third, blogs meld news reporting with commentary from very diverse sources. But Haas's own research leads him to question each of these claims. He concludes that 'there is little evidence of weblog reporters engaging in any independent, alternative news reporting ...'. Indeed Haas argues that Weblogs 'reproduce' rather than 'challenge' mainstream **journalism** and that there are 'distinct similarities' between mainstream media and the blogosphere and 'between the journalistic norms and practices of mainstream **news** organisations and individual Weblogs' (2005: 387).

Wall concurs in her study of blogs during the Second Gulf War, which revealed: (1) that bloggers obey mainstream conventions in war coverage; (2) bloggers see themselves as superior reporting mechanisms to mainstream coverage; and (3) they promote blogs as a means to improve existing war reporting (2006: 111–26). Arianna Huffington, writer and editor of the authoritative and widely read blog 'HuffingtonPost.com' concurs arguing that blogs promise the salvation not destruction of traditional media. 'Big media,' she claims 'are critically ill but will actually be saved by the transfusion of passion and immediacy of the blogging revolution' (2006: 30). She argues that blogs are: (1) transforming the ways in which news is disseminated; (2) personal and written with passion; and (3) generating conversation as much as providing information and thereby creating a 'close bond between blogger and audience'. This is why blogs will not wholly replace print media but they are nonetheless 'the most vital source of news in America' (2006: 30).

Blogs are not necessarily political and are important outlets for discussing some commercial goods and services. In particular, products aimed at the youth market need coverage in blogs and online communities and these

blog (blogger, blogging, blogosphere)

media are heavily targeted by businesses operating in the sports apparel, computer gaming, music and many other sectors.

The anonymity of blogging creates clear ethical issues for PR. The largest independent PR consultancy, Edelman, was exposed in 2006 for a fake blog (or flog) on behalf of its client, Walmart. The flog purported to be by a couple travelling across the USA parking in Walmart carparks. The couple reported universally good experiences dealing with Walmart staff, all of whom seemed to be delighted to be working for the retail giant. This aroused suspicion and investigations uncovered that the couple were being paid by Edelman – a connection that had never been divulged. The PRSA has long had an ethical policy condemning 'astro-turfing' or the creation of fake grass roots campaigns or producing any material where a financial interest is not declared.

FURTHER READING

Haas, T. (2005) 'From "public journalism" to the "public's journalism"? Rhetoric and reality in the discourse on Weblogs', *Journalism Studies*, 6 (3): 387–96.

Huffington, A. (2006) 'Now the little guy is the true pit bull of journalism', *Guardian*, 14 March: 30.

Johnson, T. and Kay, B. (2004) 'Wag the blog: how reliance on traditional media and the Internet influence credibility perception of weblogs among blog users', *Journalism and Mass Communication Quarterly*, 81: 622–42.

Postrel, V. (1999) *The Future and Its Enemies: The Growing Conflict Over Creativity, Enterprise and Progress*. New York: Touchstone.

Surowiecki, J. (2005) *The Wisdom of Crowds*. London: Abacus

Wall, M. (2006) 'Blogging Gulf War 11', *Journalism Studies*, 7 (1): 111–26.

BF & QL

Bottom Line

Also described as net income, the bottom line is a financial performance measure and is equal to the income that a firm has after subtracting costs and expenses from the total revenue. Expenses will typically include tax expense. For a retail firm, subtracted costs may be the cost of goods sold, sales discounts, and sales returns and allowances. For a product company **advertising**, manufacturing, and design and development costs are included.

Net income is sometimes called the bottom line because it is typically found on the last line of a company's income statement. This can be found in a public company's annual report. Another term that is closely related to bottom line is top line. As the total revenue forms the first line of the account statement, it is often called top line. Both terms are used widely in business language. Bottom line is used to describe the heart or reality of a business situation while a top line account is used to describe a quick snapshot of a situation. In the mid-1990s the term **triple bottom line** was introduced to take into account the environmental and social performance of an organisation. Triple bottom line reporting developed from a view that organisations needed not only to satisfy the needs of shareholders but also stakeholders. Stakeholders being any person or group directly or indirectly affected by the actions of the business.

In **public relations** terms, the reporting of non-financial items on the balance sheet is now a legal requirement in the UK and as a result there has been a dramatic development of corporate social responsibility programmes designed to address the needs of triple bottom line reporting. This new legislation means that larger companies now have to report not only on financial matters but factors such as stakeholder relationships, environmental impacts and risk management: produce an operating financial review (OFR). By making the reporting of non-financial performance mandatory, the PR industry would seem to have an opportunity to demonstrate the strategic role PR can play at the heart of corporate governance.

FURTHER READING

Elkington, J. (1994) 'Towards the sustainable corporation: win-win-win business strategies for sustainable development', *Californian Management Review*, 36 (2): 126–143.

Fairchild, F. and O'Connor, N. (2003) Reputation and the Bottom Line: A Communications Guide to Reporting on Corporate Reputations. London: CIPR, Mori and Business in the Community.

Proctor, R. (1994) *Finance for the Perplexed Executive*. London: Harper Collins.

Spiro, H.T. (1996) *Finance for the Non Financial Manager*. New York: John Wiley and Sons.

bottom line

EP

A concept describing the role a **public relations** practitioner adopts within an organisation. If strategy is a means by which an organisation adapts to its environment, there is a clear need for an understanding of that external environment. In strategic planning terms, this environmental scanning function is performed by a **boundary spanner**.

White and Dozier (1992) argue that in this role, PR practitioners are able to make a significant contribution to the strategic decision-making process within an organisation. By operating at the touching point between an organisation and its environment, the boundary spanner is able to identify how internal change and strategic decisions could affect important stakeholder groups and the relationships they have with them.

The boundary-spanning role describes the importance of external stakeholder analysis and how this analysis needs to be brought inside the organisation and then imparted to senior decision makers. It comprises two key functions: information gathering and processing; external representation. It allows the public relations practitioner to act as the eyes and ears of an organisation to ensure it understands the perceptions stakeholders may or may not have of the central organisation. In this way, the boundary spanner works as an early warning system for the organisation, highlighting emerging issues that may affect the organisation's current or future strategies.

FURTHER READING

Grunig, J.E. and Repper, F.C. (1992) 'Strategic management, publics and issues', in J.E. Grunig (ed.), *Excellence in Public Relations and Communications Management*. Hillsdale, NJ: Lawrence Erlbaum. pp. 117–57.

White, J. and Dozier, D.M. (1992) 'Public relations and management decisions making', in J.E. Grunig (ed.), *Excellence in Public Relations and Communications Management*. Hillsdale, NJ: Lawrence Erlbaum. pp. 91–108.

EP

Brand Stretching

See **convergence**.

Branding

Branding is the process by which companies differentiate their products from their competition. In developing a unique identity, which may include a name, packaging and design, a brand is developed. In developing and managing this unique identity, the branding process allows organisations to develop strong emotional and psychological connections with a product, goods or service. This, in turn, eases the purchasing decision. Branding affects stakeholder perceptions and the marketing task is to ensure these perceptions are positive. The stronger the branding position, the higher the price you can charge for that product with a corresponding increase in sales volume.

Branding is an important element in consumer markets and also allows the development of a new product by facilitating new product lines or product extensions by building on the consumer's perceptions of the values and character represented by the brand name. Brassington and Pettitt (2000) maintain this points to the most important function of branding which is to create and communicate a three-dimensional character for a product that is not easily copied or damaged by competitors. A brand therefore is understood to be any name, design, style, words or symbols, singly or in any combination that distinguish a product from another in the eyes of the customer.

In the UK in 1998 the three biggest brands were Coca-Cola, Walker's crisps and Nescafe coffee. Sales and advertising spend for each brand was in excess of £580m and £31.41m for Coca-Cola; £400–5m and £6.88m for Walker's crisps; £285–90m and £6.24m for Nescafe coffee.

Barbie® is an iconic global brand. Born in 1959, she is now approaching early middle age and her 50th birthday. This has been achieved through a process of rebranding which has seen the original Barbie® go through three facelifts in 1967, 1977 and 2000 reflecting women's changing role in society.

FURTHER READING

Bainbridge, J. and Curtis, J. (1998a) 'The UK's biggest brands, part 1', *Marketing*, 30 July: 22–5.

Brassington, F. and Pettit, S. (2000) *Principles of Marketing*. London: Pearson.

Carpenter, P. (2000) *e-Brands*. Cambridge, MA: Harvard Business School Press.

Hussey, M. (1998) 'Seriously, it's Barbie', *Express*, 26 January: 19.

Jobber, D. (1995) *Principles and Practice of Marketing*. New York: McGraw-Hill.

EP

Budget

The budget, in **public relations** terms, is the amount of money an organisation is prepared to spend on a PR programme across a period of time communicating messages to target stakeholders.

PR consultancies develop their budgets for clients by dividing their time between fees and costs. Fees are related to the time it takes a consultant or team of consultants to advise on and deliver a particular message or campaign. Fees are also described as the charge out rate. Charge out rates relate to the cost a consultant charges for one hour of time. This varies from anything between £60 per hour through to more than £300 per hour depending on expertise and experience. Costs are related to all other additional monies spent in delivering the campaign. Costs may include, design, printing, distribution, venue hire, **celebrity** payment, mobile phone costs, travel and accommodation.

By combining the total fees and the total costs for the campaign you have your total budget. Budgets are then reconciled on a monthly basis to see what has been delivered against the agreed budget. One of the real issues in PR consultancy is the concept of over-servicing. Over-servicing occurs when the consultant puts in more fee time than has been budgeted for. In some cases this is charged back to the client if there is a valid reason for the increased fee time. However, in most cases the additional work is not charged back and this erodes the profitability of the work.

FURTHER READING

Davis, A. (2003) *Everything You Should Know About Public Relations*. London: Kogan Page.
Gregory. A. (2000) *Planning and Managing Public Relations Campaigns*. London: Kogan Page.

EP

Business to Business (B2B)

B2B is PR aimed mainly at business customers. The phrase is contrasted with business to consumer (B2C). While a great many products – especially in the ICT field – are plainly aimed at both markets – B2B and B2C are often seen as alternative career pathways in PR consultancies. Many consultancies focus solely on one or the other while larger consultancies often have different divisions for these two areas. B2B is also often referred to as corporate PR as distinct from consumer PR.

FURTHER READING

Haywood, R. (1991) *All About Public Relations: How To Build Business Success On Good Communications*. London: McGraw-Hill.
Kitchen, P. (1997) *Public Relations: Principles and Practice*. London: Thomson.

QL

Campaign

Campaign is the umbrella title for any activity designed to produce a planned outcome. Most often a campaign will make use of **media relations** and **lobbying** to achieve its ends. The campaign can be single issue, for example, 'Save the Whale', or multi-purpose, for example 'Make Poverty History'. Many scholars believe that a campaign has many of the hallmarks of a life cycle. Tench and Yeomans (2006) suggest five stages in this cycle. (1) Strain, where the issue becomes recognized and accepted for action. (2) Mobilisation, suggest where campaigning organisations are put together. (3) Confrontation, as campaigners lobby for action. (4) Negotiation, during which compromises are sought and the (5) resolution stage, where the campaign is successful or abandoned.

One of the most high profile campaigns in recent years has been that challenging the globalisation of the world economy. Demonstrations, often violent, have dogged meetings of the World Trade Organisation (WTO) and the G8 group of developed countries. In each case, the demonstrations have been geared to achieving maximum worldwide coverage to prompt debate on the global economy. On a more local scale, many campaigns have been directed at road building – the A34 Newbury bypass being one of the most famous – or the erection of mobile phone masts on school buildings. Common to all campaigns is the need to seek publicity to apply pressure to decision makers and so move from strain to resolution.

In consultancy terms the word 'campaign' relates to the planning mode adopted to ensure the target for key deliverables is met. Ideally this should involve: approval of objectives; budgeting; provision of creative brief; response to the brief; agreement on key messages; determination of delivery systems; execution of plan; review and evaluation. In some circumstances the campaign may be delivered as what is known as '**pro bono**' work; in other words the agency would not get a fee for its operation but would deliver the campaign for the public good. This is most often encountered in work for charity and **NGO** sectors.

FURTHER READING

Cutlip, S.M. (2000) *Effective Public Relations*, 8th edn. Upper Saddle River, NJ: Prentice Hall.

Klein, N. (2000) *No Logo.* London: Flamingo.

Tench, R. and Yeomans, L. (2006) *Exploring Public Relations.* Harlow: Pearson.

Wilson, D. and Andrews, L. (1993) *Campaigning: The A–Z of Public Advocacy.* London: Hawksmere.

MH

Celebrity

A celebrity is a person who is widely recognised in a society and who commands **public** and media attention. The word stems from the Latin adjective *celeber*, meaning famous and celebrated. While fame is generally considered to be the major prerequisite for celebrity status, it is not always sufficient. There has to be a level of public interest in the person which may or may not be connected to the reason they are famous. For example, a public figure such as a politician or industry leader may be famous but not a celebrity unless something else triggers public and mass media interest. Other types of fame, particularly those connected with mass entertainment are almost guaranteed to lead to celebrity even if the person deliberately avoids media attention. Examples of these are performers such as actors, musicians and athletes.

Each nation or cultural community has its own largely independent celebrity system. For example individuals who are extremely well known in India might be unknown abroad: Bollywood actors are a good example of this. sub-national entities or regions will also have their own celebrity system. Locally, regional newscasters, politicians or community leaders could be considered celebrities: Thus celebrity is relative, depending on geographic scale. A celebrity will be known only by those audiences that are reached by the media in which the celebrity features. In a smaller country, linguistic or cultural community, a figure will be less likely to gain worldwide celebrity.

Some celebrities can be considered global and are known across the world. These will almost all be high-powered religious, political figures, entertainment and sports stars. Many people will refer to celebrities as A-list,

celebrity

37

B-list, C-list or Z-list. These indicate a placing within the hierarchy, though due to differing levels of celebrity in different regions, it is difficult to place people within one bracket.

FURTHER READING

Breitbat, A. and Ebner, M. (2005) Hollywood Interrupted: Insanity Chi in Babylon. The Case Against Celebrity. New York: John Willey & Sons.
Holmes, S. and Redmond, S. (eds) (2006). Framing Celebrity. London: Routledge.
Klein, N. (2000) No Logo. London: Flamingo.
Ries, A. and Ries, L. (2001) The Fall of Advertising and the Rise of PR. New York: Harper Collins.

EP

Censorship

Censorship is typically defined broadly to include:

> the control of information that is given out ... Censors are not just people with big black pens cutting out information which they don't like from books or letters, or with scissors chopping out bits of film or video. As well as government officials, they can be owners of publications, judges, editors, advertisers or even the writers themselves. Nor are they always in far-off countries ruled by dictatorships. (Woolmar, 1990: 7)

This definition highlights a number of interesting features of censorship.

First, while censorship is most readily defined negatively as withholding information, Woolmar's phrase 'control of information that is given out' suggests that censorship may also involve a more proactive distribution of information. The 'over-provision' of information can be a useful strategy for information management. According to a probably apocryphal story, a KGB officer commented to a CIA agent, 'We keep our people in the dark by telling them nothing, you keep yours in the dark by telling them everything' (cited in Franklin, 1994: 5)

Second, censorship is not limited to governments and public authorities but can result from the actions of private individuals and organisations: journalistic self-censorship being an example. Herman and Chomsky's **propaganda** model, moreover, argues that the corporate and monopoly ownership of media institutions, along with the actions of powerful **advertisers** serve not only to limit the diversity of expressed views but construct a '**manufactured consent**' among readers and viewers, although such media are not officially censored (Herman and Chomsky, 1988: ch. 1).

Finally, Woolmar's definition notes that censorship is a function of *all* governments no matter how liberal: especially at times of war (Miller, 2004). In the UK context such censorship involves the system of DA Notices (http://www.dnotice.org.uk/system.htm and Sadler 2001), the restrictions imposed by the Official Secrets Act (Machon, 2005) and, occasionally, the formal censorship of news agencies forbidding them from reporting particular events and processes such as the political problems and paramilitary **campaigns** in Northern Ireland (Article 19, 2000).

On 19 October 1988, the Home Secretary banned 11 political and paramilitary groups, including the legally constituted party Sinn Fein, from television and radio but not from newspapers (Article 19, 2000). Notices were issued to the BBC and the IBA requesting that they 'refrain at all times from sending any broadcast matter which consists of or includes any words spoken ... by a person who ... represents an organisation specified ... below, or when the words support or solicit or invite support for such an organisation'. The ban applied retrospectively and resulted in the absurdity of broadcasters having to re-edit educational programmes to remove footage of the Nationalist politician Connelly. The ban was eventually lifted in 1994.

The most recent and striking example of **journalists'** self censorship emerged following the decision by the Danish newspaper *Jyllands Posten* to publish cartoons of the Islamic Prophet Mohammed. The publication of the cartoons triggered widespread complaints, public demonstrations and even physical attacks on Danish journalists and public officials around the world, including demonstrations in London throughout February 2006. During the ensuing debate about press freedom versus press responsiblity, no UK newspaper republished the cartoons (Williams, 2006: 2). But websites and **blogs** proliferated. Journalist Hans Henrik Lichtenberg, for example, at Newspaperindex.com, a 'daily blog on newspapers and free speech' reproduced the offending cartoons and orchestrated a debate on journalistic autonomy and self censorship (http://blog.newspaperindex.com/2005/12/10/un-to-investigate-jyllands-posten-racism/).

FURTHER READING

Article 19 (1989) *No Comment: Censorship, Secrecy and the Irish Troubles.* London: The Internatioal Centre on Censorship.

Machon, A. (2005) *Spies, Lies and Whistleblowers: MI5 and the David Shayler Affair.* London: Pluto.

Sadler, P. (2001) *National Security and the D Notice System.* Aldershot: Ashgate.

Williams, G. (2006) 'The Danish cartoon controversy', *Free Press* No 151 (March/April): 2–3.

Woolmar, C. (1990) *Censorship.* London: Hodder Wayland.

BF

Circulation (Newspapers)

These figures signal the number of copies of newspapers and magazines that are sold or distributed during a given time period. In the UK the largest selling national newspaper is *The News Of The World* (3.28m copies approx), with the popular mid-market tabloid *Mail on Sunday* (2.32m) and *Sunday Mirror* (1.36m) coming second and third, respectively, in the competitive Sunday market. The most popular daily newspaper remains the *Sun* with a circulation of 3.08m. Since 2003, the *Daily Mail* (2.32m) has superseded the *Mirror* (1.51m) as the paper with the second largest circulation. 'Quality' dailies like the *Telegraph* can achieve wide circulations (882,000) although figures for the *Independent* (233,000) and the *Financial Times* (444,000) are more typical (all figures ABC November 2007).

Circulation figures are significant because they are closely connected to **advertising** revenues, which typically constitute between 40–60 per cent of national newspapers' income and 80 per cent of local newspapers' revenues; approximately 50 per cent of local newspapers are distributed free and are consequently wholly reliant on advertising income (Franklin, 2006: 4–8). Circulation is the main determinant in the setting of a newspaper's advertising rates. Expressed broadly, the greater the readership, the higher the advertising revenues. But advertisers are not simply interested in *how many* readers will see their advertisement but *what kind* of readers. Circulation figures therefore try to indicate circulation within certain desirable social groups such as the A, B and C1 socio-economic categories and the high-spending age groups comprising 22–44-year-olds.

Given this crucial connection between circulation and advertising, two independent bodies, The Audit Bureau of Circulation (ABC) and Verified Free Distribution (VFD), produce quarterly circulation figures for all national, regional and local newspapers and assess readership changes across the previous quarter. Recently, ABC announced that figures will be available for online editions so long as: readers have opted to receive the e-publication; proof of reader subscription is available; the audited edition has been available across the audit period, and subscribers have been notified about particular categories of additional, free publications (Richardson, 2005: 36).

The bad news for all hard copy newspapers is that circulation figures are declining; in some sectors the decline is rapid. Aggregate circulation figures for all national and Sunday titles fell from 38.4m in 1965 to 29m in 1995 (Franklin, 1997: 88) and 22.7m in 2007; a loss of 15.8m copies representing 41 per cent of the market with losses accruing at an accelerating rate (Franklin, 2008: 9). Certain sectors, significantly local and regional newspapers, have witnessed plummeting circulations; see Table 1. In the final quarter of 2005, 18 of the 20 top selling local newspapers were suffering circulation declines (Newspaper Society, 2006).

Explanations for this decline involve a round up of the usual suspects; the expansion of television and radio news services, 24-hour news channels, news online and the availability of news via mobile telephony in what Hargreaves has described as the age of 'ambient news' (Hargreaves and Thomas, 2002). For their part, newspaper publishers and editors have responded with a number of marketing strategies to offset these trends, including bulk and discount sales (including a 10-year price war initiated by Rupert Murdoch with the 10p *Sun* in 1993), television advertising, redesigned and more numerous supplements and wheelbarrow loads of free DVDs. The recent major redesign of national newspapers with *The Times* and *Independent* moving to 'compact' editions and the *Guardian* moving to Berliner formats all express, at least in part, the editors' relentless search for new readers, new advertisers and sustained, if not increased, circulation. Variations in newspaper circulations reflect,

Table 1. Circulation of selected evening and morning titles, 1995–2005

(Newspaper title (evening)	Circulation		
	1995	2000	2005
Manchester Evening News	193,063	176,051 (−8.8%)	144,201 (−18.1%)
Birmingham Evening Mail	201,476	136,743 (−32.1%)	93,339 (−31.7%)
Leicester Mercury	118,594	111,652 (−5.9%)	82,232 (−26.3%)
Yorkshire Evening Post	106,794	100,794 (−5.6%)	68,767 (−31.8 %)
Sheffield Star	100,971	84,327 (−16.3%)	62,850 (−25.5%)
Newspaper title (morning)			
Yorkshire Post	79,094	76,424 (−3.4%)	50,541 (−33.9%)
Western Mail	64,602	55,273 (−14.4%)	42,981 (−22.2%)
Newcastle Journal	57,677	50,295 (−12.8%)	38,187 (−24.1%)
Ulster Newsletter	33,233	33,435 (+0.6%)	26,270 (−21.4%)
Birmingham Post	28,054	20,922 (−25.4%)	14,256 (−31.9%)

Source: Franklin (2006. 7).

Note: Figures in brackets in the 2000 column represent circulation decline between 1995 and 2000 expressed as a percentage. Bracketed figures in the column 2005 represent percentage circulation declines for the period 2000 to 2005).

at least in part, broader patterns of media consumption and the size of audiences for **radio**, **television** and **Internet** services.

FURTHER READING

Audit Bureau of Circulation: http://www.abc.org.uk

Franklin, B. (2008) *Pulling Newspapers Apart: Analysing Print Journalism*. London: Routledge.

Richardson, J.E.R. (2005) 'Circulation', in *Journalism Studies: Key Concepts*. London: Sage. pp. 36–7.

Hargreaves, I. and Thomas, J. (2002) *New News, Old News*. London: ITC/BSC.

Newspaper Society (2006) http://www.newspapersoc.org.uk/Default.aspx?page=951

key concepts in
public relations

Circulation (Internet)

According to the web traffic ranking service Alexa (accessed on 5 May 2008) half of the top 10 websites globally are search engines or directories: Yahoo.com (1), Google (2), Windows Live (4), MSN (5) and Yahoo.jp. The top content-based site is YouTube, ranked third, with social networking sites MySpace (6) and Facebook (8) also scoring highly. The other entries in the top 10 are Wikipedia (7) and Blogger (9). It is noteworthy that all the content-based entries in the top 10 are highly interactive websites with a mass of user-generated content. The most highly rated sites that are principally concerned with the one-way transmission of information are Microsoft.com (14) and imdb.com (27 – the Internet movie database). While news is available on both Yahoo! and Google, the top rated site that is news-driven (and an offshoot of the MSM) is BBC News (46). CNN (50) and ESPN Sportszone (65) are not far behind, but the only newspaper website in the top 100 is the *New York Times* (97). Among British users, the BBC News makes the top 10 (7) and the top newspaper is the *Guardian* (27).

FURTHER READING

Alexa: http://www.alexa.com

QL

Client

As in other professional practices, a client is the paying customer. A client relationship normally differs from ordinary customer relationships in that it implies a degree of professional trust and is bounded by professional ethics. In particular public relations professionals, like lawyers and accountants, owe their clients integrity of advice and confidentiality. It is a PR professional's duty to offer a client the best advice, in the client's interest. It would be unprofessional to bias advice in favour of that which maximises ongoing business.

Respecting the confidentiality of business information is fundamental to good PR practice. PR professionals will normally be privy to market-sensitive information long before it is made public, and absolute trust is essential for this relationship to succeed. In financial PR the ordinary professional duty of confidentiality is reinforced by legal restrictions on the release of market sensitive information and on insider trading.

Client handling skills and the ability to find new business are central to success in PR consultancy. To reach the highest level it is not normally sufficient to excel at PR practice. Generating new business is usually considered a prerequisite for appointment as a board director. Client contracts normally come in two types: retained contracts, usually renewed for a year at a time; and project contracts, which are for a fixed term or for the completion of specified tasks.

Consultancies usually bill clients by the hour at an agreed rate for each team member. Hourly rates are calculated on the assumption that employees should generate three times their annual salary (sometimes discounted to twice the salary for consultants seconded full-time to a client). PR teams employed **in-house** (qv) frequently replicate the client–consultancy relationship to create accountable management structures.

FURTHER READING

Beard, M. (2001) *Running a Public Relations Department*. London, CIPR.
Kitchen, P. (1997) *Public Relations: Principles and Practice*. London: Thomson.

QL

Codes of Conduct

There are two principal standards for defining a professional: one is the opposite of amateur, someone who is paid for the task; the other is a member of a learned trade governed by appropriate standards of behaviour (Dictionary.com, accessed 19 September 2007). It is an objective of professional institutes such as the Chartered Institute of Public Relations and the Public Relations Society of America that PR should be seen to be a profession in the sense of the second definition given above, and not merely the first. Both institutes therefore publish codes of conduct, binding on all members and enforced by the institutes acting in a quasi-judicial manner. The CIPR Code requires members to, first:

- Maintain the highest standards of professional endeavour, integrity, confidentiality, financial propriety and personal conduct.
- Deal honestly and fairly in business with employers, employees, clients, fellow professionals, other professions and the **public**.

The Code also sets out three principles of good practice: integrity, competence and confidentiality. It should be noted that these principles, and the similar ones promulgated by PRSA, are general principles and, within the traditions of Anglo-American Common Law, and are interpreted by qualified professionals according to precedent. There are potential conflicts between the principles. Conflict could arise between the obligation to deal honestly and fairly with the public and the obligation to maintain confidentiality, if, for example, a client were behaving in a dishonest or unprincipled way. It is the obligation of individual professionals, perhaps taking advice from their professional institute, to reconcile such conflicts using their own judgement.

The PRSA Code gives examples of unacceptable behaviour, but does not seek to lay down rigid prescriptions in the manner of a Civil Law jurisdiction, and so remove the judgement from the individual professional. In their operation, these codes are similar to those of other learned professions such as the law. Indeed, following the Enron scandal and the consequent demise of international accounting firm Andersen, it has been suggested that accountancy regulation in the USA should shift to one based on ethical principles (like the codes of the PRSA and CIPR, and British accounting institutes) rather than being rule-based. It should be noted that, although both CIPR and PRSA are able to expel members for breaching their codes, it is not necessary to be a member of a professional organisation in order to practice. (This is also true for most accountants, but not for lawyers.) This means that anyone expelled can continue to practice. Indeed, rather than be formally expelled, practitioners have found it expedient to resign from the institute while investigation is still proceeding.

FURTHER READING

CIPR: http://www.cipr.co.uk/direct/membership.asp?v1=code
Gregory, A. (2006) 'Ethics and professionalism in public relations', in R. Tench and
  L. Yeomans (eds), *Exploring Public Relations*. London: Prentice Hall. pp. 288–308.
PRSA: http://prsa.org/_About/ethics/preamble.asp?ident=eth3

QL

Commercial Speech

Although corporate speech on issues relating to political and social policies receives full First Amendment protection, speech related to a company's business may be considered commercial speech and subject to government regulation. Commercial speech has been defined in the USA by the Supreme Court as either speech that does 'no more than propose a commercial transaction' or as expression 'solely motivated by the desire for profit'.

This is potentially a major issue for the global **public relations** industry as the editorial boundaries between PR practitioners as information providers and the media as information mediators becomes blurred.

Advertisements promoting a product or service are not difficult to classify as commercial speech. They satisfy either definition used by the courts in the USA. But communication materials developed by PR practitioners as part of an information campaign for a client or organisation such as brochures, direct mail and information sheets are harder to classify.

From a PR perspective, the goal would be to have PR materials considered political or corporate speech, warranting high protection from government regulation. PR campaigns are designed to foster relationships with publics. However many campaigns now lead the **communications** process and are specifically designed to sell a product, service or goods to a selected audience. Therefore, restricting commercial speech to speech that does no more than propose a commercial transaction works to the PR professionals' advantage. However, when the Court uses the

key concepts in public relations

economic motivation definition, a great deal of PR speech falls under the commercial speech umbrella and becomes subject to **regulation.**

Even a PR consultant's economic report has been held to be commercial speech because it was prepared for a **client** 'embarking on a marketing campaign'. In May 2002 the California Supreme Court held that Nike's efforts to refute allegations that its foreign factories were sweatshops constituted commercial, not corporate, speech and were therefore subject to state laws prohibiting false and misleading advertising.

Nike had sought to counter the allegations concerning its labour practices by issuing statements defending its record in 'press releases, in letters to newspapers, in a letter to university presidents and athletic directors, and in other documents distributed for public relations purposes'. According to the Court, Nike's messages were commercial speech because they were directed by a commercial speaker to a commercial audience, and because they made representations about the speaker's own business operations for the purpose of promoting sales of its products. The court's opinion should serve as a reminder to public relations professionals that their efforts may well be considered commercial speech and subject to government regulation.

FURTHER READING

Gower, K. (2003) Legal and Ethical Restraints on Public Relations. Chicago, IL: Waveland Press.
Kasky v *Nike*, Inc, 27 CFal. 4th 939 (2002).

EP

Communication

The transmission of information and meaning through speech, text, symbols or images, and behaviour. As 'social animals' (Aronson, 1972), communication is essential for human society.

Within the **public relations** context, communication is an integral function, perhaps definitive, of the profession, whether this is internal within an organisation (to employees or key **stakeholders**), or to external stakeholders and **publics.**

Indeed the concept forms some of the key definitions of the profession – the Department of Trade and Industry (a government department in the UK), in conjunction with the Chartered Institute of Public Relations, recently defined PR as 'influencing behaviour to achieve objectives through the effective management of relationships and communications' (2003: 10).

Much of what is now PR theory originated from academic schools of management and **communication**, and the ways in which organisations communicate to stakeholders and publics forms the basis of much of the work of James Grunig, one of the most recognised PR theorists.

FURTHER READING

Aronson, E. (1972) *The Social Animal*. New York: Viking.

Grunig, J.E. (1992) *Excellence in Public Relations and Communication Management*. Hillsdale, NJ: Lawrence Erlbaum Associates.

Grunig, J.E. and Hunt, T. (1984) *Managing Public Relations*. New York: Holt, Rinehart and Winstone.

Tench, R. and Yeomans, L. (2006) *Exploring Public Relations*. Harlow: Prentice Hall.

NM

Communications Audit

Communications audit is the name given to a thorough analysis of the **communications** processes (internal and external) of an organisation. The aim is to compare the communications objectives (as understood by senior management) with both the output (messages transmitted) and the outcomes (messages received) in all target audiences. The audit should provide the strategic leadership of the organisation with credible and actionable information about the scope, reliability, efficiency, credibility and economy of communications practices and programmes.

Like financial audits, communications audits can be conducted internally or externally, but an external audit is likely to have greater credibility. External auditors will have a stronger focus on the task, the time to devote to it, and core stakeholder groups (especially staff) are more likely to believe in their confidentiality, and thus be more direct. Some practitioners recommend that a full communications audit should be conducted every five to seven years, provided effective research and evaluation practices are in place to provide interim feedback; audits may also be desirable following mergers, acquisitions, or other strategic reviews or repositioning.

An audit starts with the organisation's communications philosophy, if any, including any written policies. From there it proceeds to the goals and objectives, before examining specific communication vehicles, which will include not merely those under the control of the **public relations** department (such as **media relations**, website, etc.) but also such things as word of mouth communications by all external facing staff, internal noticeboards, and the practices of management with regard to internal briefings.

A comprehensive assessment of communications outcomes involves detailed research based on surveys, **focus groups** and one-to-one interviews. These would be conducted with all of Haywood's six target publics (see **public relations** qv). After a series of in-depth meetings with senior management, which would define long- and short-term goals, and specific objectives for the organisation's communication, there would be two phases. The internal phase would look at all communication channels, and conduct surveys, focus groups and interviews with staff. Ideally, all staff would be covered by the survey, and there would be a focus group and interviews in each functional group. The external phase would replicate the internal with external target audiences. Normally, a communications audit concludes with recommendations.

FURTHER READING

Haywood, R. (1991) *All About Public Relations: How to Build Business Success on Good Communications.* London: McGraw-Hill.

Kitchen, P. (1997) *Public Relations: Principles and Practice.* London: Thomson.

Kopec Associates: http://kopecassociates.com/audits.aspx

communications audit

49

Communications Strategy

Communications strategy is the device which delivers the **key messages** to the target **audience**. To arrive at that strategy, which is essentially a pipeline or conduit for transmission, five steps have to be undertaken. First, the target for the **communications** has to be identified – one discrete group or multi-location – as this will have an impact on the techniques used. For example, a direct mail approach to animal owners offering pet insurance would be more effective than a broad-based **advertising campaign**. Second, **horizon scanning** needs to be initiated. What is the current public perception of the company/organisation? Is there anything in sight which could derail the strategy such as a television documentary alleging slave labour wages in supplier factories? Third, the components of the communication need to be examined. Is this a major press launch; behind the scenes **lobbying**, or simply the **Friday night drop?** Fourth, the strategy roll-out where all the above elements come together. And finally there is **evaluation** – did we hit the target? How often and how successfully? Two elements can interfere with the smooth running of a communications strategy: noise and feedback. Noise occurs not just in the physical sense but has more to do with external distortion, either deliberate or accidental, of the key messages. Feedback is where the receiver of the communications responds in a way which might indicate the need to alter the output at a later date. In both cases continuous measurement is the only way of ensuring a strategy is delivering on its targets.

FURTHER READING

Harrison, S. (1995) *Public Relations: An Introduction*. London: Routledge.

MH

key concepts in public relations

Conflict of Interest

Conflicts of interest often arise in **public relations** practice and are dealt with under a range of codes of behaviour. The Chartered Institute of Public Relations (CIPR) says that conflicts of interest must be declared to clients. They must be expressed in written form along with the circumstances that give rise to them. The **Code** then allows the client or employer to decide to consent to work being continued.

In practice conflicts of interest are usually clear cut. For example a consultancy could be working with one brand in a competitive market and one of the brands' competitors asks for the agency to pitch for their business. This is a clear conflict and must be highlighted to either the approaching organisation or the client. However there are situations where the boundaries are blurred or where a change in the business environment can create a conflict.

A PR professional, for example, might represent a sports retailer targeting different sections of the sports market and different stakeholders and media. The consultancy could also appoint a different team of consultants to work on each account. So long as both **clients** are comfortable with the arrangement then the consultancy is free to represent both brands.

There could also be situations in which a consultancy represents, for example, a computer retailer and a mobile phone company. Due to market opportunity, the computer retailer moves into the mobile phones market and you then have a clear conflict within the consultancy. In practice, fee income generation and long-term opportunity usually wins the day and management decisions are made accordingly. It may include resigning one of the accounts but not before all attempts are made to allow the consultancy to represent both companies.

In the long run, even if the clients accept the conflict, there can be clashes and operational difficulties. One organisation may pay a higher fee to the consultancy and therefore expect greater care and attention is given to their business. That organisation may demand the most knowledgeable staff with all the best media contacts works for their business only.

There are further issues of confidentiality and sensitive market information. For example, if a consultancy is representing two competitor brands, staff are privy to confidential marketing and sales information for each client. There could be pressure from the client on junior staff to reveal market sensitive information about their competitor. Again the CIPR code says that 'insider' information must not be disclosed.

Conflicts of interest may also arise at an individual level where consultants may feel uncomfortable working with a particular client in a particular market. For example, consultants may feel unhappy representing tobacco, drinks or fast food companies based on a personal moral and ethical code. Many consultancies do have clauses that allow employees to opt out of working with such companies but in reality, if the **brand** is strong and the fee income impressive, pressure can be placed on staff to work on high income accounts even if they are unhappy about the product the client markets.

FURTHER READING

Bevins, T.H. (1993) 'Public relations, professionalism, and the public interest', *Journal of Business Ethics*, 12: 117–26.

Cutlip, S.M., Center, A.H. and Broom, G.M. (2000) *Effective Public Relations*, 8th edn. Upper Saddle River, NJ: Prentice Hall.

MORI (2004) *Annual Corporate Social Responsibility Study*. London: MORI.

Tench, R. and Yeomans, L. (2006) *Exploring Public Relations*. Upper Saddle River, NJ: Prentice Hall.

EP

Consultancy

PR consultancies, also known as agencies, are businesses that provide specialist **public relations** and marketing **communications** services to a range of clients. Consultancies broadly take two forms – **full service** or specialist and they range in size from a one-person owner manager to multi-national organisations offering clients global reach. Often, these global consultancies are subsidiaries of larger marketing communications consultancies, which also offer **advertising**, market research, design and an array of other specialist communications services.

Full service consultancies offer **clients** the full range of PR services across a range of business and industry sectors. These services offer expertise in marketing communications, consumer branding, business to business, corporate or City, **lobbying**, crisis, healthcare, issues, Internet, sports marketing and training. The specialist firms are smaller and focus on particular markets such as **consumer PR**, healthcare and publicity.

Consultants sell their time to clients and charge by the hour for their expertise. They are represented in the UK by the Public Relations Consultancy Association and members are bound by a code of conduct. The largest global PR consultancy **brands** include Hill & Knowlton, Porter Novelli and Weber Shandwick

FURTHER READING

Culbertson, H.M. and Chen, N. (1996) *International Public Relations: A Comparative Analysis*. Mahwah, NJ: Lawrence Erlbaum.
Vercic, D. and Krishnamurthy, S. (ed.) (2003) *The Global Public Relations Handbook: Theory, Research, Practice*. Mahwah, NJ: Lawrence Erlbaum.

EP

Consumer
Public Relations

Consumer PR tends to be a commercially driven service which aims to connect a **brand**, product or service with its core purchasers. The aim of consumer **public relations** is to surround the target consumer with information and publicity in order to inform those purchasers and potential purchasers of the unique selling points of the product in a bid to create positive impressions of the brand, service, product or goods. Good consumer impressions mean increased sales volume.

Consumer PR has long been considered the 'public face' of the industry and often branded lightweight and fluffy. While that element exists, in truth, great consumer PR is the heartbeat of any leading PR consultancy. At the core of consumer PR is the ability to develop great publicity ideas and 'sell' them to journalists in order to get media coverage to target **audiences**. By 'sell', we mean pitch story ideas in order for the **journalist** to get an idea of how that story can fit in with the editorial agenda of the publication or programme. This involves creating news, developing a press release and then phoning or e-mailing journalists with the story idea. It tends to involve a short conversation highlighting the key 'headline' of the story and developing the interest of the journalist. One of the biggest complaints from journalists is that the news stories are not relevant, they are poorly written, sent to the wrong journalist and include too much corporate information.

Tactics used by consumer PR practitioners to manufacture news include creating research on behalf of a client which allows the consultant to develop a range of 'stories' with branded messages. This gives the journalist a good story angle and the client branded coverage; using a **celebrity** to 'front' a campaign. Celebrities are used for their ability to generate media coverage. PR practitioners buy the time of leading celebrities to act as endorsers of a product. This tactic is used when launching a new product to gain as much publicity as possible in order to put the product at the front of the consumer's mind and differentiated from its competitors.

FURTHER READING

Green, A. (1999) *Creativity in Public Relations*. London: Kogan Page.

Kotler, P. (2003) *Marketing Insights from A to Z: 80 Concepts Every Manager Needs to Know*. New York: John Wiley & Sons.

Lewis, D. and Bridger, D. (2003) *The Soul of the New Consumer*. London: Nicholas Brealey.

Tench, R. and Yeomans, L. (2006) *Exploring Public Relations*. Harlow: Pearson.

EP

key concepts in
public relations

Contacts

The process of **networking** will result in a number of contacts (individuals or organisations) that are vital to effective **communication**. The idea of the long 'business lunch' is a familiar stereotype in **public relations** but can in fact produce more subtle and targeted results than blanket information releases.

Contacts may be individuals with a shared background (such as education – known as the 'old school tie' network in the UK), or with whom there is a mutual respect and trust (see **Guanxi**). In reality, they are more likely to be those who have a particular knowledge or sympathy concerning particular issues.

In a practical context a practitioner is likely to have a range of individual contacts to approach for information or to target specifically when releasing information, such as specialist analysts or commentators, or particular **journalists**.

NM

Content Analysis

Content analysis is a **quantitative** research method that is used to describe the content of texts. These can be written, audio, visual or multimedia – for example, newspaper clippings, television broadcasts, radio broadcasts, **advertisements**, company reports or websites.

The origins can be traced to the Second World War during which Allied intelligence units monitored texts as diverse as enemy communications and the kinds of music played on popular radio to estimate changes in troop concentrations. The technique became popular in communications research after the war in an attempt to investigate the success of techniques of **persuasion** and **propaganda**. Following this, but particularly in the 1970s and 1980s, content analysis figured prominently in research into popular entertainment, particularly that relating to **regulation** of television, print and radio as a result of concerns over levels of violence and sexual content (see, for example, the works of George Gerbner et al. [1969, 1979]).

As with other quantitative methods the parameters of the research must be carefully established before beginning the analysis. In content analysis the researcher must define the *unit of analysis* – the specific text (or part of it) to be considered. To take the example of print journalism, this could be all of the articles in a particular newspaper, all of the articles on the front page or all of the headlines on the front page.

The *units of measurement* must also be predetermined – these are the specific instances that are being counted. Some examples might include those analogous to **demographics** – the publication itself; date; article length, position in the newspaper and so on, and those specific to the research – for example, the sources that are quoted (directly or indirectly); references to commercial competitors/rival organisations; the **key messages** that appear; the kinds of imagery used.

These elements should ideally be agreed by more than one researcher to remove any possibility of subjectively assessing the material under consideration. Testing that several observers would quantify the same text in the same way is known as *inter-coder reliability*.

As a quantitative technique, a large amount of data can be collected and quickly analysed using simple statistics, and content analysis can also span a considerable time period, allowing comparisons across weeks, months, years or decades. This will often require the construction of a representative sample – a subsection of all the material available. Some considerations specific to content analysis are discussed in the section under **sampling**.

Content analysis can be used simply to describe **communication** content to give a context in which a particular topic or issue is portrayed. It may also be used to compare media content to the 'real world' to investigate the representation of particular issues or sections of society.

In terms of **public relations** research, the technique is often used to assess the sheer volume of media coverage that a particular **campaign** generates, or to gauge the ways in which the media are reacting to specific **key messages**. This simple analysis of press clippings (for example) is often used in the **evaluation** of a particular campaign, while other independent media monitoring organisations provide publicly available data on business and political topics (for example *Media Tenor*).

Essentially this is a descriptive technique and it is important to note the limitations of the technique. The fact that 70 per cent of peak-time television programming featured advertisements for a particular soft drink does not necessarily mean that the **audience** of those programmes had an overwhelming desire to purchase the product. This is one of the prominent criticisms of media effects research – incidences of violence on television cannot be said to make the viewer violent. For this reason, content analysis is often used in combination with other research techniques – see the section under **methodology**.

FURTHER READING

Davies, M.M. and Mosdell, N. (2006) *Practical Research Methods for Media and Cultural Studies: Making People Count*. Edinburgh: Edinburgh University Press.

Deacon, D., Pickering, M., Golding, P. and Murdock, G. (1999) *Researching Communications: A Practical Guide to Methods in Media and Cultural Analysis*. London: Arnold.

Media Tenor: http://www.mediatenor.com/

Wimmer, R.D. and Dominick, J.R. (2006) Mass *Media Research: An Introduction*. Belmont CA: Wadsworth.

NM

Continuous Professional Development

Continuous professional development (CPD) is the name for the schemes run by a variety of professional institutes, including the Chartered Institute of Public Relations (CIPR). In the USA the Public Relations Society of America's (PRSA) scheme is simply called Professional Development. CIPR's CPD scheme is branded as 'Developing Excellence'. CPD schemes are not qualifications. Most, including Developing Excellence, require keeping a record of developmental activities such as attending training events and involvement with professional institutes. In general, institutes without compulsory CPD find that enrollment of around 25 per cent is normal. In some professional institutes CPD enrollment is compulsory. The Institute of Chartered Accountants England and Wales (ICAEW), for example, has this requirement. Without it, professional practice certificates will not be renewed and a member cannot progress to Fellowship. In public relations, however, no professional practice certificate or membership of a professional institute is required in law. It should be noted that, even in the case of ICAEW, professional practice certificates are

CPD

57

only required for accountants who conduct the audit of public companies, a very specific task which most accountants are not called upon to perform.

Developing Excellence divides goals into three areas: professional practice; education and training and personal development. Specific success criteria are required for the plan. Some levels of CIPR membership – including accredited practitioner – require CPD enrolment. In the USA, accredited practitioner status depends on passing exams, something which the UK scheme does not require, though the CIPR Diploma qualifies associate members for faster track admission to full membership and, ultimately, accredited practitioner status. CIPR has announced a new Chartered Practitioner status, in accordance with the institute's new status as a chartered body.

FURTHER READING

CIPR: http://www.cipr.co.uk/member_area/cpd/main.asp
PRSA: http://www.prsa.org/_Advance/main/index.asp

QL

Convergence

Convergence and **brand stretching** are core themes in the development of the media in the digital world. New media channels create new outlets for existing media **brands**, thus leading to new areas in which previously niche brands now compete against each other. This is true in both geographic and technological senses. For example, the journalism of the *New York Times* is now available much more widely, where the hard copy ('dead tree' version, in web-parlance) is not easily obtained. This puts the paper in direct competition with non-American newspapers. But it is not only newspapers which are providing written news services online – television and radio stations do the same. So nytimes.com now directly competes with news.bbc.co.uk even though they are historically based in different media channels and in different countries.

An interesting example of media products now planning their content on a multi-media basis is the photo competition run in 2004 by *Today* the premier news and current affairs programme on BBC Radio 4, UK. The BBC claimed it as the first instance of a photo competition on a radio programme.

In 2006, the *Daily Telegraph* reorganised its newsroom and required journalists to produce all stories in written, audio and video form for its website as well as a written version for the dead tree edition.

Just as news organisations have stretched their brands into online offerings, online organisations have stretched theirs into offering news. Search engines such as Yahoo! and Google permanently scan the web for news stories and post them on their news sites. Sophisticated algorithms analyse the stories and rank them according to their news-worthiness. This enables the sites to provide competitive, up-to-date news offerings without employing journalists.

As of 2004, one difficulty for the algorithms was in distinguishing satirical items from real news. On 30 November 2004 the lead story on Google News was that President George W Bush had been arrested in Ottawa for war crimes, during his state visit to Canada. The story, which seems to have originated from a site called Axis of Logic, was, in its original form, clearly labelled as satire, but Google's computers nonetheless ranked the story as the most significant of the day.

QL

Copyright

All unique literary and artistic work in English law is automatically covered by copyright. It is not necessary to register copyright as it is with patents and trademarks, though it may be necessary to prove the date of creation in order to enforce the right. Copyright covers writing, painting, photography, music, dance and a host of other fields of art.

It is not necessary to prove that the work is of any merit, merely that the creator made judgements, such as selecting a camera angle or choosing words. It is not necessary in the UK or in America to display the international copyright symbol '©' for work to be covered by copyright law, however doing so ensures the work is protected (at least theoretically) in all countries which are signatories to the Universal Copyright Convention.

Copyright does not protect a concept or idea – as was recently reaffirmed in the Da Vinci Code case. The plaintiffs in this case alleged that author, Dan Brown, used ideas from their book *The Holy Blood and the Holy Grail*, for his bestselling novel. That Brown was influenced by their ideas was not in dispute, but the plaintiffs nonetheless lost the case. This is because it is the way the idea is expressed that is the property of the copyright owner. Copyright in the EU normally persists until 70 years after the death of the creator. In the case of a film, it is for 70 years after the death of the last surviving of the principal director, authors of the screenplay and dialogue, and composer of any music especially commissioned for the film.

Copyright is normally owned by the creator(s), though this is not always the case for employees who created the work on their employer's time. For employees and contractors, contracts should state who owns copyright in any work created. If the contract does not explicitly resolve the issue a range of factors will be considered including the norm for the industry and the extent to which the employee was directly controlled by the employer.

In commissioning work on behalf of a **client** from a contractor there are three possible owners of the copyright: the client who paid for the work, the agent who commissioned the work and the contractor who created the work. Contracts should be explicit and consistent with one another: that is, an agent who promises to provide copyright to a client must ensure that contracts with suppliers allow for this.

FURTHER READING

Intellectual Property Office: http://www.ipo.gov.uk/whatis-copy.htm

Corporate Communication

Corporate communication is the umbrella expression to describe how an organisation talks to itself and to the outside world. It is grounded in corporate **reputation** and grows out of corporate identity; the core purpose of the organisation. Core purpose has been defined by one CEO of a multi-national as 'what gets me up in the morning and off to work'. Quite literally, it is what the corporation stands for and knowledge of this is an essential prerequisite to any corporate communications strategy.

Typically the corporate communications function embraces reputation management including **Crisis PR, media relations,** investor relations, internal communications, social programmes **(CSR)** and advertising. Central to the success of corporate communications is its integration with the rest of the business putting it on an equal footing with other lead departments such as marketing and finance. The success or otherwise of a corporate communications strategy depends on where the communications function sits within the organisation. If it forms part of the 'dominant coalition' or the inner circle of decision makers an effective strategy is assured. Being part of that circle provides what has been called 'top cover'; or demonstrable support from main board, which central to the delivery of corporate communications.

FURTHER READING

Gregory, A. (1997) *Planning and Managing a Public Relations Campaign.* London: Routledge.

Harrison, S. (1995) *Public Relations: An Introduction.* London: Routledge.

Tench, R. and Yeomans, L. (2006) *Exploring Public Relations.* Harlow: Pearson

corporate communication

MH

Corporate Social Responsibility

Corporate social responsibility (CSR) is predicated on the belief that there is more to business than business. It is supported by the idea that trade brings obligations. In capitalist economics a company must return a profit to the shareholders but CSR argues that there are responsibilities to other stakeholder groups as well as to the environment and social justice. Arguably, CSR is not telling society what is good for society, but responding to what society tells the firm it wants and expects from it. Underlying this is the so-called **licence to operate**, which spells out the contract with society, a corporation's most valuable asset. Expressed broadly, CSR implies a company operates in a wider interest than just the narrow goal of increasing shareholder value; it aims to demonstrate that the positives of corporate activity outweigh the negatives.

The debate currently centres on whether CSR is a must have or just a nice to have. Critics argue it is no more than a corporate cosmetic, a **public relations** fig leaf, designed to cover up alleged bad behaviour by diverting attention to good works such as environmental remediation and the defence of human rights. What is certainly influencing the argument at the moment is the **24/7** world of globalised media where international companies quite literally have no hiding place in terms of worldwide **reputation**.

A global brand brings threats as well as opportunities. Many commentators agree that the key to acceptance or rejection of CSR has to be its measurability and the application of the **triple bottom line**. In parallel with this society's expectations have changed; corporations are no longer just about making money. Some corporations have already drawn up their own checklist of how the value of CSR can be judged. The Royal Dutch Shell Group argues that the application of CSR policies can reduce risk by meeting expectations; reduce costs by being more eco-efficient; evolve portfolios by anticipating market changes; influence innovation; attract more loyal customers; recruit and keep the brightest brains, and overall enhance the reputation of the **brand**. An ambitious list but one which many other multinationals will certainly sign up to.

FURTHER READING

Clutterbuck, D. (1992) *Actions Speak Louder: A Management Guide to CSR*. London: Kogan Page.

Schwartz, P. (1999) *When Good Companies Do bad Things*. New York; John Wiley and Sons.

MH

Creativity

A definition of creativity in relation to **public relations** is found in Andy Green's (1999) excellent *Creativity in Public Relations*. Green says, 'Creativity is the ability each of us has to create something new by bringing together two or more different elements in a new context, in order to provide added value to a task. A creative act consists of not only originating but also evaluating the added value it contributes. It is not novelty for its own sake, but it must produce some form of value that can be recognised by a third party 1999: 8.'

More broadly creativity is a mental process involving the generation of new ideas or concepts, or new associations between existing ideas or concepts. The products of creative thought usually have both originality and appropriateness. Although intuitively a simple phenomenon, it is in fact quite complex. It has been studied from the perspectives of others.

Unlike many phenomena in science, there is no single authoritative perspective or definition of creativity. Unlike many phenomena in psychology, there is no standardised measurement technique. Despite, or perhaps because of, the ambiguity and multi-dimensional nature of creativity, entire industries have been spawned from the pursuit of creative ideas and the development of creative techniques. This mysterious phenomenon, though undeniably important and constantly visible, seems to lie tantalizingly beyond the grasp of most people. It is nonetheless considered to be one of the most important elements in PR consultancy in providing clients with communications campaigns which differentiate products from their competitors.

A study of the importance of creativity in UK PR consultancy found that the ability to create memorable campaigns was ranked as one of the highest of abilities by some of the leading practitioners in the UK. The study also looked at the strategies firms employ to ensure creativity thrives in their respective environments (Cooper, 2002). The research identified a range of techniques most commonly used by some of the UK's leading consultancies to build distinctive campaigns. Techniques included brainstorming, Edward De Bono's Six Hats and Tony Buzan's Mind Mapping and visualisation. Taking the most widely used technique to explain more, brainstorming is designed to develop as many ideas as possible in a short period of time. The session should usually involve no fewer than four people and no more than 12 and last for no longer than one hour. Rules are applied to the group during the hour-long session which includes no idea being a bad idea and seniority being suspended. This allows for rapid idea generation and all feeling able to contribute to the session. The brainstorm is guided by a leader and a facilitator. The leader outlines the objectives of the brainstorm, while the facilitator 'captures' the ideas being discussed. In practice, this involves the facilitator writing down the ideas on a flip chart. Sometimes these ideas are displayed in the brainstorm venue to allow ideas to be connected.

One of the key concerns with the brainstorming technique is the lack of diversity within brainstorming groups and the development of group think. There is a need to build in diversity to the team and ensure the process is challenging in order to generate new and relevant ideas.

FURTHER READING

Belbin, R. (1997) *Team Roles at Work*. Oxford: Butterworth-Heinmann.
Cooper, D. (2002) 'Creativity in UK public relations, MA thesis, Cardiff University.
Green, A, (1999) *Creativity in Public Relations*. London: Kogan Page.
Kao, J. (1996) *Jamming*. London: HarperCollins.
Peters, T. (1996) *A Passion for Excellence*. London: Fontana

key concepts in
public relations

EP

Crisis Public Relations

Crisis PR, many practitioners believe, has one defining characteristic. It will happen to you. Working in the Fast Moving Consumer Goods (FMCG) area you might have to deal with a product recall after bottled water became contaminated. In travel PR, you might have the plane crash or the ferry sink. In the corporate world you could face allegations of fraud, environmental damage or government bribes. The list goes on. What is common to all such incidents is the absolute requirement for what has been described as an early yet considered response to the crisis (see **response statement**).

Textbook case histories are replete with examples of how companies got it right and got it wrong. The response of the then British Midland airline to a fatal plane crash on the M1 just short of the airport runway in the East Midlands merits a brief examination. The chairman, Sir Michael Bishop, assumed the role of main media spokesman, and delivered the first key messages. In summary they were: We regret what has happened and our thoughts are with the families. We will investigate the cause of the crash. And we will announce the results. Simple, cogent and above all appropriate to the circumstances, they have become a benchmark against which other responses can be judged.

Unfortunately many companies faced by a crisis go to a default mode which says 'no comment'. This leaves what crisis managers term the 'information vacuum', a veritable black hole which will be filled by the competition, the opposition or just plain media speculation. Crisis PR starts with the first lesson – seize the day. Normally this involves a **response statement** within the first hour of an incident; a fuller press release as soon as practicable and a strategy to get you through the next 72 hours. This may include a **press conference,** briefings **on or off the record**, a press pack and the activation of a **dark website.** Practitioners in crisis PR agree that handling the incident effectively has to be driven by speed of reaction; accuracy of information and transparency of process. In crisis mode, getting all three to line up is one of the greatest challenges PR practitioners can face.

FURTHER READING

Haywood, R. (1994) *Managing Your Reputation*. New York: McGraw Hill.
Regester, M. and Larkin, J. (2001) *Risk Issues and Crisis Management*. London: Kogan Page.

MH

Cybersquatting

Cybersquatting refers to the practice of buying Internet domain names which are, arguably, linked to trademarks or otherwise with intellectual property. There is a related practice of buying generic domain names solely for the purpose of selling them on, but cybersquatting, with the implication from the word 'squatting', refers specifically to taking possession of domain names which should properly belong to someone else. The cybersquatter's purpose is usually to sell the address or to put up an antagonistic site.

The antagonistic site may be motivated by hostility to the organisation (usually a company, sometimes a political candidate) or simply to drive the price higher. This practice has been likened to extortion.

In the early days of the Internet there was no procedure for resolving disputes as to domain name, and some were sold at a very high price. Alta-Vista – then the leading search engine and owned by computer hardware manufacturer Compaq – paid a reported US$3 million for the domain name altavista.com (without a hyphen) as many intending customers were visiting the alternative site by accident. (Reports vary as to the content on the alternative site. Some suggest it was pornography and others online gambling. Either way, it was embarrassing to Compaq.)

The courts were reluctant to become involved, being unsure as to jurisdiction. Some argued that the courts in the plaintiff's jurisdiction should hear the case, others favoured the jurisdiction of the defendant and still others that of the Internet host. It was unclear how a ruling could have been enforced in any event.

ICANN (the Internet Company for Assigned Names and Numbers) now has a disputes procedure. Where there is clear breach of a trademark and the organisation registering the domain has no particular claim on it, ICANN will normally find for the trademark owner. However an individual called Smith has as much claim to a domain as a company called Smith. Critics have suggested that by reinforcing trademark ownership, ICANN is siding with big business. A related activity called typosquatting – of which the Alta-Vista case was arguably an example – is taking possession of domain names very similar to those of established organisations, such as **www.microsofy.com**. Cybersquatting is related to the practice of establishing **rogue sites**, but is completely different from establishing **dark sites**.

FURTHER READING

ICANN: http://www.icann.org/udrp/udrp.htm

QL

Dark Sites

Dark sites should not be confused with rogue sites. A dark site is a website contained behind a firewall and not available for the public to see. Preparation of a dark site is a key task in crisis management as it enables an organisation to be fully prepared for a crisis without actually revealing information not yet in the public domain or not yet relevant. For example, a company which knows it is likely to be criticised in the media or by an NGO may have material refuting the allegations which it is expecting to be made. It would not wish to publish this material until the allegations actually have been made, so it would keep them on a dark site.

Another area of public relations in which dark sites are extremely useful is Financial Public Relations or investor relations. To avoid breaching the laws which prohibit insider trading, it is essential to release information to all shareholders (and potential investors) at exactly the same time. Privileged advance briefings of fund managers and brokers, or of staff, are no longer permitted. The precisely controlled nature of a dark site allows practitioners to prepare information in advance and in great detail, and then release it all at once with the flick of a switch.

QL

Defamation

Defamation in English law consists of two types: slander and libel. Slander is usually spoken while libel is printed or broadcast. Both slander and libel are torts, so (with very few exceptions) the aggrieved party must initiate a lawsuit.

A tort cannot be prosecuted as a crime would be. It is the responsibility of the complainant to show that the defamation took place – that is, that the words were spoken or that the material was published. The complainant must also show that the material is defamatory – that is, that it lowers the complainant's reputation in the eyes of a reasonable person. It is not enough to show that *some* people will think less of the complainant. For example, it has been suggested that calling someone gay is no longer defamatory in English law, though it undoubtedly once was. (Liberace, and others, have successfully sued for this defamation in the past. More recent actions, such as those by Jason Donovan and Robbie Williams, have focused on the implication of dishonesty.)

Defences against an action for defamation include *justification* (that the charges published are substantially true), *fair comment* (that a reasonable person could well have believed the charges on the basis of the evidence available) and *privilege* (that the defendant had a duty to publish). Qualified privilege can cover material written in, for example, a job reference or appraisal or material published by a newspaper. However a defence of qualified privilege will fail if the material was published maliciously or recklessly, and this can include, in the case of a newspaper, neglecting normal journalistic procedures.

Testimony given on oath in court and speeches given in Parliament are covered by absolute privilege and are not actionable, even when malicious. Reporting statements made in court or Parliament is also not actionable, provided it is a neutral reporting of what was said. It is the defendant's responsibility to prove the defence. All proof must be established on the balance of probability (not beyond reasonable doubt) to the satisfaction of the jury. Uniquely, in English law, the jury also assesses damages.

Some countries have a crime of libel (almost never prosecuted in the UK, though still on the statute books). The European Court of Human Rights has declared that such a criminal offence breaches the right to free speech. An action can be pursued in any jurisdiction where the complainant has a reputation and the material was published. In these days of online publishing this has led to 'jurisdiction shopping' – choosing the jurisdiction most favourable to the complainant. For example, the American boxing promoter Don King sued an American publication in England, because English libel laws are more restrictive than those in the USA.

FURTHER READING

Hadwin, S. and Bloy, D. (2007) *Law and the Media*. London: Butterworth.

QL

Demographics

A term deriving from the Greek *demos*, meaning the people, demographic information describes personal characteristics of certain segments of a population. Some typical elements include gender, age, nationality, religion, ethnicity, income level and so on.

In **marketing** and **advertising** particularly, the use of demographic profiling is a popular technique to target specific **campaigns**. This involves creating a hypothetical profile of a typical member of a particular subgroup, for example, 18–25-year-old males, in order to paint a picture of their attitudes and behaviours, and therefore to suggest particular ways in which they may be better informed, engaged or influenced.

Large databases of demographic information are publicly available, including those from census surveys that present information about entire populations. Demographics are clearly important in large-scale survey research, such as that used to gauge **public opinion**, since individual characteristics are likely to influence attitudes, behaviours and beliefs. Information about the characteristics of a population is also crucial to **sampling** techniques when constructing representative samples in order to conduct such research.

FURTHER READING

Davies, M.M. and Mosdell, N. (2006) *Practical Research Methods for Media and Cultural Studies: Making People Count.* Edinburgh: Edinburgh University Press.
Gunter, B. (2000) *Media Research Methods. Measuring Audience Reactions and Impact.* London: Sage.

NM

Destination Branding

Relatively new in terms of academic research, but with an arguably long history in geopolitical and economic examples, destination branding (also referred to as place branding or nation branding) encompasses the idea that geographical locations can benefit from the same kinds of techniques as the **branding** of commercial goods and services, in establishing analogues of unique identity and personality that attract business and consumer investment.

There are economic benefits for a destination to have a unique and appealing brand, which creates loyalty in the investors and consumers of that brand. Though some may view the branding of their own country in commercial terms as somewhat distasteful and contrary to their political and cultural history, tourism, as a fast-growing and extremely profitable global industry, can have a significant economic impact on a destination.

The World Tourism Organisation suggests that 'the twenty-first century will see the emergence of tourism destinations as fashion accessories. Indeed as style symbols, destinations can offer similar consumer benefits to highly branded lifestyle items' (Morgan et al., 2004: 4). Such benefits extend beyond the money spent in the destination by tourists themselves, but also have influence in terms of the additional development of local infrastructure, preservation of history and culture, focus of global attention and interest, attraction of overseas investment, stimulation of the reputation and export of local goods and services, and provision of an employment boost to the local economy.

Successful city brands are an obvious example of this phenomenon. National capitals such as London, Paris and Dublin have managed to create individual identities over and above those of the countries in which they are situated. Others that are not capital cities have also created 'unique destination propositions'. New York City has a clearly defined identity distinct from other American locations, and other non-capital cities such as Barcelona and Shanghai have exploited their own cultural, technological and innovative assets to establish themselves as distinctive locations within their own nations.

Global cultural and media events can also be utilised by those seeking to develop destination branding strategies. City branding initiatives can take advantage of regional and global competitions, such as the European City of Culture and World Expo events, as well as sporting tournaments such as the football, rugby and cricket world cup finals and the Olympic Games.

Destination branding can extend beyond individual cities to regions. Taking sporting events as an example, international competitions are usually distributed across several cities in a host country and can be used to highlight not only less publicised cities, but also rural areas of cultural, historic and aesthetic interest outside these individual tournament venues – for example, the use of Sydney's 2000 Olympics by Brand Western Australia. Other region branding initiatives include the recent (2007) African Cup of Nations in Ghana and the establishment of California as a regional brand offering sporting and recreational pursuits outside the well-known tourist destination cities in that area.

Destination branding can also extend to nations – the publicity of countries and the creation of, and association with, positive images or stereotypes of particular cultural, historic, aesthetic and social attributes in order to facilitate 'nation branding'. Again, global media events can play a part in this; for example, the much publicised on-location filming

of the cinematic blockbuster trilogy *Lord of the Rings* has had a significant tourism impact on 'Brand New Zealand'.

Nation branding can function not only as an attraction for tourism but
often as a socio-political imperative to create, nurture and sometimes rebrand, internal and external national identities. Perhaps not always formally
recognised as such, nonetheless, there have been strategic and sustained
branding and rebranding initiatives in former colonial and former communist countries over the last 60 years at least. This is often driven by a desire
to distance the modern image of a nation from an unpalatable history or
association, both for global political or economic reasons. Slovenia, for
example, has achieved a remarkable distance from its former communist
Yugoslavian past to become an attractive individual tourist destination in its
own right and a significant player on the European political stage (holding
the presidency of the European Union in 2008).

At the time of writing (2008), Kosovo is undergoing something of a
nation branding exercise, with the introduction of a new flag and discussions around the introduction of a new national anthem (distinct from its
ethnic ties to Albania), to reinforce its recent declaration of independence
from Serbia. The political and commercial benefits from membership of
global alliances such as the European Union and NATO are often an
incentive for nation branding initiatives that target both internal and
external **publics**.

Cities, regions and nations, just as commercial brands, are not immune
from events outside their control that may affect their brand equity. As
such, contingencies must be in place for **crisis management**. Potential
threats from recent global events such as avian flu, foot and mouth
disease and SARS, civil unrest, conflict and terrorism, and perceived
incompetence in constructing and organising events must all be
acknowledged in any destination branding strategy, whether it is at city,
regional or national level. New York City has been able to overcome
anxiety concerning security, and perhaps even capitalise on the events of
September, 11th, Athens, and by association Greece, was able to overcome accusations of mismanagement before and during the 2004
Olympic Games. At the time of writing, the potential for disastrous destination branding management for China's Beijing Olympics is ongoing.

FURTHER READING

Abimbola, T. (2006) 'Market access for developing economies: branding in Africa',
Place Branding, 2 (2): 108–17.

key concepts in
public relations

Anholt, S. (2005) Brand New Justice: The Upside of Global Branding. *Burlington, MA: Elsevier Butterworth-Heinemann.*

Anholt, S. (2006) 'The Anholt-GMI City Brands Index. How the world sees the world's cities', *Place Branding*, 2 (1): 18–31.

Chalip, L. and Costa, C.A. (2005) 'Sport event tourism and the destination brand: towards a general theory', *Sport in Society*, 8 (2): 218–37.

Konecnik, M. (2004) 'Evaluating Slovenia's image as a tourism destination: a self-analysis process towards building a destination brand', *The Journal of Brand Management*, 11 (4): 307–16.

Fall, L.T. (2004) 'The increasing role of public relations as a crisis management function: an empirical examination of communication restrategising efforts among destination organisation managers in the wake of 11th September, 2001', *Journal of Vacation Marketing*, 10 (3): 238–53.

Morgan, N., Pritchard, A. and Pride, R. (2004) *Destination Branding: Creating the unique destination proposition.* Oxford: Elsevier Butterworth-Heinemann.

NM

Diversity

The Chartered Institute of Public Relations (CIPR) in the UK launched its diversity action programme in 2005 at the World PR Conference in Trieste. It follows work developed by the Public Relations Society of America (PRSA) and considerable work by the advertising industry in the UK to attract an ethnically diverse workforce into the creative industries.

At the same time as the **public relations** profession grows, it simultaneously becomes more diverse and inclusive. Recent surveys show that there are already considerably more women working in PR than there are men. And, if anything, this trend is likely to accelerate – the vast majority of PR university students and new entrants to the PR profession are female. PR moreover remains an overwhelmingly 'white' profession, with far too few high-profile PR role models from minority groups. One of the key responsibilities borne by the CIPR is to lead the profession, and to help it face up to entrenched problems. The low visibility of minority groups is one such problem.

In broad definition terms and the social context, the term diversity refers to the presence in one population of a wide variety of cultures, languages, physical features, socio-economic backgrounds, opinions, religious beliefs, sexuality and gender identity.

At the international level, diversity refers to the existence of many peoples contributing their unique experiences to humanity's culture.

In a business context, diversity is approached as a strategy for improving employee retention and increasing consumer confidence. The 'business case for diversity', as it is often phrased, is that in a global and diverse marketplace, a company whose makeup mirrors the makeup of the marketplace it serves is better equipped to thrive in that marketplace than a company whose makeup is homogeneous.

Specifically in PR there is a long way to go in terms of addressing the diversity issue. There is no research which gives the basic facts on the ethnicity, age, social background, sexual orientation or disability of public relations practitioners in the UK. However the CIPR has anecdotal evidence of the following themes. Black and Asian candidates are not represented in PR, partly because of the image of the industry itself, but partly because there is a belief that there are barriers to promotion. There is some evidence that older graduates find it more difficult to secure a first job than 'traditional' graduates. PR still attracts middle-class people, although there is some evidence that candidates from working-class backgrounds are now entering the profession and doing well.

FURTHER READING

CIPR: http://www.cipr.co.uk/diversity

Graen, G.B. (ed.) (2003) *Dealing with Diversity*. Champaign-Urbana, IL: IAP.

Harvard Business Review (2001) *Managing Diversity*. Boston, MA: Harvard Business School Press.

Benson, R., Rainbird, D., Midgley, N., Braddock, K. and Stasler, B. (2005) *Creativeworld: The Fish Can Sing's Guide to the New Creative Economy*. London: The Fish Can Sing Ltd.

Mace, R., Holden, C.J. and Shennan, S. (2005) *The Evolution of Cultural Diversity. A Phylogenetic Approach*. London: Routledge Cavendish.

PRSA: http://www.prsa-ncc.org

EP

Dumbing Down

Advocates and opponents of the 'dumbing down debate' argued about the extent to which changing news values and news formats, evident in print and broadcast **journalism** during the 1980s and 1990s, were resulting in a 'dumbing down' of the reporting of news and current affairs. The debate engaged media academics (Sampson, 1996; Franklin, 1997), as well as print (Engel, 1996) and broadcast journalists (Clarke, 2003; Humphrys, 2005), who criticised national and local media for 'dumbing down', moving to 'tabloid' formats and stories and offering trivial 'infotainment' or 'Newszak' rather than 'high quality' programming and **news** and current affairs. Distinguished **editor** Harold Evans warned fellow **journalists** against 'the drift from substantive news to celebrity hunting, from news to entertainment' (1996: 1). But the debate about changing **news values** engaged both those who 'lament' the alleged decline in traditional journalism (Engel, 1996) as well as those enthusiasts, typically cultural theorists, who wished to celebrate the emergence of more popular cultural forms (Langer, 1998).

Proponents of the dumbing down thesis argued that recent trends in news presentation and content marked: (1) a retreat from investigative journalism and 'hard' news to the preferred terrain of 'softer' consumer or life style stories; (2) a focus on entertainment rather than information resulting in 'infotainment'; (3) journalists' preferences for human interest above the public interest; (4) news reports characterised by sensationalism rather than measured judgement; (5) the triumph of the trivial above the weighty which guaranteed that gossip about celebrities from soaps, sport and the Royal family assumed greater news salience than significant events of public consequence; and (6) the neglect of international affairs and the foregrounding of a domestic **agenda** typically dominated by crime stories. In summary, the 'dumbed down' news agenda reflects journalists' preference for 'stories which interest the **public** above stories which are in the public interest' (Franklin, 1997: 4); what McNair designates 'bonk journalism' (1999: 145) and Andrew Marr describes as 'bite-sized McNugget journalism' (cited in Morgan, 1996: 14).

The factors responsible for this alleged 'dumbing down' are identified as: (1) the increasingly competitive markets in which news media operate exacerbating the relentless search for readers and audiences; (2) government media policies which favour the proliferation of broadcast news services and enhanced competition for viewers and advertisers, as well as the regulation of content with a 'lighter touch'; (3) new technologies for print and broadcast media, which prompt de-skilling, multi-tasking, casualisation and job cuts along with the burgeoning of radio and television stations on satellite and digital platforms; and finally (4) the growth in **freelance** journalism and public and private sector **public relations** which, for the first time since the earliest days of journalism, have placed a large part of news production outside news media organisations and specifically the newsroom; in brief PR professionals are increasingly significant as a source of news stories for print, broadcast and online media (Franklin 1997: ch. 1).

The evidence to support the dumbing down thesis is hotly contested. Winston (2002), for example, compared television news contents and formats from the early *Bad News* studies of 1975 with an equivalent sample of broadcast news during 2000–2001 but noted no significant shifts. By contrast Barnett and Seymour's (1999) study of television across 20 years (1977–1997), observed striking changes especially the decline in the foreign news components of current affairs programming.

Newspaper editors, such as Alan Rusbridger of the *Guardian*, have counter-argued for a 'dumbing up' of news and a retreat from reports of celebrities and reality television. For their part, other academics, have suggested that recent developments signal the extent to which mainstream understandings of 'quality' news have too frequently been gendered (Costera Meijer, 2001) or the degree to which there has been a 'dumbing down of the workforce' in certain key respects (Ursell, 2003).

FURTHER READING

Barnett, S. and Seymour, E. (1999) *A Shrinking Iceberg Slowly Travelling South: Changing Trends in British Television – A Case Study of Drama and Current Affairs.* London: Campaign for Quality Television.

Franklin, B. (1997) *Newszak and News Media.* London: Arnold.

Humphrys, J. (2005) 'First do no harm', B. Franklin (ed.), *Television Policy: The MacTaggart Lectures.* Edinburgh: Edinburgh University Press. pp. 265–74.

Langer, J. (1998) *Tabloid Television: Popular Journalism and the 'Other News'.* London: Routledge.

Ursell, G. (2003) 'Creating value and valuing creation in contemporary UK television: or dumbing down the workforce', *Journalism Studies*, 4 (1): 31–46.

Winston, B. (2001) 'Towards tabloidisation? Glasgow revisited 1975–2001', *Journalism Studies*, 3 (1): 5–20.

BF

The readers of *British Journalism Review* pronounced Harold Evans, former Editor of the *Sunday Times, The Times* and the legendary *Northern Echo*, the most distinguished editor in UK **journalism** history; C.P. Scott (*Manchester Guardian* 1872–1929) came second. Twenty editors received at least a single vote, although no female editors received votes. This is perhaps unsurprising given that only a handful of women have occupied the editor's chair in national newspapers. Rosie Boycott at the *Express*, Janet Street Porter at the *Independent on Sunday* and Rebekah Wade, the first woman editor of a tabloid, at the *Sun* (since January 2003) have each blazed a trail for others to follow. Current editors were told not to vote for themselves; one found the temptation irresistible! (Hagerty, 2002: 6).

The editor is the most senior member of the editorial staff of any **news** organisation and is consequently judged accountable for all editorial decisions (Hadwin, 2006: 144–5). In truth, the editor sits at the top of a hierarchy of editors each with allocated responsibility for a distinctive area of the paper's editorial coverage – fashion, news, sport, politics – or production – sub-editor, night editor and picture editor.

In a newspaper, the editor typically stamps his or her authority on the paper and his or her judgement of what constitutes news predominates in the paper: David English's radical revamp of the *Daily Mail* and J.L. Garvin's transformation of the *Sunday Observer* offer obvious examples here (Evans, 2002: 7). But most significantly, the editor is the lynchpin which connects the editorial with the business side of the paper, linking **journalists**, readers, distributors, the owner, **advertisers** and even the humble newspaper street vendors; although most significantly editors must be 'close to the readers' (Hadwin, 2006: 143). Consequently, editors must achieve a delicate balancing act. As Evans notes 'if you lend one ear to staff and the other to readership, where do you find the third ear for ownership?' (2002: 11). Occasionally editors lose their balance, especially in their relationships with owners; they usually fall before retiring injured!

Two areas have proved especially destabilising. First, some owners try to intervene in the editorial affairs of their papers, insisting on a particular approach or 'party line' to the paper's editorial. Murdoch's

editor

insistence that the *Sun* should support new Labour in 1997, after many years backing the Conservative Party, attests to the influence of owners in shaping the editorial content and line of their papers. Murdoch has engaged in some very public spats with his editors, typically recorded in the editors' memoirs after they were sacked (Evans, 1994; Neil, 1997); Maxwell enjoyed a similar reputation. The Scott Trust, established by editor C. P. Scott, manages the financial affairs of the *Guardian* and offers a unique but ingenious way to resolve such disputes.

Second, editors and owners may find themselves structurally at loggerheads. The editor's role is to promote and protect the editorial quality and integrity of the newspaper while the owner is driven by the 'bottom line'; profitability and editorial integrity may collide. The editor, Hadwin claims 'is the custodian of the newspaper and must put the newspaper and its readers first ... the editor's decisions and judgements make the newspaper what it is' (2006: 148). They need 'to move beyond increasing profit margins into raising the sights of their journalists and their titles. Otherwise they are hastening the day when those margins collapse' while 'selling themselves' and 'their readers short' (Hadwin, 2006: 148). This is a dilemma which many editors of local and regional newspapers confront (Franklin, 2006: ch. 1)

FURTHER READING

Evans, H. (1994) *Good Times, Bad Times*. London: Coronet Books.

Franklin, B. (2006) 'Attacking the devil: local journalists and local newspapers in the UK', in *Local Journalism and Local Media: Making the Local News*. London: Routledge. pp. 3–16.

Hadwin, S. (2006) 'Real readers, real news: the work of a local newspaper editor', in B. Franklin (ed.), *Local Journalism and Local Media: Making the Local News*. London: Routledge. pp. 140–9.

Hagerty, B. (2002) 'Announcing the greatest editor of all time', *British Journalism Review*, 13 (4): 6.

Neil, A. (1997) *Full Disclosure*. London: Pan Books.

BF

Embargo

At 12.35 p.m. on 12 May 2006, the House of Commons' Select Committee on Public Affairs (PASC) issued a press release (Press Notice 42, Session 2005–6), headed 'PASC to hear from Sir Gus O'Donnell and the House of Lords Appointments Commission about Honours and Peerages', which announced that 'On Tuesday 16 May the Public Administration Select Committee will be taking evidence in public for its inquiry into Ethics and Standards in Public Life'. The press notice offered details of the intended line of questioning of the witnesses, provided the broad context for the ongoing inquiry as well as the alleged 'honours for cash' scandal, widely reported in the national press, which had triggered the specific focus for this particular meeting of the PASC. The notice concluded by offering a contact telephone and email for 'Media Enquiries' alongside the injunction 'Embargoed until 0001 Tuesday May 16'.

The embargo means that journalists are requested not to publish any information contained in the press release until after the time and date specified by the information provider. This 'prohibition' lacks any formal or statutory authority, and hence any obligation for journalists to comply – even though, on this occasion, the release emanates from a Parliamentary Select Committee – but it serves to illustrate neatly the often collaborative character of the relationships between **journalists** and news **sources** that characterises many of their mutually beneficial day-to-day working practices. Journalists and their sources of news are 'inextricably linked' (Blumler and Gurevitch, 1981: 473).

The embargo allows journalists, for example, to file a story with their news desk ahead of its planned publication date and provides both time and opportunity to complement the original release with additional interview(s), picture and quotation materials. With increasing **newsroom** pressures of time and cost, the embargo allows journalists to schedule their work across the news week. It also delivers an often detailed and complex story 'on a plate'; and to order! For the information source, the embargo offers the prospect of controlling the timing as well as the content of the information released. News coverage will be closely focused on a particular day rather than published across different news days and consequently its impact will be maximised, allowing the source a more comprehensive 'management' of the news agenda. **News management**, of course, is not a precise science but if a **public relations**

embargo

professional is able to time the release of information adverse to an organisation's interests this may allow them to release more favourable **news** to mask or offset the initial 'bad news'.

However, as noted above, there is no formal requirement for journalists to comply with embargoes and in a competitive market for news, journalists may be tempted to break the embargo and publish ahead of their rivals. Embargoes are unlikely to prove a sufficient brake on journalists' enthusiasm for a strong and breaking story; embargoes are effective in the context of routine news stories. But when journalists break an embargo in this way, they risk undermining what Mancini identifies as the 'trust' which is central to their effective working relationships with sources and public relations professionals (1993: 33). Blumler and Gurevitch claim such conflicts will be resolved promptly since the professional ambitions of both journalists and sources require a more peaceful and routinised coexistence (1981: 472).

FURTHER READING

Blumler, J.G. and Gurevitch, M. (1981) 'Politicians and the press: an essay on role relationships', D. Nimmo and L. Saunders (eds), *Handbook of Political Communication*. London: Sage. pp. 467–97.

Mancini, P. (1993) 'Between trust and suspicion: how political journalists solve the dilemma', *European Journal of Communication*, 8 (March): 33–53.

BF

Ethics

See **Codes of Conduct.**

key concepts in public relations

Evaluation

Like any other business, **public relations** needs to demonstrate its value. Evaluation is a fundamental way of doing this but historically evaluation has taken a back seat to delivery in the PR industry. In a sense, the industry has become its own worst enemy, failing to develop meaningful evaluation strategies at a price marketers are willing to bare. However, this picture is changing. As the marketing **communications model** changes in line with fracturing audiences and growth in media channels, no longer is it taken for granted that advertising leads the **communications** programme and therefore clients and businesses are investing in evaluation techniques which will assess the true value of a public relations campaign.

Anne Gregory (2000) describes three elements of programme evaluation – input, output and outcome. Input is the measure of what the PR professional does and how their work is distributed. An output measure maps how the inputs are used such as media mentions, readership, circulation and content analysis. An outcome measure is the end effect of the communication and is measured in three ways: changes at the thinking or awareness levels; changes in the attitude or opinion level; and changes in behaviour.

Evaluation **methodologies** include media **content analysis** to highlight positive and negative media coverage. Assessment of the reach of a campaign by adding up the total opportunities to see (OTS). This is a measure of the total number of target consumers who may see the communications message. Assessment of the column inches a campaign managed to achieve in newspaper coverage. This is a measurement of the amount of editorial coverage achieved by a campaign. A crude assessment measure used by practitioners is a comparison between the number of column inches of editorial coverage and the equivalent advertising spend.

Evaluation in PR, however, is becoming far more specialised with companies such as Echo Research and Mori using a range of quantitative and qualitative research techniques to analyse specific corporate messaging, editorial coverage and public opinion. Furthermore, in the UK the Chartered Institute of Public Relations (CIPR) has produced a number of guides that can assist in framing a suitable evaluation methodology for a given **campaign**. The global industry is working on a common standard but it is proving hard to apply with various organisations adopting different approaches to evaluation from the objective-led to measuring the quality of relationships.

FURTHER READING

Beard, M. (2001) *Running a Public Relations Department*, 2nd edn. London: Kogan Page.

Echo Research: http://www.echoresearch.co.uk

Gregory, A. (2000) *Planning and Managing Public Relations Campaigns*, 2nd edn. London: Kogan Page.

Kitchen, P.J. (1997) *Public Relations Principles and Practice*. London: International Thomson Business Press.

Fairchild, M. (1999) *The Public Relations Research and Evaluation Toolkit: How to Measure the Effectiveness of PR*. London: Institute of Public Relations and Public Relations Consultants Association with PR Week.

Mori: http://www.mori.co.uk

EP

Event Management

American writer Daniel Boorstin has described what he termed the pseudo event; and one of the founding fathers of PR, Edward Bernays, has written about creating 'events as news'. In other words events might not be events after all in the sense of a spontaneous happening, but a creation to max-imise coverage. The essence of the PR event, quite simply, is to achieve pub-licity and the management of such events is a key part of the PR skillset.

In **Model** theory the most obvious user of events is the publicist: the Oscar ceremony; the product launch or the celebrity interview. Events are frequently used in **Financial Public Relations** such as the annual general meeting or quarterly presentations of results. Another way of looking at the event is to think of it in terms of the 'photo opportunity'. A good picture may indeed be worth a thousand words and nowhere is this more apposite than in event management.

Careful planning with an eye to the picture and **Soundbite** as well as skilful managing on the day are prerequisites. Of course, some events will not require being 'manufactured'. A new signing for a soccer club or a factory opening for example. But mostly the creative ingenuity of the PR professional will be required to create an 'event as news'.

MH

Excellence Theory

Excellence theory suggests that the two-way symmetric **model** of PR is best practice. Grunig wrote that:

> **Public Relations** contributes to organisational effectiveness when it helps to reconcile the organisation's goals with the expectations of its strategic constituencies. This contribution has monetary value to the organisation's.
>
> PR contributes to effectiveness by building quality long-term relationships with strategic constituencies. PR is most likely to contribute to its effectiveness when the senior PR manager is a member of the dominant coalition (… of decision makers) where he or she is able to help shape the organisation's goals and to help determine which external **publics** are most strategic.' (Dozier et al., 1995)

Grunig identified four levels of excellence: the programme level where PR is managed strategically; the departmental level that tracks how PR fits within the business; the organisational level that considers the various processes of communications both internally and externally, and finally the business level that tracks the commercial benefits to the organisation of excellent PR.

FURTHER READING

83

Grunig, J. (1992) *Excellence in Public Relations and Communication Management*. Hillsdale, NJ: Lawrence Erlbaum.
Heath, R.L. (2001) *Handbook of Public Relations*. Thousand Oaks, CA: Sage.
Moss, D. (1991) *Public Relations in Practice*. New York: Routledge.

MH

The phrase 'fifth estate' was neologised by Baistow in his highly critical book *Fourth Rate Estate: An Anatomy of Fleet Street* to describe the expansive **public relations** industry in the UK and what he believed to be the undesirable consequences of that growth (1985: 67–76). Drawing on the 18th-century notion of the press as the **fourth estate** of the realm, an indispensable critic and watchdog holding government publicly accountable for its actions, Baistow argued that a fifth estate of PR specialists had emerged and was being used by political and economic elites to offset the critical oversight that journalists previously provided to protect the public interest. 'Everyone from the Prime Minister to the latest rock star, and not least big business, has something they want to sell, from ideas and personal images to consumer goods and services', he claimed. 'Manipulation of the news media by the fifth estate is rampant' (1985: 67–8).

Baistow's claims about the political implications of the PR industry remain highly contentious, but his suggestions concerning the growth of the industry are indisputable. PR has expanded rapidly in the UK since 1945 in terms of its numbers of practitioners (Miller and Dinan, 2000; Davis, 2002: 173), their levels of professional education and training increasingly provided by universities, and their professional organisation in bodies such as the Institute of Public Relations (IPR) (Fedorcio et al., 1991; Mitchie 1998: 17). In 1997, Franklin estimated the number of practitioners working in the private and public sectors of public relations to be approximately 25,000 (1997: 19). Mitchie confirms this number and echoes Baistow's concern that this trend is 'deeply undemocratic' (1998: 17). However, by November 2005 a survey by the CIPR revealed that the UK PR industry employed 43,000 people in a business worth a total of £6.2b. Public and not for profit sectors are among the heaviest users of PR, accounting for 36 per cent of the turnover of all PR consultancies and employing 52 per cent of all in-house PR professionals, reported *PR Week* (11 November 2005).

What seems to concern observers is the apparent ease with which this 'fifth estate' is able to generate and place stories in news media

key concepts in public relations

reflecting the sectional interests of client groups; what concerns journalists is that PR copy is increasingly replacing stories written by journalists and may lack the objectivity that they argue characterises their editorial copy. The editor of *PR Week* estimated that a minimum 50 per cent of broadsheets' copy and 'more for tabloids' is now provided by 'PRs' who now 'do a lot of journalists' thinking for them' (*Guardian*, 13 May 1996: 10). As **sources** become increasingly influential in shaping newspaper content, the tail begins to wag the dog (Tunstall, 1983; Franklin, 1997): the fifth estate of PR practitioners is taking over. Davis claims, 'the liberal description of the fourth estate media, based on an image of independent autonomous **journalists** seeking out news, has been severely undermined by the growth of the PR sector' (2002: 173).

Public, as well as academic, discourses have similarly been critical and increasingly associated PR with **propaganda, spin** and **spin doctors**. Franklin (1988, 2004), for example, has illustrated the effectiveness of PR practitioners, especially in local government, in **agenda setting** key areas of democratic debate, while Gandy's (1982) concept of **information subsidies** illustrates how structural inequalities are reinforced by PR practice. McNair (1996), Schlesinger (1990) and Miller (1998) have explored media-source relations and criticised the implications of public relations for citizen access to the public sphere.

FURTHER READING

Baistow, T. (1985) *Fourth Rate Estate: An Anatomy of Fleet Street*. London: Macmillan.
Fedorcio, D., Heaton, P. and Madden, K. (1991) *Public Relations in Local Government*. Harlow: Longman.
Mitchie, D. (1998) *The Invisible Persuaders*. London: Bantam Press.
Franklin, B. (1988) *Public Relations Activity in Local Government*. London: Charles Knight.
Miller, D. and Dinan, W. (2000) 'The Rise of the PR Industry in Britain 1979–98', *European Journal of Communication*, 15 (1): 5–35.

BF

fifth estate

Financial
Public Relations

The Public Relations Society of America (PRSA) first outlined the specialist role of the financial PR practitioner in 1988 and clarified its definition in 2002. It says FPR is an area of PR which relates to the dissemination of information that affects the understanding of the stockholder and investors generally concerning the financial position and prospects of a company, and includes the improvement of relations between corporations and stockholders.

Investor relations is a strand of FPR which looks at the relationship between private stockholders and the corporation while FPR encompasses relationships with the wider financial and community, such as financial analysts, potential investors and financial journalists. Tools of communication include the annual report in which the company outlines its financial performance against set objectives and looks at future prospects and business strategy. The annual report is supported by the **Annual General Meeting** (AGM).

There are tight restrictions on the way financial information is distributed to the financial markets. In the UK for example and with companies floated on the London Stock Exchange (LSE), any information which could have a material affect on company stock values must be distributed via the Regulatory News Service (RNS). This ensures the information is distributed rapidly to all key stakeholders. Year end or half year results are always distributed in this way.

FPR is also important in building and maintaining good relations with key stakeholders in times of crisis such as a company takeover or if an organisation is looking to raise further finance in order to expand into different markets. It is also important in bringing a company to market. A rapidly growing private company may seek to list as a private company in order to raise investor finance to expand. As part of this listing process, the organisation would seek to outline to key financial analysts and City institutions the future direction of the organisation, the leaders of the business and its profitability.

FURTHER READING

Baines, P., Egan, J., Jefkins, F. and Jefkins, F.W. (2003) *Public Relations: Contemporary Issues and Techniques*. London: Butterworth-Heinmann.

Davis, A. (2007) *Mastering Public Relations*. New York: Palgrave Macmillan.

L'Etang, J. (2008) *Public Relations, Concepts, Practice and Critique*. London: Sage.

EP

Focus Groups

Popular in social science research and communications studies, as well as in **marketing, advertising, public opinion** and **public relations**, focus groups involve a topic-based discussion led by a *moderator* (the researcher).

They offer a **qualitative** method of data gathering and can produce extremely rich and interesting results. This technique differs from **key figure interviews** in that it is the ways in which the group discusses the issues that provide the most insight, rather than the views that specific individuals express. In a strict methodological sense, this technique also differs from some market/public opinion research strategies using group discussion – sometimes known as *Delphi groups* or *consensus groups* – that aim to produce a specific outcome, in that it is the process of discussion that is the feature of interest, rather than any agreed opinion or policy recommendation that may be reached as an outcome of the process.

Focus groups are often used during the initial stages of research to explore in detail issues that the participants feel are important to the central research topic. More often than not they are used as a complement to other **methodologies**, either to inform the design of research instruments such as surveys/content analyses that can subsequently involve a greater number of research participants or items, or to shed light on findings from data obtained from such large-scale and objective, but less detailed, means.

Two elements are crucial to the success of the experience and to the quality of the data obtained. The first is the skill of the moderator. As with other qualitative methods, the researcher plays an integral role in the

focus groups

87

process of data collection. Their task is essentially to act as a chairperson for a discussion, guiding the topic and retaining the focus, while remaining as impartial and objective as possible, in order to allow the group participants to express their own views freely and to challenge the views of others in a constructive way.

Due consideration should be paid to common-sense but easily overlooked details that really only come with experience and considerable preparation. How will a researcher who is obviously wearing a wedding ring influence a discussion of the issues that concern divorcees or single-parent families, for example?

The ways in which the discussion is prompted and kept within the confines of the research topic are also dependent on a certain amount of skill and imagination. Popular techniques for stimulating discussion include the use of visual or verbal cues in order to focus the discussion and the participants' thoughts (for example, video clips or flash cards), or the use of tasks such as sorting material into categories by group discussion. More commercial uses of this method might pass around a product prototype for discussion, or display a video clip inviting group participants to 'vote' using particular electronic responses or colour-coded cards.

A second consideration is the participants themselves. Topics that might be considered to be emotionally neutral (requiring less self-revelation on the part of participants) can frequently be discussed in groups of eight to 12 people, other more sensitive topics may require a smaller, more intimate number. This will also depend to an extent on the moderator's skill and comfort levels in dealing with groups that are intended to be lively and opinionated.

Cultural and sociological factors also play an important role here. Males and females may speak more or less freely in mixed- or same-gender groups (depending on the topic). Similar considerations must be taken into account with other **demographics** such as age, religion, ethnicity and so on.

The outcomes of research-oriented focus groups may be used in a variety of ways. Sometimes particular quotes that the researcher feels are representative of segments of the debate may be used as primary data in support of a particular hypothesis. More detailed examination of the ways in which participants agree or disagree with others (and sometimes express contradictory viewpoints in their own opinions), and the ways in which the group functions as a whole can be conducted using other more detailed qualitative analysis techniques.

FURTHER READING

Barbour, R.S. and Kitzinger, J. (2001) *Developing Focus Group Research: Politics, Theory and Practice*. London: Sage.

Deacon, D., Pickering, M., Golding, P. and Murdock, G. (1999) *Researching Communications: A Practical Guide to Methods in Media and Cultural Analysis*. London: Arnold.

Gunter, B. (2000) *Media Research Methods. Measuring Audience Reactions and Impact*. London: Sage.

Wimmer, R.D. and Dominick, J.R. (2006) *Mass Media Research: An Introduction*. Belmont CA: Wadsworth.

NM

Fourth Estate

The liberal notion that **journalists** and the press constitute a critical 'fourth estate' of the realm, protecting the public interest by serving as a 'watchdog' on governments, reporting their policies and activities and thereby making them publicly accountable, has a considerable pedigree dating back to at least the 18th century. Those who argue for the press as a fourth estate suggest that in addition to acting as a check on executive power, the press has a duty to inform and articulate public opinion. This 'fourth estate of the realm' complemented the three original 'estates' constituted by the clergy (Lords Spiritual) who sat in the House of Lords, the Lords Temporal and the 'Commoners' in the lower chamber. Indeed, some observers attributed a leading role to this new 'fourth' estate with a commentator in the mid-19th century suggesting that 'journalism is now truly an estate of the realm; more powerful than any of the other estates' (cited in Boyce *et al.*, 1978). On this account, the clatter of journalists' typewriters becomes an essential sound in the cacophony of competing voices which constitute pluralist democracy.

From its earliest articulation, the notion has been contested by critics who (1) suggest that the 'fourth estate' has increasingly been corrupted and replaced by a '**fifth estate**' of **public relations** practitioners

fourth estate

89

who are becoming increasingly influential in news making and reporting (Baistow, 1985: 67–76; Davis, 2002: 173), or (2) those critics who suggest that journalists are more akin to 'lapdogs' ('mere poodles of governments') than 'watchdogs' because of their support and endorsement of governments and corporate interests rather than any opposition to them (Franklin, 1997: 38); Donohue et al. (1995: 117), for example, describe journalists as 'guard dogs' protecting particular group interests within power elites.

Critics have challenged other assumptions of the 'press as fourth estate model' suggesting that it requires: (1) a press free from state/political **censorship** and journalists' self censorship (Sadler, 2001); (2) journalistic autonomy which is undermined by corporate media ownership and management (Herman and Chomsky, 1988; Evans, 1994); (3) objectivity in news coverage which is difficult to achieve in the face of growing **news management** by governments (Franklin, 2004); (4) a sustained journalistic commitment to editorial coverage of significant public/political issues which is less likely in an increasingly competitive market for **news** which encourage a greater focus on 'soft news and entertainment' (Franklin, 1997).

Despite these sustained criticisms, the idea of the press as a fourth estate of the realm enjoys a continuing popularity – not least among journalists (Marr, 2004)

FURTHER READING

Baistow, T. (1985) *Fourth Rate Estate: An Anatomy of Fleet Street*. London: Macmillan.

Boyce, G., Curran, J. and Wingate, P. (eds) (1978) *Newspaper History from the 17th Century to the Present Day*. London: Constable.

Davis, A. (2002) *Public Relations Democracy: Public Relations, Politics and the Mass Media in Britain*. London: Sage.

Donoghue, G.A. Tichenor, P.J. and Olien, C.N. (1995) 'A guard dog perspective on the role of the media', *Journal of Communication*, 45 (2): 115–32.

Marr, A. (2004) *My Trade: A Short History of British Journalism*. Basingstoke: Macmillan.

BF

Freelance

A freelancer is an independent contractor selling his or her services individually. A freelance **public relations** practitioner will seek clients in exactly the same way as a larger consultancy, indeed this is how many larger businesses began. Some freelancers, however, have made a specific lifestyle choice and are not intending to build a larger business. Freelancers sometimes work in networks or 'virtual' companies, subcontracting some tasks to others.

A freelancer may be, for tax purposes, a sole trader or own a small business. A freelance journalist is one not employed by any particular medium, but selling material to a range of media. Freelance journalists are very useful outlets for PR practitioners. In general freelancers will be happy to take on any story they think they can sell, and will have a good eye for what will sell, and suitable markets for it. Many editors will be more responsive to a pitch from a freelance journalist than they would be from a PR practitioner.

It should not be assumed that a freelancer is necessarily trying to break into full-time employment or filling time while looking for a job – though some are. Some people prefer the lifestyle for its flexibility. Freelancing can also be more profitable than running a business.

Freelance PR practitioners often fill particular niches for a number of **clients**, including consultancies. Freelancers – both PR practitioners and journalists – are often people with substantial reputations and able to command high fees while being selective about the work they undertake.

FURTHER READING

PRSA: http://www.prsa.org/_Networking/ipa/index.asp?ident=ec1
Richards, P. (1998) *Be Your Own Spin Doctor*. London: Take That Ltd.

freelance

Friday Night Drop

The Friday Night drop (FND) originated in **financial public relations**. Its aim was to 'drop' or leak on an exclusive basis a piece of company information to a chosen City journalist on a Friday evening after the markets had closed. The information would then be written up in a Sunday paper in order to influence the markets, and by definition share price, when they reopened on Monday morning for trading.

The practise is now widespread in the political world with government information departments as well as opposition parties leaking, or trailing, policies on Friday, often to several journalists, in order to test public reaction following publication on Sunday. On the basis of that reaction, policy could be adopted, diluted, or even in some extreme cases, denied. Critics of the process (Jones, 2006) believe it helps bypass traditional Parliamentary scrutiny with debate on policy increasingly taking place in the Sunday papers, on the growing numbers of Sunday morning television political chat shows, and radio programmes such as BBC Radio 4's *Today*. So common is FND that it has become an integral part of the governing process (Franklin, 2004).

Some journalists resolutely oppose the system because they believe it compromises their independence and interferes with their ability to report. However, many politicians and their advisers argue it encourages wider public debate.

Key to the survival of the technique is the changing geography and relationship between journalists and government **spin doctors**. Fewer and fewer reporters with more space to fill face and increasing number of **special advisers** (Blick, 2004; Lewis et al., 2008a, 2008b). In such circumstances the future of the FND seems assured.

FURTHER READING

Blick, A. (2004) *People Who Live in the Dark: The History of the Special Adviser in British Politics.* London: Politicos.

Lewis, J., Williams, A. and Franklin, B. (2008a) 'Four rumours and an explanation: a political economic account of journalists' news gathering and reporting practices', *Journalism Practice*, 2 (1): 27–45.

key concepts in
public relations

Lewis, J., Williams, A. and Franklin, B. (2008b) 'A compromised fourth estate: UK news journalism, public relations and news sources', *Journalism Studies*, 9 (1): 1–20.

Jones, N. (2002) *The Control Freaks*. London: Politicos.

MH

Full Service

Full service is a term used to describe a **public relations** consultancy that provides **clients** with a full range of PR services. It has value in offering existing and potential clients a one-stop shop for shaping **communications** goals.

Hill and Knowlton is one of the world's largest marketing communications consultancies and specialises in delivering global communication campaigns for a number of the world's largest organisations. It maintains that brands, companies, governments and organisations face tough challenges and the need for powerful, compelling communications has never been greater. It adds that communication is harder to achieve because of the fragility of **reputation**, media fragmentation, **audience** proliferation and information overload.

This complex external business environment means that full service consultancies provide clients in four global regions with a range of services across a variety of sectors. Hill and Knowlton is divided into four regions: Asia-Pacific; Europe, Middle East and Africa (EMEA); United States; and Latin America. Within these regions it offers clients seven sector-specific services. These comprise: corporate and financial; **crisis management**; **healthcare** and pharmaceutical; marketing communications; online; public affairs; and technology.

Within each of these service sectors the consultancy will offer specialist PR tactics which include: media relations; research; third party endorsement; **celebrity** management; sponsorship; media training; event

full service

93

management; design and print; web development; content development; **evaluation**, and market reports.

Full service agencies offer clients the ease of only having to manage one external relationship for all their PR needs but can be criticised for being expensive and lacking the dynamism of specialist, smaller agencies that focus of specific sectors of the industry and tend to have lower overheads with corresponding lower fees. However this is not always the case in the healthcare, crisis and financial PR sectors.

FURTHER READING

Lattimore, L.L., Baskin, O.W., Heiman, S.T., Toth, E.L. and Van Leuven, J.K (2004) *Public Relations: The Practice and the Profession*. New York: McGraw Hill.
Marconi, J. (2004) *PR: the Complete Guide*. London: Thomson.
McCusker, G. (2004) *Talespin*. London: Kogan Page.
Van Ruler, B. and Vervic, D. (ed.) (2004) *Public Relations and Communications Management in Europe*. Amsterdam: Walter de Gruyter.

EP

Gatekeeper

A term which has its origins in social and organisational psychology of the 1940s and 1950s (Lewin, 1947) and essentially refers to a person who controls the flow of some commodity to the intended receiver through a series of 'gates'.

In a media context, the concept has become associated with a role as a filter of information, deciding what kinds of material are suitable for mass publication. Lewin's original work was applied to a **journalism** context by White (1950) who studied the impact of editorial decisions and personal bias on coverage of particular issues and individuals.

The idea was later extended by McCombs and Shaw (1976) to add weight to the theory of **agenda setting**, in which the media have a crucial role to play in influencing the audience's perceived importance of certain news stories, by placing more or less emphasis on those stories.

An individual gatekeeper functions to decide which stories are allowed onto the news agenda and which are left out. This can function at several levels and will be affected by a media organisation's ownership, overall editorial policy, **regulations** and further down to the individual decisions of editors, sub-editors and reporters themselves.

Effective **public relations** professionals will seek information about who the key gatekeepers are in any given organisation, and this concept will have a role in the selection of target publications, specialist **journalists** or **communications** personnel and the crafting of **key messages**.

FURTHER READING

McCombs, M. and Shaw, D. (1972) 'The agenda setting function of mass media', *Public Opinion Quarterly*, 36: 176–87.

NM

Globalisation

Originated from the rapid increase in international trade in the mid-20th century, and globalisation has now become a buzzword in a plethora of contexts, with supporters and critics in equal numbers. Essentially the term has come to refer to a shrinkage, but also an expansion, of the world as economic, communications and social networks become more interconnected and instantaneous.

Critics suggest that the phenomenon is little more than imperialism, based on a Western (primarily American) model of business and culture that undermines less powerful nations and forces a global uniform identity of image and behaviour, increasing the gap between rich and poor.

Others argue that this interconnectivity can be a force for good, challenging the power of individual nation states and establishing more influence for international intergovernmental and non-governmental organisations, particularly those that seek to redress economic and social inequality around the world through pressure on the more developed countries.

A driving force behind globalisation is the rapid change in the international communications landscape. Increasingly sophisticated recording and broadcast technology, coupled with the expansion of the Internet, has transformed the world into what Marshall McLuhan (1964, 2006), writing in the 1960s, foresaw as a 'global village'. Again this idea has detractors and supporters. The rise of multinational cross-platform media organisations could be accused of providing a limited, one-dimensional information source. The dominant language of the Internet is English.

The increased ease of access to information, and proliferation of forums in which users can generate and deliver content, can however potentially act as a challenge to multinational commerce and information providers and bring economic benefits to less developed countries' infrastructure.

Public relations as a profession is increasingly international, with growing numbers of international agencies, as well as clients drawn from multinational companies and the rise of specialist areas such as public diplomacy and cultural diplomacy.

One of the challenges for international public relations is the extent to which **communications campaigns** are internationally standard or are adapted to suit local cultures and environments – the clichéd 'think global, act local' mantra.

Though the discipline has a largely Western history, the increase in international and cultural research is testament to the growing interest in how effective PR can function globally.

FURTHER READING

Culbertson, H.M. and Chen, N. (1996) *International Public Relations: A Comparative Analysis*. Mahwah, NJ: Lawrence Erlbaum.

Emmott, B., Crook, C. and Michlethwait, J. (2002) *Globalisation: Making Sense of an Integrating World: Reasons, Effects and Challenges*. London: Economist.

Szondi, G. (2006) 'International context of public relations', in R. Tench and L. Yeomans (eds), *Exploring Public Relations*. Harlow: Prentice Hall. pp. 112–40.

Vercic, D. and Sriramesh, K. (2003) *The Global Public Relations Handbook: Theory, Research and Practice*. Mahwah, NJ: Lawrence Erlbaum.

NM

Googledance

At the time of writing Google has become the most important Internet search engine and faces no obvious and immediate challenge. It does, however, continue to attract criticism. The process of ranking matches to a particular search term may be automated, but the decision making behind the algorithm remains editorial. Battelle draws attention to the controversy surrounding the so called Googledance, when the company shifts the algorithm and causes some websites to crash down from high positions on particular search terms to much lower matches. He gives the example of 2bigfeet.com, which suffered badly from the 14 November 2003 review nicknamed 'Florida'. The site, which is a retail outlet for oversized shoes, had previously been first match for the search term 'big feet' and fell out of the top 100 for the same search term after Florida. Google is such an important driver of business for websites that such changes can be catastrophic for smaller businesses. Some critics cited by Battelle have suggested that Google's periodic tweaking of the algorithm and reordering of the matches is designed, at least partly, to encourage etailing businesses to buy adverts on Google rather than rely on organic matches. He gives the example of a search for 'digital camera' which, in December 2004, produced reviews in all the top match positions with etail businesses much lower, and therefore inclined to buy advertising. (In October 2006 the same search produced a mixture of reviews and e-commerce sites.) Google has now abandoned the periodic gross shifts in the algorithm in favour of more frequent smaller changes, which has somewhat muted the criticism.

googledance

FURTHER READING

Battelle: http://battellemedia.com/

Battelle, J. (2006) *The Search: How Google and Its Rivals Rewrote the Rules of Business and Transformed Our Culture*. Boston: Nicholas Brealey.

Search Engine Watch: http://searchenginewatch.com/

QL

GoogleEarth

GoogleEarth is a global mapping system, which requires users to download software to their computers. It has proved especially flexible for 'mash ups', the linking of two unrelated information sources to produce something new. For example, by linking GoogleEarth to *Craig's List* – a small ads listing in the USA – it is possible to map the location of people selling cars in a particular price bracket by reference to the user's home.

The public relations implications of such technology are potentially startling, and only in their infancy. By taking just two small and unrelated examples it should be possible to show that there are numerous potential applications, and that the market is likely to develop them over the next few years.

In the field of direct sales, telemarketers often call potential customers claiming to be 'in your area at the moment', while nonetheless exhibiting an ignorance of the area, which is unsurprising, given the tendency for call centres to relocate thousands of miles from the target markets.

A telemarketer with genuine knowledge of the area, including examples of neighbours who had recently installed new kitchens or conservatories on or in similar properties, would be at a clear advantage.

Equally, political campaigners who could mash up GoogleEarth with crime statistics and the electoral register would be able to produce tailored newsletters with detailed local information about the risk of crime.

key concepts in public relations

Environmental and municipal tax statistics could also be mashed up with GoogleEarth and the electoral roll in the same way. Local political newsletters have traditionally been produced on the ward or precinct level, but mash ups enable parties to produce different versions for each street or even each property.

These examples, while small in themselves, are evidence of the flexibility such processes bring to PR.

FURTHER READING

Battelle: http://battellemedia.com/
Battelle, J. (2006) *The Search: How Google and Its Rivals Rewrote the Rules of Business and Transformed Our Culture*. Boston: Nicholas Brealey.
Search Engine Watch: http://searchenginewatch.com/

QL

Google Games

Google is now so popular that a number of games have developed around it. The most popular remains Google bombing.

Though Google's algorithm remains secret, it has been known for some time that the text in links to a site is one of the criteria. It thus becomes possible to associate a site with a particular search term by creating links to it. For some years the top match for the term 'miserable failure' was the White House biography of President George W. Bush. This was the case on each occasion that the author has checked it for over three years until 2007 when the algorithm was changed and stories about Google bombing became the top matches. This change in the algorithm was reported in the *New York Times* on 29 January 2007.

The precise phrase 'miserable failure' seems to have originated with the presidential campaign of Congressman Richard (Dick) Gephardt,

99

who used the phrase multiple times in his speeches while seeking the Democratic nomination for president. Ironically, Gephardt's campaign crashed to a humiliating fourth place finish in the 2004 Iowa caucuses, a contest he had won in his previous presidential campaign in 1988. Despite what can only be described as a miserable failure of a presidential campaign, Gephardt's phrase lives on.

There were many attempts by supporters of Bush to remove his biography from the top slot by using the same phrase to link to other sites. The length of Bush's dominance of this search term suggests, though, that he was not pressed for the top slot (though the figures are known only to Google) and only Google's intervention removed him from it. Bush's dominance of this term may, in part, be because Bush supporters were divided as to whom they think should replace him as first match for this search.

On 20 October, 2006, the second match was the White House biography of former President Jimmy Carter, though film-maker Michael Moore also featured in the top 10. Most of the other high matches were articles in the technical or general media, either about Google bombing or about the fact that Bush consistently takes the top slot for this search.

British activists also joined in this game. Until the same changes that spared the blushes of President Bush, the top match for the term 'liar' was the Cabinet Office biography of Tony Blair and the biography of John Prescott was the top match for the search 'fuckwit'.

Another popular game is the search for Googlewhacks. A Googlewhack is a two-word search term, without the use of inverted commas, which produces exactly one match on Google. Purists insist that only words in the dictionary may be used, which excludes some, but not all, proper nouns. This author was able to discover one Googlewhack linking to his own website using the words 'psephology' and 'larque', but since 'larque' is a proper noun this has not been accepted by the whackstack, the official arbiter of Googlewhacks.

Famous Googlewhacks include 'ambidextrous scallywag' and 'unmerciless politician'. Unfortunately, the process of becoming famous automatically disqualifies a Googlewhack, as the phrase then appears on numerous sites writing about Googlewhacks.

Another game is the Googlefight, where two search terms are simultaneously tested to see which produces the largest number of matches.

FURTHER READING

Battelle: http://battellemedia.com/
Battelle, J. (2006) *The Search: How Google and Its Rivals Rewrote the Rules of Business and Transformed Our Culture*. Boston: Nicholas Brealey.
Googlewhack: http://www.googlewhack.com/
Search Engine Watch: http://searchenginewatch.com/

QL

Government Public Relations

Government PR has changed radically across the last 20 years as successive governments have become increasingly concerned with being '**on message**' and conveying messages to target audiences among the general public (especially messages favourable to their electoral fortunes) during a period in which politics and political communications has become 'mediatised': and characterised by the 'Packaging of Politics' (Franklin, 2004).

Governments, of course, have always used **media briefings, public relations, advertising, marketing** and downright **propaganda** to influence and shape **public opinion**. In that sense government PR is as old as kissing babies. But the period since the mid-1980s has marked a watershed expansion in government PR: it was marked by Lord Young's (Minister at the DTI) observation that 'The government's policies are like cornflakes. If they are not marketed, they will not sell' (*PR Week*, 16 March 1988).

Conservative administrations under Thatcher's leadership expanded government advertising from £62m in 1982/3 to £200m in 1988/9 (Cobb, 1989: 12): in that year the government replaced Unilever as the largest single purchaser of advertising. Alongside advertising, the government centralised it **news management** activities at No. 10, endowed Bernard Ingham, the Prime Minister's press secretary, with

government public relations

101

unprecedented powers over the recruitment and promotion of the government press officers and PR specialists in the Government Communications Service and the Central Office of Information and used the Parliamentary lobby in a robust fashion to set the public agenda for policy discussions.

Elected in 1997, the Blair administration expanded expenditure on advertising and strengthened government news management initiatives (especially via the lobby) to handle its relations with news media and the public. In the three months prior to the 2001 general election, for example, new Labour launched 172 marketing campaigns and spent £97m on advertising, prompting allegations that the government was using public money for propaganda.

The government's media and PR strategy was based on what Romola Christopherson – a senior government press and information officer – characterised as the 'Three 'Rs'. The first 'R' she explained is *rhetoric* – getting the message and encapsulating the message in a marketing slogan ('New Labour, New Britain', 'Peoples' Princess') all those **soundbites**, getting that rhetoric absolutely clear and right and accessible. The second 'R' is *repetition*, repetition, repetition, repetition. When you're bored with repeating it, it probably means that people are beginning to pick it up. The final 'R' is **rebuttal**, which is do not let any attack on you go without walloping back at it (Romola Christopherson in *Control Freaks*, Channel 5, 28 September 2002). Implementing this strategy since 1997 involved: the centralisation of communications at No. 10; a very assertive relationship with journalists (which Ingham called an old-fashioned game of 'carrots and sticks') and, the politicising of the Government Information and Communications Service (GICS) (Oborne, 1999; Barnett and Gaber, 2001). It was this growing concern among the public, **journalists** and academics, about government uses of '**spin**' to manage its PR, which led eventually to the resignation of the Prime Minister's Press Secretary Alastair Campbell and the appointment of the Phillis Committee to investigate government media and PR.

Phillis' summary finding was to blame Whitehall, government and the media (but especially the **Lobby**) for a 'three-way breakdown in trust between government and politicians, the media and the general public' (Phillis, 2004: 4). Three factors triggered the breakdown: the communications strategy adopted by Labour since 1997; journalists' and the media reactions to that strategy; the response of the civil service in the government information and communication service (GICS) to the new (modernising) demands that were placed on it. The Committee recommended: disbanding the GICS (now the Government Communications Network with a remit to 'Consolidate standards and good practice in government communications' [Garner, 2006: 192]); strengthening information structures within individual departments; heading up the communications service with a permanent secretary – in classic New Labour speak a 'no spin Czar' (James Howell, a friend of Peter Mandelson, was duly appointed) and the furtive meetings of the lobby should be replaced with open and televised briefings (Phillis, 2004).

Some journalists were sceptical concerning this last recommendation; *Guardian* political editor Michael White claimed that trying to eradicate politicians' briefing of **lobby journalists** was akin to trying to get rid of original sin! But there are now monthly televised briefings from No. 10. But allegations by both opposition politicians and members of the public that Blair and the Labour government were 'all spin and no substance' remain commonplace. Interestingly it is an allegation levelled by Labour politicians against the new Conservative Party leader David Cameron. Both government and opposition, it seems, need to attend to their relations with the public.

FURTHER READING

Barnett, S. and Gaber, I. (2001) Westminster Tales: The Twenty First Century Crisis in Political Journalism. London: Continuum.

Franklin, B. (2004) Packaging Politics: Political Communications in Britain's Media Democracy. London: Arnold.

Garner, B. (2006) 'Hungry media need fast food; the role of the Central Office of Information', B. Franklin (ed.), Local Journalism and Local Media: Making the Local News. London: Routledge. pp. 189–99.

Oborne, P. (1999) Alastair Campbell, New Labour and the Rise of the Media Class. London: Aurum Press.

Phillis, R. (2004) The Government Communications Review. Available at: http://www.gcreview.gov.uk

public relations · government

BF

Essentially referring to relationships and personal connections, *guanxi* is a central concept in Chinese society and one that Western organisations who operate there are increasingly encouraged to explore, understand and utilise. Part of the concept dates back to ancient philosophies and societal mores regarding respect for others and for the structure of society itself, as reflected in the roles in which an individual functions in relation to other people.

It is essentially concerned with **networking** and **contacts**, which are built up over time through mutual respect and integrity and frequent contact. In this sense, business in China is far more reliant on trusted individual relationships than the more commercially driven, cost effective concerns of the Western model.

Good *guanxi* is established through common identities, mutual acquaintances or the prospect of future relationships, as well as mutual openness and integrity in all dealings. Gifts may be part of this process, but this is more than 'oiling the wheels' of exchanges.

Establishing *guanxi* with government officials is also a useful process, though arguably declining in importance, since most organisations are reliant upon the authorities to some extent, whether this is through funding or as part of the bureaucratic requirements.

To an extent, it also relates to an individual's or organisation's **reputation**, since good *guanxi* will result in wide-ranging and long-lasting working relationships.

FURTHER READING

Buderi, R. and Huang, G.T. (2006) *Guanxi (The Art of Relationships): Microsoft, China, and Bill Gates's Plan to Win the Road Ahead.* New York: Simon and Shuster.

Chen, X. and Chen, C.C. (2004) 'On the intricacies of the Chinese *guanxi*: a process model of *guanxi* development', *Asia Pacific Journal of Management* 21: 305–24.

So, Y.L. and Walker, A. (2005) *Explaining Guanxi: The Chinese Business Network.* Abingdon: Routledge.

key concepts in
public relations

NM

Healthcare Public Relations

This is a specialist sector within the broad **public relations** industry. It covers both public and private sector practice where consultants communicate to key stakeholders on key health issues. This can range from awareness campaigns on behalf of governments to service issues on behalf of local National Health Service Trusts and from global pharmaceutical product launches to alternative forms of health treatment. Traditional PR tactics are utilised such as event management, **lobbying**, **media relations**, speaker platforms, research and press conferences but they are used to target a range of healthcare professionals such as regulators, health writers and **journalists,** doctors, analysts who specialise in the healthcare sector and scientists.

A commonly used phrase in healthcare PR is OTC or over the counter, referring to common healthcare products consumers can buy from pharmacies. An excellent case study in OTC PR has been designed and delivered by one of the leading consultancies in the UK, Lexis PR. It has a thriving healthcare section and one of its clients is Roche Consumer Health. It wanted Lexis to put Pro Plus®, the natural stimulant product, onto the news pages of the mainstream media and target the 12 million UK workers suffering from tiredness in the workplace. Lexis developed an award winning creative campaign to help Pro Plus® take time management to another level by creating a mathematical formula to predict the time of day when people would feel most tired at work.

An interactive calculator was created that allowed workers to find out the exact time of day they would feel most tired and get a profile of their alertness throughout the day. Using a third-party endorser, Lexis worked with Dr Paul Jackson from the Sleep Research Laboratory at Loughborough University to back the scientific methodology with an attitudinal survey of 1000 people.

The campaign was branded Pro Plus® 'Knacker Factor' and it hit a real chord with the UK media with branded coverage appearing in four national newspapers, 40 regional press and 15 top radio stations. Hits to the site peaked at 36,000 users on the first day of the campaign, and continues to attract 8000 a day according to the case study on its company website. By combining strong creativity, third-party expert endorsement and a **media relations** hook that appealed to target media, the agency was able to target key audiences with strong healthcare messages to link the product, Pro Plus®, directly to being the answer to midday revival.

FURTHER READING

Heath, R.L. (2001) *Handbook of Public Relations*. Thousand Oaks, CA: Sage.
Larey, K. (1995) *Public Relations in Health Care, A Guide for Professionals*. New York: Jossey-Bass.
Lexis PR: http://www.lexispr.com (accessed 20 April 2007)
Stauber, J. and Rampton, S (1995) *Toxic Sludge Is Good for You: Lies, Damn Lies and the PR Industry*. Monroe, ME: Common Courage Press.
Tench, R. and Yeomans, L. (2006) *Exploring Public Relations*. Harlow: Pearson.

EP

Hofstede

In today's multinational business and communications environment, an understanding of individual cultures is essential to effective functioning. In **public relations** theory, one of the most influential contributors to such understanding is Professor Geert Hofstede, a Dutch organisational anthropologist. In 1980, he published the results of a long-term survey into the attitudes and values of IBM workers in more than 70 countries, and this work continues to be expanded by researchers aiming to quantify the differences that exist between members of individual international cultures.

The original study identified four indices or dimensions to differentiate cultures.

Power distance – is the extent to which less powerful members of institutions or organisations accept that power and influence is distributed unequally in society.

Individualism – reflects the extent to which people act and are integrated into groups. Individualistic societies place emphasis on people acting alone or in very small groups. The opposite – collectivist – societies are those in which larger and more cohesive groups exist and function.

Masculinity – refers to the value placed on masculine or feminine activities in the culture. Masculine attributes include competitiveness or assertiveness, feminine attributes are more associated with relationships and compassion for others.

Uncertainty avoidance – refers to a society's tolerance for and comfort with ambiguity and uncertainty. This includes philosophical and emotional dimensions concerned with 'truth', rules and structure.

A fifth dimension, added after additional research using an instrument developed with Chinese academics, and reflecting an influence of Confucian philosophy, is *long-term orientation*. This is more concerned with virtues; long-term orientated societies value prudence and perseverance, short-term orientated societies place more value on tradition and fulfilling social obligation.

FURTHER READING

Hofstede, G. (1991) *Cultures and Organizations: Software of the Mind*. New York: McGraw-Hill.
Hofstede, G. (2001). *Culture's Consequences: International Differences in Work-related Values*. Thousand Oaks, CA: Sage.
Hofstede, G. and Hofstede, G.J. (2005) *Cultures and Organizations: Software of the Mind: Intercultural Cooperation and its Importance for Survival*. New York: McGraw-Hill.

NM

A Korean term often used, according to Y. Kim, as a substitute for PR. The terms are not, however, synonymous, at least not if the modern

Western understanding of **public relations** is the source of comparison. Hong bo, again according to Y. Kim, is more akin to publicity and often used to evade negative media coverage. It can therefore be considered a reactive and one-way communication process.

Kim believes that hong bo is 'deeply rooted in the collaboration between the authoritarian government and the powerful chaebol system during the 1970s' (2003: 106). The chaebol are mammoth Korean conglomerates, usually active in a range of business spheres and frequently dominated by family interests. Samsung, Hyundai and LG are all chaebol, and despite efforts under President Roh Moo-hyun and his predecessor to reform the economy the chaebol remain a powerful force.

Authoritarian rule, however, is a thing of the past. Military rule continued for some years after the assassination of President Park Chung-hee, but South Korea has become a democracy, arguably with the election of Roh Tae-woo in 1987, and more clearly since the peaceful transfer of power to the first civilian president, Kim Young-sam.

Y. Kim suggests that the hong bo system is representative of Korea's past more than its more dynamic and competitive present. In 1996, he conducted a survey of 167 PR practitioners to measure where Korean PR practice stands in terms of Grunig and Hunt's **models**. He concluded that though most practitioners are, day-to-day, focused on the press agentry and public information **models**, he found evidence that they aspire to the two-way models and that those who use the two-way models derive more job satisfaction.

Kim links these developing changes in Korean PR to developments in government and society. There has been a considerable rise in the influence of **NGOs** in Korea in recent years, with 70 per cent of the groups having been founded after the democracy movement of 1987 led to the first transfer of power at an election in several generations. Interestingly, both the Korean Public Relations Association (est. 1989) and the Korean Public Relations Consultancy Association (est. 2000) post-date this dramatic change in Korea's political development.

FURTHER READING

Kim, Y. (2003) 'Professionalism and diversification: the evolution of public relations in South Korea', K. Sriramesh and D. Vercic (eds), *Global Public Relations Handbook: Theory, Research and Practice*. Mahwah, NJ: Lawrence Erlbaum.

Horizon Scanning

The mid-1990s saw a flurry of activity in the corporate world as the capabilities of the developing Internet and a 24/7 media were utilised with great effect by **NGOs** to challenge the behaviour of multinational companies across the globe. Many cross-border companies were caught unawares by issues arising in one country having a detrimental impact on reputation and profitability in many others. The blame in part for this failure of **reputation management** can be directed at the lack of horizon scanning.

This is part of the **issues management** function and refers to the technique by which multinationals become aware of threats to their reputation, both real and apparent. The horizon can be close. For example, the local community might object to a factory extension because of fears of traffic congestion or increased pollution risk. The horizon can also be distant; for example, new regulations in Washington could affect the movement of hazardous materials through US ports, or changes in the tax regime in Brussels could harm margins in the European Union.

Horizon scanning aims at identifying, prioritising and dealing with situations before they become potentially damaging issues. Horizon scanning is not universally accepted in the corporate world; critics argue that it amounts to going looking for trouble. However, as the examples above illustrate, to ignore the technique can prove very costly.

MH

Human Resources

Large organisations typically have an HR department – what used to be called 'personnel'. Public relations teams, particularly those based in house, but also sometimes consultancies – will deal directly with HR departments over a number of core issues. One area of co-operation or conflict is internal communications. CIPR takes the view that anyone engaged principally in internal communications is a PR practitioner. The Chartered Institute of Personnel and Development (CIPD) takes a different view, and calls the practice 'employee relations'. Employees are, of course, a core stakeholder group.

In practice the co-operation of both departments is often important to achieve competent internal communications. One model is for the HR department to set goals and policies and for the PR department to undertake the actual communications. The HR department is thus the client with the PR department acting as consultancy. In-house PR departments will also need to co-operate with HR departments for their own recruitment.

FURTHER READING

Smith, L. and Mounter, P. (2005) *Effective Internal Communication.* London: CIPR.
Yeomans, L. (2006) 'Internal communications', R. Tench and L. Yeomans (eds), *Exploring Public Relations.* Upper Saddle River, NJ: Prentice Hall. pp. 332–53.

QL

In-house

(See also **Consultancy**)

A PR practitioner may be employed in-house or in a consultancy. In the former case the practitioner is employed directly by the client whose public relations he or she is managing. In freelance and secondment contracts the distinction can blur somewhat.

QL

Infotainment

A neologism combining the two words 'information' and 'entertainment' to signal the growing tendency for news and current affairs on all media platforms, to foreground entertainment above information in order to make factual reporting more accessible and increase readership/ **audience** size and reach (Franklin, 1997: 4).

The extent to which **news**, current affairs and the reporting of other subjects/topics are increasingly characterised by infotainment has become highly contested, but the term is common currency in discussions about the **dumbing down** of news media. American journalist James Fallows in his critical text *Breaking the News: How The Media Undermine American Democracy* argues that 'the most influential parts of the [US] media have lost sight of ... the essence of real journalism ... which is the search for information of use to the public' (1996: 6–7); the arrival of infotainment undermines this process.

Market pressures are typically identified as the culprit driving the development of infotainment, although such an argument rests on the contentious and wholly unsubstantiated assumption that moving 'downmarket' or **dumbing down** editorially will increase rather than diminish **audiences** and readerships. This has not been the experience of the British tabloid press, especially the Sunday tabloids, whose growing reliance on infotainment as an editorial feature has accompanied plummeting **circulations**. But some authors, exemplified by Delli Carpini and Williams (2001) in their essay 'Let us infotain you', offer a much more positive appraisal of infotainment.

FURTHER READING

Delli Carpini, M. and Williams, B. (2001) 'Let us infotain you: politics in the new media environment', in W. Lance Bennet and R. Entman (eds), *Mediated Politics: Communication in the Future of Democracy*. Cambridge: Cambridge University Press. pp. 160–81.

Fallows, J. (1996) *Breaking The News: How the Media Undermine American Democracy*. New York: Pantheon Books.

Franklin, B. (1997) *Newszak and News Media*. London: Arnold.

BF

Infotainment

Information Subsidies

Oscar Gandy's influential book *Beyond Agenda Setting* explores the rise of specialist information professionals (special advisers) within government structures in the USA. Gandy's argument is that, 'at every level of government [state and federal] ... there are information specialists whose responsibility is to ensure that the nation's public media carry the desired message forward to the general public, other government officials and key corporate leaders' (1982: 74).

The functioning of this system depends on what Gandy designates information subsidies. These include a range of strategies employed by press officers to minimise the costs of information which **journalists** require to construct, publish and report particular news stories. This provision and control of information subsidies (including **video news releases** [VNRs] and press conferences) is significant because it confers on information providers the possibility for **agenda setting** in **news** media.

Following Gandy's work, several studies have revealed the extent to which information subsidies can be effective in enabling **public relations** specialists and government information and press officers to influence and manage the news agenda in: press coverage of local/state politics in both America and Britain (Franklin and Van Slyke Turk, 1988); reports in national and local newspapers of government policy initiatives such as the Poll Tax (Deacon and Golding, 1994); local newspaper reporting of UK general elections (Franklin et al., 2006); press reporting of devolution in Northern Ireland (Fawcett, 2001); local and regional news media reporting of local government (Fedorcio et al., 1991) and many other areas of news coverage.

Some academic studies have concluded that the very successful deployment of information subsidies by information professionals working within state structures has become so endemic to modern systems of governance that it is appropriate to speak of Britain as 'a public relations state' (Deacon and Golding, 1994: 4) or a '**public relations democracy**' (Davis, 2002).

FURTHER READING

Davis, A. (2002) Public Relations Democracy, Public Relations, Politics and the Mass Media in Britain. London: Sage.

Deacon, D. and Golding, P. (1994) Taxation and Representation: The Media, Political Communication and the Poll Tax. London: John Libbey.

Franklin, B. and Van Slyke Turk, J. (1988) 'Information subsidies: agenda setting traditions', Public Relations Review Spring: 29–41.

Gandy, O. (1982) Beyond Agenda Setting: Information Subsidies and Public Policy. New York: Ablex.

BF

Internet

The history of the Internet began in the 1960s with ARPANET or DARPANET, a project of the US Department of Defense. The (Defense) Advanced Research Projects Agency Network was the world's first packet switching network. Unlike circuit switching networks, packet switching networks cannot be disabled by the dislocation of a single connector. There is always an alternative route around that connector. The Pentagon wished to develop a communications infrastructure that was invulnerable to enemy attack and could continue to operate even if the USA were occupied by an enemy. This capability is critical to the modern operation of the Internet, the linear descendent of ARPANET.

One of the key factors about the Internet is that it is very hard for governments to censor it. That is because it was designed for that exact purpose. Today the Internet consists of several levels, of which the most widely known are email and the World Wide Web. Three other levels are Usenet, or news groups, instant messaging and file transfer protocol (FTP). FTP is used mostly for downloading very large files such as computer software. Usenet, although operating independently of the web, is usually accessed using web-based technology such as Google Groups. Much of Usenet's original functionality – discussion boards for people with an astonishing range of interests – has now been superseded by the ease with which web-based blogs can be established. Instant messaging is wildly popular among some Internet users. Unlike other technologies, such as telephony and email, instant messaging does not allow users of

internet

one provider to send messages to someone using another provider, which remains a major problem.

The Internet brings several clear developments to business and the media, and thus to public relations. First, it reinforces other movement towards **globalisation**. New business models, such as selling goods and services online, and the new global reach of media products are key contributors to globalisation.

Second, it offers increased speed of dissemination in the media. 'Daily' newspapers and even 'weekly' business magazines now produce news in real time, thus **journalists** are writing to very much tighter deadlines than was common 10 years ago. Third, disintermediation is also a strong trend that the Internet has brought to business and PR. Businesses and other organisations now have direct channels of communication with core stakeholder groups such as customers, and are thus no longer as dependent on journalists. These direct channels of communication are available to communicate easily with peripheral stakeholders, such as small shareholders. This has greatly diminished the information gap between fund managers and retail shareholders in a trend called data democratisation. Combined with technology **convergence**, lack of **censorship**, globalisation, speed, interactivity, disintermediation and data democratisation are the main themes of the changes brought by the Internet.

FURTHER READING

Starr, P. (2004) *The Creation of the Media: Political Origins of Modern Communications.* New York: Basic Books.

QL

Internet Public Relations

The spread of the Internet has brought about dramatic change in public relations, just as it has in other areas of business and to the media. These changes are by no means complete. The fact that the media now operate on much faster deadlines changes the way in which PR operates. Weekly news cycles for business magazines have been wholly superseded.

The Internet also opens new channels of communication with the media. Leading practitioner Terence Fane-Saunders, of Chelgate and formerly of Burson Marstellar and Hill & Knowlton, claims that 'the fisherman has replaced the hunter'. By this he means that it is no longer sufficient for PR practitioners to seek out journalists, it is now necessary to create on your website 'bait' that will bring the journalists to you. Naturally, the aim is to ensure that your 'bait' – material of value to a journalist researching a story – will be larded with your key messages.

Other areas of PR have experienced similar stark change. While some aspects of lobbying, depending as they often do on close private relationships, have not changed, public affairs have been revolutionised. For example, public political campaigning is now led by online campaigning. Relatively small outfits are able to run highly sophisticated and influential political campaigns. (For example, see http://www.citizenoutreach.com, run by a lone activist from his home, but gathering increasing influence in Washington DC, principally by means of an effective e-newsletter.)

Monitoring and research of political trends and public policy is now conducted almost wholly online. Political candidates can use the Internet to raise money – especially via a large number of small donations, decreasing the candidate's dependence on major donors. The interactive nature of online communications increases the ability of campaigns to mobilise and motivate volunteers, as well as listen to the concerns of activists.

Internal communications, once the poor relation of PR, has also been dramatically changed. Some organisations – in particular service organisations, in which the whole staff will be online – have converted 100 per cent of their central internal communications to digital channels. The advantages of speed and a precisely controlled central message are clear. Less clear is the main disadvantage – that it can encourage managers to be lazy, and to send an email instead of talking to their staff.

Financial PR is another area where methods of communication have changed markedly. FPR practitioners usually report to the client at the highest level – MDs and FDs. Such busy clients can often be reached only by email. Aspects of research such as investor targeting – which involves checking the publicly available share registers of companies similar to your client – can now be conducted in minutes, when the work would previously have taken days or even weeks. Again, the precisely timed and controlled nature of online communications is critical (see dark sites) as releasing information other than to the agreed timetable can result in criminal prosecution.

QL

Journalism

Journalism is not considered to be much of a job: even by **journalists**! Distinguished editor H.L. Mencken described it as 'a craft to be mastered in 4 days and abandoned at the first sign of a better job' (Delano, 2000: 261). Ernest Hemingway, who worked as a reporter for the *Kansas City Star* in the 1920s, later dismissed his published work from this period as 'just journalism' even though this writing informed much of his later fictional work (Zelizer, 2004: 1).

Journalism assumes a number of meanings reflecting the different understandings made by the 'interpretive communities' of **journalists** and academics (Zelizer, 2004: 29–43), but two distinct yet connected meanings are prominent. First, journalism is a rapidly expanding industry with a global reach, which has economic, political and cultural significance. It is arguably the most significant industry in contemporary society. Second, journalism is an arena of professional practice. It is what journalists do. Journalism is the process by which journalists produce everything from magazines like *Guitar, Biker, Asian Babes* and *Women's Weekly* to Al Jazeera, *Newsnight, The South Wales Echo, CNN,* Internet **news** and literally millions of **blogs**.

As an industry, journalism is a substantial and expansive employer providing work for an estimated 70,000 journalists in the UK (Journalist Training Forum, 2002: 2). Each day, its products are accessed globally by billions of consumers eager for newspapers, magazines, Internet news and radio and television programming. The outlets for journalism's products, moreover, are expanding rapidly reflecting technological advances. The UK's four terrestrial channels in 1982 have been complemented by more than 250 channels delivered by satellite and cable, along with news online, via mobile telephony and a multitude of local and national radio stations (Franklin, 2001: 1).

However, journalism is also a profession – or is it a craft? (Cole, 2006: 75). Sidestepping that controversy, most are agreed that journalism is a revelatory activity that involves discovering and reporting previously unknown and significant matters. For Michael Schudson, journalism provides 'Information or commentary on contemporary affairs taken to be publicly important' (2002: 14) while for Denis McQuail journalism constitutes 'paid writing (and the audiovisual equivalent) for public media with reference to actual and ongoing events of public relevance' (2000: 340). But journalism involves more than the simple chronicling of events and requires commenting, criticising, clarifying, editing and interpreting events as well as simply reporting them. Consequently the journalist 'expresses a judgement on the importance of an item, engages in reporting, adopts words and metaphors, solves a narrative puzzle assesses and interprets' (Adam, 1993: 73, cited in Zelizer, 2004: 21)

McNair claims journalism has three functions: provision of information; support for public life and political debate and finally, provision of entertainment (2005). Provision of information, the key function of journalism since the early 17th century, has always been conducted in a market context and hence journalism was 'born as a commodity for sale in the cultural marketplace' (McNair, 2005: 28). This information, moreover, must be useful, reliable and inform readers about distant events of which they could not otherwise have knowledge. It must also be objective, independent and provide readers with a reasonable approximation of the truth, since subjective myths and misinformation have no value for readers.

However, journalism's support for public life and its propensity to report and comment on political events and issues has been in tension with this ambition to deliver objective information. Journalism occupies a unique position in society from which it reports, but also engages in politics, helping to influence and shape public opinion and thereby political structures, processes and outcomes (Lloyd, 2001). In the UK, constant press criticism of Prime Minister Thatcher proved corrosive of her premiership; in the USA, the investigative journalism of Woodward and Bernstein ended Nixon's presidency.

Nonetheless, journalists' desire to participate in, as well as report, political life has been a constant element within journalism. Distinguished journalist Andrew Marr, for example, argues that the 30,000 estimated political pamphleteers at the time of Cromwell, 'bear more than a passing resemblance to today's more splenetic columnists, (2004: 6).

Finally journalism has always involved a balance between entertaining and informing readers. Journalism may entertain even when it seeks to inform and consequently these should not be seen as antipathetic functions. Hence, readers enjoy articles about sport, entertainment, fashion, lifestyle, cookery, gardening and even reading their stars to see what the future holds for them. The term 'infotainment' captures much of this editorial content.

FURTHER READING

Adam, S.G. (1993) *Notes Towards a Definition of Journalism*. St Petersburg, FL: Poynter Institute.

Cole, P. (2006) 'Educating and training local journalists', B. Franklin (ed.), *Local Journalism and Local Media: Making the Local News*. London: Routledge. pp. 95–104.

Delano, A. (2000) 'No sign of a better job: 100 years of British journalism', *Journalism Studies*, 1 (2): 261–73.

Journalist Training Forum (2002) *Journalists at Work: Their Views on Training, Recruitment and Conditions*. London: The Journalists Training Forum.

Marr, A. (2004) *My Trade: A Short History of British Journalism*. Basingstoke: Macmillan.

McNair, B. (2005) 'What is journalism?', in H. de Burgh (ed.), *Making Journalists*. London: Routledge. pp. 25–43.

Zelizer, B. (2004) *Taking Journalism Seriously: News and the Academy*. London: Sage.

BF

key concepts in
public relations

Journalist

Journalists get a bad press! Their public reputation could hardly be lower. A MORI poll in 1993 discovered that while 83 per cent of respondents trusted teachers and doctors to tell the truth and 14 per cent trusted politicians, only 10 per cent trusted journalists to be honest. But a YouGov Poll in 2003 revealed the complex variety of public attitudes to journalists with 81 per cent of the public expressing trust in BBC and Channel 4 journalists, while figures for *broadsheet* journalists (65 per cent), *local* journalists (60 per cent), *mid-market tabloid* journalists (*Daily Mail, Daily Express*) (36 per cent) and journalists working on *red top tabloids* (16 per cent) displayed a marked decline (Marr, 2004: 14).

However, the Hollywood image of the journalist, exemplified in the portrayal of Bob Woodward and Carl Bernstein in *All The President's Men*, is strongly at variance with these public perceptions. The film presents an image of crusading journalists possessed with a near missionary zeal to discover the truth and identifies journalism as a **fourth estate**; that is as a challenging oppositional institution. On this account, the journalist is central to democracy, symbolises individual freedom and champions freedom of information which, once acquired, is used to expose the corruption and oppression of tyrants. Accordingly Napoleon claimed that 'four hostile newspapers are more to be feared than a thousand bayonets, (Randall, 1996: 4). This perception of the journalist as central to democratic protocols persists. Harcup claims, 'being a journalist is not like working in a baked bean factory' (2004: 2), since journalists do more than simply produce a commodity (like baked beans) for sale in a market place. The activity of being a journalist has social, political and cultural implications. Journalists, Harcup claims, '*inform* society about itself and make *public* that which would otherwise be private' (2004: 2). News is not simply a commodity like a chair or table; news has implications for society and polity, for individuals' knowledge and public opinion. This is a very flattering, possibly self serving image, but this heroic journalist is more likely to be found on the set of a Hollywood film than any newsroom.

Recent press scandals involving Jayson Blair at the *New York Times* (Hansen, 2004) and Janet Cooke at the *Washington Post* (Patterson and Urbanski, 2006), suggest that under pressures of cost cutting, understaffed newsrooms, competition for promotion and poor newspaper management, few journalists match the ideal type crusader. Moreover, changes in journalism mean that investigative journalists have all but disappeared (Foot, 1999) while 'non-news' journalism such as motoring, lifestyle and travel sections increasingly fill newspapers' columns. As Marr notes:

Some say that journalists are people who attempt to search out truths about the world around them and then inform the societies they inhabit ... But where does that leave the people writing about lawnmowers, or cheap wine offers, or even columns about their lovers. How many people who call themselves journalists have ever – in their entire careers – really found out anything much. (2004: 5)

journalist

Trying to establish the elusive identity of journalists has been a continuing academic preoccupation in the UK (Delano and Henningham, 1995), the USA (Weaver, 2005), Brazil (Herscovitz, 2004) and Indonesia (Hanitzsche, 2004). UK journalists have changed markedly in the last 20 years. *Journalists at Work* (2002) revealed there were 70,000 journalists in the UK compared with only 20,000 in the late 1960s: growth predictions suggested there would be 20,000 more UK journalists by 2010. The majority work in regional and local newspapers (30 per cent) and magazines (25 per cent), with a further 11 per cent working in national newspapers and 10 per cent each in radio and television. Half (49 per cent) of journalists are now women, although men predominate in national newspapers (55 per cent) while women are more prominent in television (55 per cent) and magazines (55 per cent). Journalists, moreover, are young (70 per cent are under 40 years of age), predominantly middle class, 98 per cent are graduates, and journalists are untypically (41 per cent) single and almost 80 per cent have no dependent children; these latter figures may speak to the long, anti-social hours worked by journalists. Significantly 96 per cent are white. Ainley's earlier study estimated that only 15 of the 8,000 journalists working the regional and local press were black or Asian (1994: 57) while the study *Diversity in the Newsroom* conducted by the Society of Editors (2004) found little had changed across the decade. Only 20 of the *Guardian's* 411 editorial staff are from ethnic minority communities while the *Leicester Mercury* with 120 staff and 38 per cent of local residents being from ethnic minority communities employs only **seven** black or Asian journalists (Society of Editors, 2004). As distinguished broadcaster Vin Ray argued 'Can a workforce like this properly reflect and understand society as a whole when it is made up of such a narrow section of it?' (2003: 167)

FURTHER READING

Ainley, B. (1994) *Blacks and Asians in the British Media: An Investigation of Discrimination*. London: London School of Economics.

Foot, P. (1999) 'The slow death of investigative journalism', in S. Glover (ed.), *Secrets of the Press: Journalists on Journalism*. London: Allen Lane. pp. 79–90.

Marr, A. (2004) *My Trade: A Short History of British Journalism*. Basingstoke: Macmillan.

Patterson, M. and Urbanski, S. (2006) 'What Jayson Blair and Janet Cooke say about the press and the erosion of public trust', *Journalism Studies*, 7 (6): 828–50.

Society of Editors (2004) *Diversity in the Newsroom: Employment of Minority Ethnic Journalists in Newspapers*. Cambridge: Society of Editors.

Weaver, D.H. (2005) 'Who are journalists?', in H. de Burgh (ed.), *Making Journalists*. London: Routledge. pp. 44–58.

Key Figure
Interviews

Key figure interviews offer a **qualitative** research technique that seeks to elicit the knowledge, beliefs or attitudes of important individuals in a particular field. They are a common and often appealing approach to communications research, but are not without their drawbacks.

There are three basic types of interview:

- Structured – in which a predetermined set of questions is posed in a set order.
- Semi-structured – in which there are some predetermined questions but there is flexibility to tailor the delivery to respondents' answers, and to add themes that were perhaps initially not anticipated.
- Unstructured – in which the role of the interviewer is minimal, simply opening up the topic of debate to the respondent and allowing the exchange to flow freely.

In the first two scenarios, a researcher will often construct an *interview schedule* – a list of the key questions or themes that are important. This not only gives some structure but can act as an important script to ensure that all issues are addressed.

It is important to realise that an interview is more than a simple conversation. Interviewing is a skill and should not be taken lightly. Clearly there is the possibility of an *interviewer effect* – the ways in which personal characteristics of the interviewer will impact on the dynamic of the situation. Some of these can not be changed – gender, age, ethnicity, regional accent, for example – but others may be worth bearing in mind prior to conducting the interview. Appropriate appearance and professional behaviour will go a long way, as will an awareness of body language and other forms of non-verbal communication, if the interview is conducted in a face-to-face situation.

When conducting a research interview, the interviewer should at all times be attentive to the respondent's answers, and respectful of the views that they express. Research interviewing should be non-judgemental and, although this may at times be difficult, the researcher should not allow his or her personal opinions to influence the respondent. Due consideration should be paid to the topic however, and therefore a range of cues and prompts should be rehearsed to avoid respondents ducking particular issues.

Questions should be challenging and interesting to the respondent, and careful research will be needed to avoid asking for information that is freely available elsewhere (for example in the company literature or on the website). This is a waste of both the researcher's and the interviewee's time.

Interviews will normally be recorded and subsequently transcribed for analysis, though care should be taken to obtain consent from the respondent for recording of the session and to establish a level of attribution for any quotes to be used in the research report.

The interview process can be difficult, time consuming and, on occasion, personally stressful. However, the data produced can be extremely rewarding and insightful, and this technique also offers valuable opportunities for **networking**.

FURTHER READING

Deacon, D., Pickering, M., Golding, P. and Murdock, G. (1999) *Researching Communications: A Practical Guide to Methods in Media and Cultural Analysis*. London: Arnold.

Denscombe, M. (2003) *The Good Research Guide*. Maidenhead, PA: Open University Press.

Gunter, B. (2000) *Media Research Methods. Measuring Audience Reactions and Impact*. London: Sage.

Wimmer, R.D. and Dominick, J.R. (2006) *Mass Media Research: An Introduction*. Belmont, CA: Wadsworth.

NM

Key Messages

Key messages are the centrepiece of any **public relations** campaign. In essence they should embrace the reasons behind what you are using PR to achieve. Derived from **excellence theory,** the key messages identify your core purpose; elaborate on how you will achieve it; and then build in a facility to evaluate the results.

Defining the key messages at the start of a **campaign** focuses attention not only on what is to be delivered, but how it will be delivered. It is also vital that the key messages have internal buy-in at all levels to ensure consistency of support throughout the life of the campaign. Most importantly, there should not be too many them, three being a popular number. Many more than this, and you will certainly not have identified clearly enough your core purpose.

FURTHER READING

Cutlip, S.M. (2000) *Effective Public Relations*, 8th edn. Upper Saddle River, NJ: Prentice Hall.

Wilson, D. and Andrews, L. (1993) *Campaigning: The A–Z of Public Advocacy.* London: Hawksmere.

MH

Lobby

The Parliamentary lobby dates back to 1884 when, because of civil disorder, public access to the members' lobby of the House of Commons was restricted to a select group of political journalists whose names were kept on a list compiled by the Sergeant-at-Arms. The Lobby is a cartel for the provision of political information. It is the formal association of the 220 or so senior political **journalists** based at Westminster, who deliver the greater part of the most authoritative political news and comment based on formal **media briefings** by senior politicians, but especially the Prime Minister's Official Spokesperson (PMOS) (McNair, 2000: 43–4). Recent reforms opened briefings to include all London-based foreign correspondents and, since October 2002, the 11.30 a.m. briefings are conducted at the Foreign Press Association rather than the basement at No 10: the 4 p.m. briefing is still conducted in the lobby room in the House.

The Lobby has been criticised because of the secrecy that characterises its operations, with political commentator Roy Hattersley alleging it 'promotes the politics of rumour, innuendo and gossip' (2001: 234). Distinguished journalists like Peter Kellner claim that the lobby packages political news for journalists, and 'produces lazy journalism undertaken by lazy journalists' (1983: 281). Horgan suggests that journalists' description of the briefing of the Irish lobby as 'the feed' underscores this journalistic reliance on government sources for political news (2001: 259). Broadcaster and academic Ivor Gaber argues that the lobby is used to 'fly kites' allowing politicians to gauge public responses to potential policies (2000: 67). Worse, during the Thatcher administrations of the 1980s and the early Blair governments of the late 1990s, the lobby was used to brief against the PM's opponents in Cabinet (Franklin, 2004: ch. 3). Criticisms by political journalists and the public that the lobby was being used by government for **spin** and **news management**, prompted the establishment of the Phillis Committee which reported in January 2004 that the lobby was 'no longer working for the government or the media' and that it was in part responsible for the three-way breakdown in trust between politicians, the **public** and the media (Phillis, 2004).

Advocates of the lobby system argue that it provides journalists with authoritative political comment and news, that journalists are too diverse in their political affiliations and journalistic backgrounds to be vulnerable to **spin doctors** or the spin of politicians and special advisers. Critics, advocates suggest, subscribe to a simplistic view of how the lobby works: an official briefing provides only the starting point for a journalist's story, rarely the terminus (Barnett and Gaber, 2001: 41).

In this new millennium, the lobby has been reformed in response to these criticisms, technological developments and the information and news management requirements of the government. Since 1997, journalists have been allowed to identify the Prime Minister's Official Spokesperson in their reports, while previously circumlocutions such as '**sources** close to the Prime Minister' protected the anonymity of senior government sources (Cockerell et al., 1984). Widespread public access to the web triggered the launch of the No. 10 website on 11 February 2002 (http://www.number-10.gov.uk) with edited extracts from the previous day's lobby briefing, while Michael Cockerell's film *News From No. 10*, broadcast in July 2000, shattered the tradition of lobby secrecy by featuring unprecedented pictures of a lobby briefing including the arrival of the PMOS and his communications advisers. Journalists' reporting protocols for the lobby were also revised. In July 2000, *Guardian* editor Alan Rusbridger announced that a stricter code for journalists would 'encourage reporters to be as specific as possible about the source of any anonymous quotation' (2000: 20), in order to prevent special advisers and press officers using the anonymity of the lobby to brief against cabinet critics of the Prime Minister. Finally, in 2002, the Prime Minister's Press Secretary, Alastair Campbell, announced that the morning briefings would be opened to all journalists, including London-based foreign correspondents, to question officials, government experts and sometimes even ministers: since that date some briefings have been televised. In the first instalment of his published diaries Alastair Campbell downplayed the role of the lobby in shaping political news agendas.

FURTHER READING

Campbell, A. (2007) *The Blair Years*. London: Hutchinson.

Cockerell, M. Hennessey, P. and Walker, D. (1984) *Sources Close to the Prime Minister: Inside the Hidden World of the News Manipulators*. London: Macmillan.

Franklin, B. (2004) *Packaging Politics: Political Communication in Britain's Media Democracy*. London: Arnold.

Hattersley, R. (2001) 'The unholy alliance: the relationship between members of parliament and the press', James Cameron Lecture 1996, in H. Stephenson (ed.), *Media Voices; The James Cameron Memorial Lectures*. London: Polity. pp. 227–45.

Horgan, J. (2001) 'Government sources said last night ... the development of the parliamentary press lobby in modern Ireland', in H. Morgan (ed.), *Information, Media and Power Through the Ages*. Dublin: University College Dublin Press. pp. 259–71.

Kellner, P. (1983) 'The lobby, official secrets and good government', *Parliamentary Affairs*, 36 (3): 275–82.

Phillis, R. (2004) The Government Communications Review. Available at: http://www.gcreview.gov.uk

lobby

125

BF

Lobbying

Lobbying refers to a consistent and directed attempt to influence government policy. In that sense, it is very wide ranging, embracing government at a national and local level as well as other organisations which can influence decisions. It is part of **public affairs** and whilst it makes use of the techniques of **media relations**, it has a broader role.

Four categories of lobbying are usually identified. First, there is straightforward political lobbying, which aims to drive policy by the **reputation management** of an organisation. For example, oil companies would want to stress their actions on reducing greenhouse gas emissions. Second, there is regulatory lobbying, which involves dealing with law-making agencies, for example where competition is concerned. Third, there is policy campaigning, which uses **public relations** techniques to influence the formulation and passage of policy. Finally, there is negotiation, dealing with contracts, and so forth. Many believe this is the most effective form of lobbying for, although it lacks the perceived glamour of media relations and public profile engagement, it does tend to deliver the results.

Lobbyists have often had to endure a bad press for their, obviously, partisan campaigns, and because of such scandals as 'cash for questions' where MPs were paid by interest groups to ask parliamentary questions. However lobbyists argue with some merit that their role is to provide information. Others make the decisions.

FURTHER READING

Miller, C. (2000) *Political Lobbying*. London: Politicos.
Oborne, P. (2005) *The Rise of Political Lying*. London: The Free Press.

key concepts in public relations

MH

Manufacturing Consent

In their highly influential study *Manufacturing Consent: The Political Economy of the Mass Media,* distinguished American intellectuals Edward Herman and Noam Chomsky set out what they term the 'propaganda model' of communication. American media, they argue, are **propaganda** agencies that are used systematically to mobilise ideological support for state policies. While media function to 'amuse, entertain and inform', Herman and Chomsky argue their essential function is 'to inculcate individuals with the values, beliefs and codes of behaviour that will integrate them into the institutional structures of the larger society. In a world of concentrated wealth and major conflicts of class interest, to fulfil this role requires systematic propaganda' (Herman and Chomsky, 1988: 1).

The significant argument here is the suggestion that while the private ownership of the media in the USA and the absence of any formal **censorship** makes this system of propaganda less evident, it is no less effective than in single party political systems where the media are directly controlled by the state.

Herman and Chomsky argue that all potentially newsworthy events must pass through five filters that leave only a 'residue', which has been 'cleansed' of dissenting opinions, available for broadcast and publication in the media. By filtering the **news** in this way, the media 'marginalise dissent and allow the government and dominant private interests to get their messages across to the public' (Herman and Chomsky, 1988: 2).

They identify five such filters: (1) The *private and concentrated ownership of the major media industries* among a limited and socio-culturally homogenous group; (2) the *media reliance on **advertising*** as their prime source of income; (3) US *media reliance on government, business and other semi-official sources* and **public relations** to deliver an expansive part of published news; (4) the use of *flak* – negative responses to media output – to discipline and control media; and (5) the *ideology of anticommunism,* reflecting the suspicion which communism or any 'progressive' or even 'liberal' ideology evokes among 'property owners' in America (Herman and Chomsky, 1988: 29). These filters select and structure news in ways that mobilise ideological support among the public for the 'national interest', which Herman and Chomsky argue constitutes little more than a euphemism for the interests of the powerful among corporate, military and political elites.

The propaganda model was designed to explain media behaviour in the USA but its relevance for the UK is evident: and equally contentious. But consider the 'flak' filter in the context of Alastair Campbell's attack on the BBC in 2003 for its criticisms of the government's policy on Iraq War (Franklin, 2004: 54–73).

The propaganda model has been widely criticised for: (1) offering a version of the good old-fashioned conspiracy theory (Entman, 1990: 126); (2) failing adequately to incorporate **journalists'** accounts of the news gathering and reporting process in the model (Romano, 1989); failing to take account of media professionalism and jour-nalistic objectivity (Hallin, 1994: 4); and, failing to explain contin-ued opposition to government policies articulated both by journalists and the public (Schlesinger 1989: 301). But the **propa-ganda** model continues to offer a stimulating and provocative account of media behaviour in reporting key political events and policies. In a later essay Herman confronts his critics and attempts to refute their objections (Herman, 2000: 101–13) while a recent collection by Klaehn (2005) offers a new assessment of the propa-ganda model and illustrates the relevance of its application to news media reporting of Iraq, the Palestine–Israel conflict and the civil war in El Salvador.

FURTHER READING

Entman, R. (1990) 'News as propaganda', *Journal of Communication*, 40: 124–7.
Franklin, B. (2004) *Packaging Politics: Political Communication in Britain's Media Democracy.* London: Arnold.
Hallin, D. (1994) *We Keep America on Top Of the World.* New York: Routledge.
Herman, E. and Chomsky, N. (1988) *Manufacturing Consent.* New York: Pantheon.
Klaehn, J. (2005) *Filtering the News: Essays on Herman and Chomsky's Propaganda Model.* New York: Black Rose Books.

key concepts in public relations

BF

Marketing (Mix)

The Chartered Institute of Marketing (CIM) describes marketing as the management process which identifies, anticipates and supplies customer requirements efficiently and profitably. The American Marketing Association (AMA) describes marketing as the process of planning and executing the conception, pricing, promotion and distribution of ideas, goods and services to create, exchange and satisfy individual and organisational objectives. Inherent in both descriptions are the facts that marketing is a management process. It is about giving customers what they want and anticipating customer needs both efficiently and profitably.

In the late 19th and early 20th centuries goods were relatively scarce with little competition and products did not need marketing support. Manufacturers of goods could easily sell what was produced. As markets and technology developed, competition became more serious and companies began to produce more than they could sell. In the 1950s and 1960s we saw the rise of the sales era in which organisations developed more aggressive and forceful ways of advertising their products to customers.

The 1970s saw the rise of the marketing concept through which organisations began to move away from the emphasis on heavy selling and **advertising** and the attitude of sell what we can make, to the marketing focus of find out what the customer wants and we will make it for them. Marketing gradually became a key element in corporate strategy and customers became the centre of the organisation's universe. In the 1980s marketing was widely accepted as a strategic business concept and remains at the heart of business strategy. Understanding customer need, of course, is only the starting point as the organisation then needs to act on that information in order to develop and implement marketing activities.

These activities are turned into reality by utilising the marketing mix. Borden (1964) defined the marketing mix as the combination of four major tools of marketing; otherwise known as 'the 4Ps'. The four Ps refers to: product, price, promotion and place. It is described as a mix as successful marketing relies on a balance between all four elements as part of any campaign. For success you need the right product at the right price with strong promotion and in a place where customers can buy it easily. Häagen

Dazs® ice cream offers one illustrative exemplar. A perfectly good product but it is only ice cream. Its huge success came after a daring advertising **campaign** emphasising the raunchy side of the product. A good product with bad **communication** will not work, and similarly a bad product with good communication will not work as the elements of the marketing mix all rely on each other.

FURTHER READING

Akehurst, G. and Alexander, N. (1996) *Retail Marketing*. London: Routledge.
Brassington, F. and Pettitt, S. (2000) *Principles of Marketing*. Harlow: Pearson.
Carpenter, P. (2000) *eBrands: Building an Internet Business at Breakneck Speed*. Boston, MA: Harvard Business School Press.
Smith, C. (2006) *Marketing For Dummies*. Chichester: John Wiley and Son.

EP

Mass Communication

The sending of a message or information by an individual or organisation to a large **audience**, typically through modern **communication** channels.

Mass communications is a popular field of academic research that concerns itself with the messages themselves, the communication channel, and the ways in which the audience receive and perceive that message. Characteristics of the message to be analysed touch upon theories of **persuasion** and **propaganda**.

These will clearly interact with the medium by which the message is transferred, and this has undoubtedly been influenced by the information revolution since the 1980s. With the apparent privatisation of the public sphere, through the commercial development of communication media, and subsequent pressures on journalism practice, many would argue that **public relations** has had an increasing influence on mass communication content, particularly in news media (e.g. Habermas, 1989; Franklin, 1997; Gregory, 2003).

The 'mass' in question tends to refer to the receiver of the message, and therefore to some extent assumes a homogenous and passive **audience**. Initial concepts of media effects, many of which were proposed in the 1970s (e.g. McCombs and Shaw, 1972; Blumler and Katz, 1974; Gerbner and Gross, 1976) have been revised and adapted to take account of a more active and selective audience, and further, to take account of the proliferation of news and information sources, not only as a result of **globalisation**, but also as a result of the diversity of media platforms on which mass communications takes place in the 21st century.

FURTHER READING

McQuail, D. (2005) *Mass Communication Theory.* London: Sage.
Moloney, K. (2006) *Rethinking Public Relations.* London: Routledge.

NM

Media Briefing

Media briefing and interviews are key parts of the toolkit of most **public relations** professionals. The media have many roles as part of a **communications** strategy since they can act as 'gatekeepers' – guardians of access to the wider distribution of the **key messages** – and serve an **agenda setting** function by trying to direct how the strategy is informed. This latter area is the subject of some contention since it is arguable that the media does not tell people *what* to think, but rather what to think *about*.

Two ways of relating to the media are via briefings and interviews. (See also **press conferences**). Briefings are supplanting conferences in many areas. They can be **on** or **off the record** and can be conducted in groups or singly with selected, favoured **journalists**. For PR practitioners they offer a much greater degree of positive input than that provided by the sending out of a press release or the organising of a conference.

Media interviews should always be regarded as being on the record; they should be used sparingly and only after the participants have undergone **media training**. At best, live transmission of a radio or television interview offers to the trained interviewee a unique opportunity of sending out the key messages in an unexpurgated way, not subject to 'noise' (see **excellence theory**) or editing. At worst, in inexperienced hands it can be a disaster both for the interviewee and the PR advisor. Caution should always be applied to granting such an interview. Even more caution should be exercised for a recorded interview; always ascertain the context; check who else is involved, such as a well-known critic; find out how much time is allocated and remember, this is about risk assessment. Does the possible gain outweigh concerns about balance and objectivity?

While 'no comment' should rarely be an option in PR, denying interviews with senior executives can often be the best course of action unless there are adequate safeguards in place. And that, after all, is one of the many jobs of the PR professional.

FURTHER READING

Cutlip, S.M. (2000) *Effective Public Relations*, 8th edn. Upper Saddle River, NJ: Prentice Hall.
Klein, N. (2000) *No Logo*. London: Flamingo.
Wilson, D. and Andrews, L. (1993) *Campaigning: The A–Z of Public Advocacy*. London: Hawksmere.

MH

Media Relations

Media relations is an umbrella title embracing all aspects of dealing with the press and broadcasting. It can be visualised as an iceberg. At the broad base, there is the portion relating to relationship building – getting to know journalists in a social context the better to understand and interpret their way of working. Further up the iceberg there is a narrower area where **public relations** professionals will be on hand to take calls, provide background briefings and generally facilitate the needs of the working **journalist**. Assuming this proves satisfactory for both parties, the next segment is where the PR operator would consciously go out to sell a story; offer interviews with senior executives; provide site visits;

and, when appropriate, off the record briefings. This active phase is key to successful media relations. Following on from this, the tip of the iceberg is where crisis PR happens – and it will.

If the sections down the iceberg have been laid correctly and tended, at this point of exposure the PR professional would hope to be informed of a story affecting a **client** and be invited to comment before printing or transmission. The pinnacle of successful media relations is to have your say before the story goes public. See also **Agenda Setting.**

FURTHER READING

Dilenschneider, R. (1990) *Power and Influence.* New York: Prentice Hall Press.
Gruning, J.E. and Hunt T. (1984) *Managing Public Relations.* New York: Holt, Rheinhart and Winston.
McNair, B. (1999) *News and Journalism in the UK.* London: Routledge.

MH

Media Training

Training clients (including in-house clients) to deal with the media is often a core activity for **public relations** professionals. **Journalists** frequently prefer to deal with expert spokespeople rather than with PR practitioners, and for detailed interviews or profiles, it is often essential that journalists deal with clients directly. But some clients fear media interviews, especially for broadcast, recognising that they lack the appropriate skills. A subject expertise, after all, is quite separate from the fluency and confidence needed to deal with journalists. There is no particular reason the two should go together.

Media training can take many forms. Sometimes it is little more than a pep talk before the journalist arrives, when the **client** needs to be reminded of the **key messages.** For broadcast interviews it may take the form of a practice interview beforehand, conducted by the PR professional. In some cases it is wise to bring in specialist media trainers who can run all-day sessions at broadcast studios.

media training

133

Clients are particularly nervous of live broadcast interviews, though these have many advantages over pre-recorded interviews, which can be, and often are, edited with the express purpose of making a fluent interviewee seem awkward or even dishonest. A live interview has the distinct advantage that in this case, the camera really does not lie. There are numerous techniques that can be imparted to clients very quickly, such as remaining silent to force a journalist (especially on radio) to fill the gap or the QTM (question transfer message) technique. QTM involves acknowledging the question, creating a bridge or transfer, then stating the key message that the interviewee planned to state all along. For example, a politician might respond to a question on immigration by saying: 'that's a very good question. You are right that a great many people want to come and live in the UK. That's mainly because the economy has been so successful under our management ....'

FURTHER READING

Haywood, R. (1991) *All About Public Relations: How to Build Business Success on Good Communications.* London: McGraw-Hill.
Richards, P. (1998) *Be Your Own Spin Doctor.* London: Take That Ltd.

QL

Methodology

The instruments that are employed in conducting research will depend on the research question or hypothesis under investigation, as well as practical considerations such as the constraints on time and resources.

A research question is a broad, non-directive enquiry about the topic under investigation, for example: What is company X's stance on corporate social responsibility?

A hypothesis (plural hypotheses) is a predictive statement that can be supported or rejected on the basis of evidence gathered, for example: Company X's corporate social responsibility policies are effective and welcomed by stakeholders within the specific location in which they operate.

The scientific approach is to construct hypotheses with their negative opposite, known as null hypotheses, in this case that the corporate social responsibility initiatives are not effective and not welcomed. Evidence is then collected in order to accept or reject this null hypothesis. Although this may seem counterintuitive and pessimistic, it is important to note that the majority of research in social sciences, media and communications will not be able to *prove* that something is correct, only to give support to an argument – something along the lines of eliminating as many wrong answers as possible in order to suggest that the remaining alternatives are likely to be the case.

For this reason, all terms within the hypothesis must be carefully and tightly defined to reflect exactly what the researcher means by them. This is known as creating operational definitions.

The majority of research techniques fall into one of two main categories – **quantitative and qualitative methods.**

Quantitative methods provide relatively large data sets that can be subject to statistical analysis and are intended to be generalisable to all instances, through a process known as **sampling**. Quantitative techniques include **content analysis** and surveys or questionnaires.

Qualitative methods provide more specific investigation of an issue that will be less widely applicable to other instances, but the data is rich and in-depth, aiming to give a deeper understanding of the reasons behind the issues. Qualitative techniques include **key figure interviews** and **focus groups**.

While each kind of approach has supporters and detractors, the arguments about their relative merits have moved on and are now relatively obsolete as more and more researchers use a combination of methods in their work, known as *triangulation* or a *mixed-methods* approach.

The traditional scientific research paradigm operates from a theoretical basis in which existing knowledge about a topic logically informs the creation of hypotheses and null hypotheses. This is known as *deductive* research.

In academic **public relations** research, there is a relative paucity of existing theoretical knowledge, and therefore research is more likely to take an exploratory direction, using research techniques to collect data first, which is then analysed to provide patterns of observation that may later form the basis of theory. This is known as *inductive* research.

Broom, G.M. and Dozier, D.M. (1990) *Using Research in Public Relations: Applications to Program Management*. Eaglewood Cliffs, NJ: Prentice Hall.

Gunter, B. (2000) *Media Research Methods: Measuring Audience Reactions and Impact*. London: Sage.

Kitchen, P.J. (1997) 'Developing a research framework: inductive vs deductive?', in P.J. Kitchen (ed.), *Public Relations: Principles and Practice*. London: Thomson International Business Press. pp. 272–82.

Theilmann, R. and Szondi, G. (2006) 'Public relations research and evaluation', in R. Tench and L. Yeomans (eds), *Exploring Public Relations*. Harlow: Prentice Hall. pp. 208–33.

Wimmer, R.D. and Dominick, J.R. (2006) *Mass Media Research: An Introduction*. Belmont, CA: Wadsworth.

NM

Military Public Relations/Embedded Journalists

While there is nothing new about **journalists** accompanying the military onto the battlefield, the 2003 war in Iraq saw an unprecedented **public relations** effort on the part of the Coalition forces (principally the USA and UK), and the coining of a new term in military-media relations – 'embedded journalist'.

An embedded journalist (or 'embed' as opposed to a 'unilateral') was an accredited correspondent who travelled with and reported exclusively on the activities of one particular military unit, often units directly engaged in combat. In terms of the US operation, the person most widely credited with the initial idea for this arrangement was former Hill and Knowlton board director Victoria Clarke, in her capacity as

Assistant Secretary for Defense (Public Affairs). Though critics accused their respective media, governments and militaries of overt **propaganda**, embedded journalists were able to report objectively and on several occasions were in a position to correct or directly counter official reports of controversial incidents, and coverage was less reliant on military briefings than in previous conflicts (for example, the 1991 Gulf War).

Nonetheless, the spectacular and compelling footage that embedded journalists could file led to an overall reliance on reporting of the conduct of individual operations, rather than a broader strategic analysis. In this respect, the media operation contributed to Coalition PR efforts to focus **public opinion** on support for the troops, rather than to continue debate and speculation concerning the legality and morality of the invasion. This was particularly pertinent in the UK where domestic opposition to the war was considerable.

The 2003 war was also noteworthy for the unprecedented casualty rates among independent journalists – the so-called 'unilaterals' – who were free from military restrictions on reporting and travel arrangements, but subsequently did not enjoy the associated protection. How conflict reporting develops in future is open to speculation but the effort and resources dedicated to the embedding process by the military and governments represent a significant shift away from overt **censorship** to more subtle techniques of media management.

FURTHER READING

Brandenberg, H. (2007) "Security at the source' embedding journalists as a superior strategy to military censorship', *Journalism Studies*, 8(6): 948–63.

Katovsky, B. and Carlson, T. (2003) *Embedded: The Media at War in Iraq: An Oral History*. Guilford, CT: The Lyons Press.

Lewis, J., Brookes, R., Mosdell, N. and Threadgold, T. (2006) *Shoot First and Ask Questions Later: Media Coverage of the 2003 Iraq War*. New York: Peter Lang.

Miller, D. (2004) *Tell Me Lies: Propaganda and Media Distortion in the Attack on Iraq*. London: Pluto Press.

Thussu, D.K. and Freedman, D. (eds) (2003) *War and the Media*. London: Sage.

Tumber, H. and Palmer, J. (2004) *Media at War: The Iraq Crisis*. London: Sage.

NM

Mission Statement

According to the Centre for Business Planning, a mission statement needs to be 'a clear and succinct representation of the enterprise's purpose for existence'. This means that it will include core aims for the organisation, which may include making money but will also look at the ways in which the organisation plans to do so, including focusing on customer needs. The mission statement will therefore be very different in a diversified conglomerate that has been built by acquisition compared with one for a non-profit organisation or an enterprise with a strong social purpose.

Famous mission statements include that of the Walt Disney Corporation 'to make people happy'. **Google**'s mission statement is no less ambitious: 'Google's mission is to organize the world's information and make it universally accessible and useful.' (The famous motto 'Don't be evil' is not a mission statement, it is a summary of the company's **corporate social responsibility [CSR]** policy).

Mission statements are easily mocked as being content-free marketing gobbledegook. Indeed, dilbert.com has a mission statement generator, which randomly shuffles adverbs like 'efficiently', 'proactively' and 'seamlessly' with nouns like 'data', 'paradigms' and 'leadership'. A well-written mission statement can, nonetheless, be an important focus for an organisation.

Mission statements usually define the organisation's values. For example, Shell's *Statement of General Business Principles* performs the role of both mission statement and CSR statement. In format, mission statements often begin with a simple, memorable, sentence, but frequently also include clarifying and qualifying terms below.

Other famous mission statements:

Ford: 'To become the world's leading consumer company for automotive products and services.'

Amazon: 'To build a place where people can come to find and discover anything they might want to buy online.'

eBay: 'eBay's mission is to provide a global trading platform where practically anyone can trade practically anything.'

Apple (1984): 'To produce high-quality, low cost, easy to use products that incorporate high technology for the individual. We are proving that high technology does not have to be intimidating for noncomputer experts.'

FURTHER READING

Centre for Business Planning: http://www.businessplans.org/Mission.html

QL

Models in Public Relations

This is not as many might think, an excuse for a photo opportunity. Rather it is an attempt to define the practise of **public relations** from a theoretical basis. Essentially, there are four models: press agentry; public information; two-way asymmetric; and two-way symmetric.

Press agentry is by any other definition propaganda. It exists as one-way traffic from, usually, a publicist to the media and engages in little original research. Telling the truth is not thought to be a prerequisite.

Public information is again one-way, but truth is essential as this model is most used by government agencies.

Two-way asymmetric is all about persuasion and is normally used by **NGOs** and other pressure groups to produce agreement or, at the very least, reduce dissent.

Finally, two-way symmetric is the doyen of PR. It aims to create mutual understanding by using feedback to influence the behaviour of the sender and so create changes in the behaviour of the receiver. (See **excellence theory**.)

FURTHER READING

Grunig, J. (1992) *Excellence in Public Relations and Communication Management* Hillsdale, NJ: Lawrence Erlbaum.

Moss, D. (1991) *Public Relations in Practice*. New York: Routledge.

models in public relations

MH

Networking

Social networking in PR is a key way of developing opportunities. **Public relations** consultants tend to have strong media and business networks to assist in the development of communications campaigns and the development of new business. A social network is a social structure made of hubs, which are generally individuals or organisations. It indicates the ways in which they are connected through various social familiarities ranging from casual acquaintance to close familial bonds.

Research in a number of academic fields has demonstrated that social networks operate on many levels, from families up to the level of nations, and play a critical role in determining the way problems are solved, organisations are run, and the degree to which individuals succeed in achieving their goals.

Social networking also refers to a category of Internet **social media** applications to help connect friends, business partners or other individuals together using a variety of tools such as Hotmail, YouTube, Bebo, MSN Messenger, Hi5 and Facebook.

In PR terms, social networking is a key business requirement to further career prospects. Practitioners develop 'little black books' of contact lists outlining key media and business contacts. The wider and deeper your network the greater the opportunity the practitioner has to deliver communication campaigns at speed.

FURTHER READING

Cross, R.L., Cross, R. and Parker, A. (2004) The Hidden Power of Social Networks: Understanding How Work Really Gets Done in Organisations. Boston, MA: Harvard Business School Press.

Stewart, A.S. (1998) Intellectual Capital: The New Wealth of Organizations. London: Nicholas Brearley.

EP

Harcup suggests that if people were asked to define news, most responses would include a mention of novelty; news must be new. News is information about a recent event that the hearer did not know about previously (Harcup, 2004). To cite a journalistic adage, 'there's nothing older than yesterday's news'. But news must also be about the unusual rather than the everyday. To cite a second journalistic rule of thumb, 'Dog bites man is NOT news, but man bites dog IS news'. News also typically tends to emphasise the negative aspects of life: tragedies, natural disasters, train and plane crashes, factory closures and redundancies rather than factory openings and the new jobs they bring. To cite a final adage attributed to **journalist** Ian Jacks, 'Bad news is to **journalism** what dung is to rhubarb!'

This emphasis on what is new, what is unusual and what is negative constitute what journalists call **news values**; that is, the attributes that an event must possess if it is to become news. Two Swedish sociologists, Galtung and Ruge, wrote a classic essay identifying 12 factors that gave events news value, which included a focus on elite nations, elite people and the scale of the event (Galtung and Ruge, 1965). In an update, as well as a critique of their theory, Harcup and O'Neill (2001) added celebrity and sensation to Galtung and Ruge's initial list, but also restated two very important criticisms of news values attributed to Stuart Hall. First, Galtung and Ruge's approach to news assumes there is a reality external to journalists that has to meet their criteria for newsworthiness. But in truth journalists are not simply reporters of some external reality but are actively involved in creating that reality; hence many scholarly studies refer to news 'making' rather than news 'reporting'. The inference here is that news is artifice and something constructed by journalists. Second, news values do not constitute a neutral set of criteria but articulate ideological commitments – news values are a 'cultural map' that journalists use to help them make sense of the world.

This understanding of news is closely associated with the Glasgow Media Group (GMG) which is well known for a series of studies of news beginning in the 1970s with *Bad News* (1976) and most recently

Bad News from Israel (Philo and Berry, 2004). *Bad News* made explicit the Group's guiding assumption which was that 'contrary to the claims, conventions and culture of television journalism the news is not a neutral product … Television news is a cultural artifact: it is a sequence of socially manufactured messages, which carry many of the culturally dominant assumptions of our society' (GMG, 1976: 1). Consequently, despite the claims to objectivity and impartiality made by Tuchman (1972), the *Bad News* series of books alleged a systematic skew in news programming which reflected dominant interests in society and favoured those interests. Studies of industrial relations in the UK, for example, used transcribed news reports from the period to argue for a favourable prominence in reports for management above trades unions in industrial coverage.

The advent of the converged digital newsroom and newspapers' adoption of a 'web first' policy has significant consequences for journalists' assessment of news values but also for the way in which news is reported. An evening newspaper which goes on sale at 4 p.m. but which breaks its lead story in the paper's online edition at 1 p.m. is not offering the 'new' news identified as central to the definition of news in the opening paragraph above. Consequently journalists are increasingly changing their news reporting styles away from using the inverted pyramid ideal for breaking news into a more discursive style which reviews in detail and offers context to stories rather than breaking them; a trend described as the 'featurisation' of news (Williams and Franklin, 2007).

FURTHER READING

Galtung, J. and Ruge, M. (1965) 'The structure of foreign news: the presentation of the Congo, Cuba and Cyprus crises in four Norwegian newspapers', *Journal of International Peace Research*, 1: 64–91.

Harcup, T. and O'Neill, D. (2001) 'What is news? Galtung and Ruge revisited', *Journalism Studies*, 2 (2): 261–80.

Philo, G. and Berry, M. (2004) *Bad News From Israel*. London: Pluto.

Tuchman, G. (1972) 'Objectivity as a strategic ritual: an examination of newsmen's notion of objectivity', *American Journal of Sociology*, 77 (4): 660–70.

Williams, A. and Franklin, B. (2007) *Turning the Tanker Around: Trinity Mirror's Online Strategy*. Cardiff: Cardiff University.

BF

News Agency/Press Association

News agencies or wire services ('the wires') are organisations that employ **journalists** and **editors** to gather and write **news** reports, not for direct publication in their own news outlets, but for distribution and sale to conventional news media (newspapers, radio, television and online news services) who pay an agreed rate for the right to publish them. Typically the article will be bylined to the agency – for example, the Press Association ('the PA') – although some newspapers will attribute them to 'our political correspondent' or 'our industrial correspondent' to create the impression that the paper employs a good number of specialist **journalists** (Moncrieff, 2001). Many of these published articles are **nibs** (news in brief – short items of around 50 words) although a recent research study revealed that the greater part are fairly substantial articles of up to 800 words; even in the 'quality' or 'broadsheet' papers (Lewis et al., 2006).

Local newspapers may buy complete camera ready pages of news composed by the PA with the rate reflecting whether the content is a generic page which might fit into any regional newspaper or 'bespoke' news tailored to the requirements of a specific paper and its circulation area. The output of copy is certainly prolific: half a million words a day on news, sport, foreign affairs, business news and weather. This special evening newspaper service PACE (PA Choice for Evenings), delivers a daily average of 30,000 words between 6 a.m. and 3 p.m. (Hamer, 2000: 12): the PA's ambition has always been to 'give newspapers the kind of news they wanted, when they wanted it, at the length they wanted it' but, significantly 'at a congenial price' (Scott, 1968: 41).

The PA is a national service, although there are local agencies which specialise in selling local news to local and regional newspapers (Hamer, 2006: 215–16), but the 'big four' – United Press International (UPI), Agence Presse-France (APF), Associated Press (AP) and Reuters – operate and sell news globally. Consequently they have been 'historically … one of the most formative influences in the very concept of "news" in the western world' with an ambition to 'satisfy the appetite of many daily retail media' (Boyd Barrett, 1980: 19).

One side effect of newspapers' growing reliance on wire copy to inform and shape their editorial is a growing homogenisation, standard-isation or even McDonaldisation of newspaper contents (Franklin, 2005). The editorial significance of PA activities was acknowledged in a tribute by the chair of the *Yorkshire Post* group who claimed 'the trusti-ness of the PA is one of the supreme merits of British **Journalism** … the fact is that most of our newspapers contain so much news wired from the PA that it would look monotonous if every message from its giant building … had a Press Association by-line or label' (Linton, *Yorkshire Post*, 13 March 1968). Established in 1868, the PA has recently moved to Howden, a small town outside Leeds, where its activities now include generating copy for sale for print, broadcast, teletext and online media.

FURTHER READING

Boyd Barrett, O. (1980) *The International News Agencies.* London: Sage.
Franklin, B. (2005) 'McJournalism? The McDonaldization thesis, local newspapers and local journalism in the UK', in S. Allan (ed.), *Journalism Studies: Critical Essays.* Milton Keynes: Open University Press. pp. 110–21.
Hamer, M. (2006) 'Trading on trust: news agencies, local journalism and local media', in B. Franklin (ed.), *Local Journalism and Local Media: Making the Local News.* London: Routledge. pp. 210–19.
Lewis, J. Williams, A. and Franklin, B. (2006) *Final Report on the Independence of British Journalism.* Cardiff: Cardiff University.
Moncrieff, C. (2001) *Living on a Deadline: A History of the Press Association.* London: Virgin Books.

BF

key concepts in
public relations

News Angle

News angle is what the media judge to be newsworthy. Edward Bernays, nephew of Sigmund Freud and one of the founders of modern **public** relations, wrote in the 1920s about producing events that then became news. Later American philosopher Daniel Boorstin described the **photo opportunity**, a manufactured occasion which provided a picture – and hence a story – for the news media.

Any student of the media and PR could on any day pick out literally dozens of examples of how news is 'made', not just reported. The ministerial visit to a school to announce changes to education policy (see **spin doctor**); the photo opportunity for the celebrity endorsement of a new product; royalty going about its task of opening a building or an event or unveiling something else.

To the outsider, judging what is a news angle can seem to be something of an inexact science. To the insider it is much more straightforward. What do the readers or viewers want or expect? What are their current concerns – health provision, immigration, education? In addition, the media takes on two other roles, that of **gatekeeper** and **agenda setter** (see also **media briefing** and **interviews**).

The PR professional, through the practice of **media relations**, will be well aware of what constitutes the news angle for a particular **journalist** and will attempt to provide information which will secure coverage in an increasingly competitive and fragmented marketplace.

FURTHER READING

Dilenschneider, R. (1990) *Power and Influence.* New York: Prentice Hall Press.
Gruning, J.E. and Hunt T. (1984) *Managing Public Relations.* New York: Holt, Rheinhart and Winston.
McNair, B. (1999) *News and Journalism in the UK.* London: Routledge.

MH

News Management

The phrase news management is broadly self-explanatory and refers to the various techniques that organisations and individuals deploy in their efforts to 'manage' the **news** and influence media coverage of their activities. The ambition is typically to create favourable news coverage although in circumstances of very bad news, the goal may be damage limitation. Weapons in the news management armoury include informal **press** briefings, drafting and distributing press releases, holding press **conferences**, withholding or timing the release of information (see **embargo**). Typically and perhaps predictably, the most consummate practitioners of news management deny their ability to influence or even help to shape news coverage of events; some even challenge **journalists** by declaring them to be the real **spin doctors** or news managers (Campbell, 2007)

Since the mid-1990s, news management has become closely associated with **spin** as political parties, pressure groups, parliament and government increasingly compete for highly contested space in news media to promote favourable images and reports of their major policies and leading politicians: a process described as the 'packaging of politics, (Franklin, 2004).

Governments enjoy unique access to a number of institutional mechanisms that offer them possibilities for managing media coverage as part of their broader **government public relations** strategy. These range from the use of DA Notices, formal **censorship** and the less sinister sounding briefings of the **lobby**. Post 1997, Labour created a number of governmental organisations specifically designed to assist its news management ambitions including a centralised and expanded press office and a Strategic Communications Unit at Number 10 (to plan and orchestrate media reporting of government policy), the Media Monitoring Unit (to provide 24-hour surveillance and analysis of media coverage of government and policy) in the Cabinet Office, as well as recruiting unprecedented numbers of special advisers with a specific brief for **media relations** and news management (Franklin, 1998; Oborne and Walters, 2004).

The Labour government became so enthusiastic about the possibilities for managing news media discussions of its affairs that journalists increasingly began to complain about government's bullying and disdainful attitude towards the **lobby** (Oborne, 1999: 181), with one senior journalist describing the government and its Director of Communications as 'control freaks' (Jones, 2003). The efforts of government **spin doctors** to manage the news eventually became a serious issue for the government reflecting widespread public criticism. Prime Minister Blair announced the 'end of spin' (many times) but the *Guardian*'s political editor announced wearily 'no spin is the new spin' (*Guardian*, 16 December 2002: 2–3). Eventually the Prime Minister's press secretary Alastair Campbell resigned on 29 August 2003. *The Times* seemed uncertain about the implications of Campbell's resignation for the future of news management: its front page headline queried 'The End of Labour's Spin Cycle?' (*The Times*, 30 August 2003).

FURTHER READING

Campbell, A. (2007) *The Blair Years.* London: Hutchinson.
Franklin, B. (1998) *Tough on Soundbites, Tough on the Causes of Soundbites: New Labour and News Management.* London: The Catalyst Trust.
Franklin, B. (2004) *Packaging Politics: Political Communication in Britain's Media Democracy.* London: Arnold.
Jones, N. (2003) *The Control Freaks*, 2nd edn. London: Politicos.
Oborne, P. and Walters, S. (2004) *Alastair Campbell.* London: Aurum Press.

BF

News Values

News values provide one answer to the question 'What is news?' They explain why journalists select a small handful of events from the millions which happen in the world every day and designate them 'news', while ignoring others and thereby consigning them to the dust heap of history. They vary over time, across societies, journalistic cultures and audience interests. They are not written down in any formal code but for the journalist they are almost instinctive; like their ability to 'sniff out' a good story using their 'nose' for news. Former *Guardian* editor Alastair Hetherington claimed that deciding what's news was like riding a bike; think about it too hard and you risk falling off (Hetherington, 1985). But the apparently simple question 'What is news?' raises perennial difficulties. John Pilger, for example, posed the following conundrum following the death of newspaper owner Robert Maxwell.

On the day Robert Maxwell died an estimated 6000 people were killed in a typhoon in the Philippines, most of them in one town. Maxwell's death consumed the British media ... The death of the Philippinos [sic], the equivalent of the extinction of a Welsh mining village, with many more children killed than at Aberfan, was mentioned in passing, if at all. On the BBC's *Nine O'Clock News*, Maxwell was the first item: the disaster in the Philippines was one of the last in the round up of fillers. (Pilger: 1992: 63)

Why do journalists' news values allocate so little news salience to the death of so many people overseas yet so much to the life of a single British person? During the Iraq War Phillip Knightley related an iron law of journalism to explain this journalistic exchange rate. For US journalists, he claimed, the death of one American soldier is worth 10 British and 100 Arabs (Knightley, 2003).

The classic study of news values, 'The structure of foreign news', was published by Johann Galtung and Mari Ruge in 1965; 40 years on, it remains for some observers 'the most influential explanation' of news values (McQuail, 1994: 270). The study analysed news coverage of three international crises and tried to identify the factors informing journalists' news judgements. They listed 12 factors including: frequency (news is about *events* not *processes*); threshold or intensity (a child killed in a road accident compared to 30 children killed in a school bus crash); meaningfulness signalling cultural proximity – UK citizens involved in events abroad 'Tsunami; Cardiff man dies'; consonance or predictability, and unexpectedness; in the classic example 'Man bites dog is news – dog bites man is not'. Other identified news values include continuity or follow-up stories); composition; references to elite nations; personification; negativity references to elite peoples; Jane Bloggs has baby compared to Victoria Beckham has baby. Galtung and Ruge suggest that the greater consonance between an event and these news values the more likely that it will be reported as news.

Harcup and O'Neill in their recent study of news values, review the critical literature on Galtung and Ruge's work (Tunstall, 1971; Hall, 1973; Curran and Seaton, 1997), and support Tunstall's observation that by focusing on major international crises, Galtung and Ruge ignored 'day-to-day coverage of lesser events' (Tunstall, 1971: 21). Harcup and O'Neill decide to establish a new list of news values derived from a content analysis of 1276 stories published in the *Daily Mail*, the *Sun* and the *Daily Telegraph* during March 1999. They identify three types of story not recognised by Galtung and Ruge: entertainment; good news stories; and stories expressing the newspaper's ideological agenda – for example *Sun* stories against the BBC. Harcup and O'Neill's list has 10 news values including stories about: the power elite; celebrity; entertainment; surprise; good news; bad news; magnitude; relevance; follow-up stories; the newspaper's political/ideological agenda.

They conclude that 'A story with a good picture or picture opportunity combined with any reference to an A-list celebrity, royalty, sex, TV or cuddly animal appears to make a heady brew that news editors find almost impossible to resist' (Harcup and O'Neill, 2001: 276).

FURTHER READING

Galtung, J. and Ruge, M. (1965) 'The structure of foreign news: the presentation of the Congo, Cuba and Cyprus crises in four Norwegian newspapers', *Journal of International Peace Research*, 1: 64–91.

Harcup, T. and O'Neill, D. (2001) 'What is news? Galtung and Ruge revisited', *Journalism Studies*, 2 (2): 261–80.

Hetherington, A. (1985) *News, Newspapers and Television*. London: Macmillan.

Pilger, J. (1991) *Heroes*. London: Cape.

BF

Newsrooms

Newsrooms constitute the **news** gathering and reporting centre of all news organisations. In fictionalised Hollywood accounts of **journalism** exemplified by Billy Wilder's *Ace in The Hole*, newsrooms are presented as chaotic, busy and noisy places where the ceaseless clatter of typewriter keys is punctuated only occasionally by the arrival of a journalist, with trilby hat, trailing coat and arms held high in the air announcing the immortal phrase 'Hold the front page'; as late as the 1990s, Michael Keaton's character who is an ambitious, 'scoop crazy' tabloid **journalist** in *The Paper*, offers a similar utterance (Franklin, 1997: 26).

In truth, newsrooms are very organised workplaces, carefully structured and designed to bring together distinctive groupings of journalists and **editors,** as well as various sources of news from wire services and **public relations** practitioners, to maximise the effectiveness of the news operation (Meier, 2007). In their classic study of *The Form of News*, John

Nerone and Kevin Barnhurst (2003) identify six distinctive types of newspaper and newsroom organisation reflecting different newspaper *styles* (The visual characteristics of the paper), *types* (everything that is involved in making a newspaper – machinery, business plan, the division of labour) and *ideals* (the dominant notion of what the paper is intended to do). The layout and culture of newsrooms developed historically and varied according to these three elements.

The earliest newspapers, the 'printer's paper', articulated the characteristic dominance of printers in newspaper production across the 18th century, which gave way to the 'editor's paper' (1820) reflecting the emergence or mass politics and daily publication. From 1850, the 'publisher's paper' developed a distinctive newsrooms which was supplanted by the industrial paper of the 1880 following the industrialisation of society. The developing journalistic professionalism with its ideal of objectivity triggered the 'professional paper' (1910), which has been replaced since the 1950s by the 'corporate paper' shaped by a distinctive pattern of ownership (Nerone and Barnhurst, 2003: 435–51). But the development of newspapers and newsrooms has been extremely uneven across Europe. The first newspaper in Sweden was launched in 1645, in Germany in 1610 and in Denmark 1657, with Norway (1763) and Finland (1771) trailing almost a century behind (Hoyer, 2003: 456).

The impact of emerging and new technologies on newsrooms and news production has been obvious across their historical development, not least with the arrival of the telegraph (Pottker, 2003: 501), but the emergence of the Internet, email and online production of news makes more explicit than previously the role of new technology in shaping newsrooms. In the UK in late 2006, for example, the *Telegraph* newspaper invested more than £600m in a new 'hub' design for its newsroom which placed editors and journalist in new spatial and working arrangements with each other in order to facilitate newswork in the digital age.

America has blazed the trail in constructing 'converged newsrooms' where journalists work in a single newsroom across the distinctive media platforms of print, broadcast and online. The Tampa News Centre, for example, houses the *Tampa Tribune* (newspaper), *Tampa Bay Online*, the online site and *WFLA-TV*, a local television station. Stories are assigned to reporters who gather news, and then the information gathered is packaged for distribution via any of the media outlets. This combined news gathering operation is highly efficient and cost effective (Thelen, 2003: 513).

The *Orem (Utah) Daily Journal* was the first daily newspaper to go online after only nine months of publishing a printed product (http://www.ucjournal.com/); the implications for newsroom organisation are evident. The growth of **blogs** and the arrival of citizen journalism offer an even more radical prospect; the newsroom might become redundant. A blogger requires only a laptop and a web connection. Jurgen Wilke anticipates the possible end of the newsroom and the return of journalists to their initial state of homelessness – the days when (the printers' and publishers') newspapers were produced by printers and publishers who simply pasted together news from European papers without any need for a newsroom (Wilke, 2003: 465–79). Wilke's provocative suggestion is that the newsroom might prove to be an ephemeral phenomenon: a place where for a short period of its history, journalism was conducted.

FURTHER READING

Hoyer, S. (2003) 'Newspapers without journalists', *Journalism Studies*, 4 (4): 451–65.
Meier, K. (2007) 'Innovations in Central European newsrooms: a case study and overview', *Journalism Practice*, 1 (1): 4–19.
Nerone, J. and Barnhurst, K. (2003) 'US newspaper types, the newsroom and the division of labour 1750–2000', *Journalism Studies*, 4 (4): 435–50.
Thelen, G. (2003) 'For convergence', *Journalism Studies*, 4 (4): 513–16.
Wilke, J. (2003) 'The history and culture of the newsroom in Germany', *Journalism Studies*, 4 (4): 465–78.

BF

NGOs

NGOs or non-governmental organisations have only relatively recently become significant players in **public relations**. Most often they are single-issue lobbyists, concerned for example with the environment, world poverty, or abuse of prisoners, and are largely funded by public subscription. Understandably, this leads them to seek a high media profile.

One factor that has helped their growth and perceived success is they have hired communication professionals with a live knowledge of **media relations** techniques including **soundbites** and **photo opportunities**. Coupled with the appetite for stories provided by 24/7 **rolling news**,

NGOs have been able to punch above their weight in many campaigns. They have also become adept at **celebrity endorsement** and using **infotainment** to achieve coverage.

Market leaders include Greenpeace, who harassed Shell over its decision to sink the oil storage platform Brent Spar in the North Sea; Save the Children Fund, which has successfully used Princess Anne to drive home its messages on child poverty, Landmine, which had a campaign to stop the use of such devices led by Princess Diana, and Amnesty International, which called on the services of many well-know entertainers to stage regular shows such as The Secret Policeman's Ball to raise awareness about the torture of prisoners.

FURTHER READING

Grunig, J.E. and Pepper, F.C. (1992) *Excellence in Public Relations and Communication Management*. Mahwah, NJ: Lawrence Erlbaum.

Heath, R.L. (ed.) (2001) *Handbook of Public Relations*. Thousand Oaks, CA: Sage.

Tench, R. and Yeomans, L. (eds) (2006) *Exploring Public Relations*. Harlow: Pearson.

MH

NIBs (News in Brief)

NIBs or news in brief, is a digest used in both print and broadcast. It does exactly what it says; provides a summary of stories lower down the **news** running order, which by definition do not merit a significant place of their own. An accomplished sub-**editor** can get a NIB down to one paragraph of copy or a 15-second **soundbite**. Cynics in the **public relations** industry say the NIB is the equivalent of circular file 13 – the bin, the destination of badly written press releases rescued by a news editor in desperate need of fillers.

MH

On Message

On message refers to the practice in political **public relations** of ensuring that all party members understand what the current view is of policy. The present Labour government is credited with taking this to new heights when MPs were issued with electronic pagers that delivered a constant, and changing, supply of **key messages.** In this way they could be kept informed about the daily impact of policy and so where, literally, on message.

The central aim was to ensure consistency of key messages and demonstrate party unity. For example, a constituency interview by an MP in the local paper was echoed by a ministerial appearance on *Newsnight*. Critics claim it has reduced MPs to mere **soundbite** politicians, endlessly repeating the central policy mantra. Proponents argue that in the era of 24/7, it is an inevitable consequence of feeding the huge appetite of rolling news bulletins.

FURTHER READING

Jones, N. (1999) *Sultans of Spin*. London: Orion Books.
Nyan, B. (2004) *All the President's Spin*. New York: Touchstone.

MH

On/Off the Record

Being on or off the record is one of the central tenets of **media relations.** At its core is the prospect that a PR practitioner can give information to a **journalist** without being quoted directly. This technique has many uses and pitfalls. At its most developed it is a way of getting material out into the public domain without the **source** being identified. Often, as in the case of official secrets, this might be the only way possible without compromising the informant. Crucially it depends on the level of trust between the parties.

At times it is essential to be on the record, for example in **financial public relations** where regulatory services are involved such as a stock exchange when dealing with a publicly quoted company. At other times when the PR practitioner is attempting to paint in the background to a situation, anonymity may be preferred. In **media relations** many engagements with journalists can shift between on and off the record within the same conversation. What is key is that at the outset ground rules are established as to what can be quoted directly and what is strictly for deep background. A variation on this are the so-called Chatham House Rules, named after an independent think tank based in London. Here information may be quoted directly but the source remains anonymous. For the PR practitioner an easy rule of thumb is to assume everything you say is on the record. The essential guideline before any conversation is to take a view of the impact of what you say appearing directly in the media.

For many years **lobby** briefings, which are a key feature of political PR in the UK, were conducted by an anonymous government spokesmen. Now the daily briefings are by a named individual and are on the record. The benchmark remains the same; journalists prefer to quote a named source where possible. For the PR practitioner that might be subject to careful – and on the record – negotiation.

FURTHER READING

Barnett, S. and Gaber, I. (2001) *Westminster Tales: The Twenty First Century Crisis in Political Journalism*. London: Continuum.

Franklin, B. (2004) *Packaging Politics: Political Communication in Britain's Media Democracy*. London: Arnold.

Jones, N. (2008) 'Politics', in B. Franklin (ed.), *Pulling Newspapers Apart: Analysing Print Journalism*. London: Routledge. pp. 172–80.

MH

Party Conferences

The autumn political conference season usually kicks off with the Trades Union Congress (TUC) in the first half of September, though the conferences of the smaller parties including the Green Party, Plaid Cymru and the SNP are often around the same time. The Liberal Democrat Party conference is usually in mid-September. The Labour Party is traditionally the last week of September, and the Conservatives in the first week of October.

While the LibDems have a wider range of venues, only Brighton, Bournemouth and Blackpool have traditionally had the combination of a large enough conference space and sufficient off-peak hotel space to suit Labour and the Conservatives. Labour broke with that tradition for the first time in a generation in 2006, holding its conference in Manchester, to which it returned in 2008. In the same year the Conservatives returned to Birmingham for the first time in many decades.

For Labour and the LibDems the conference retains, at least theoretically, a policy-making role. However, major set-piece battles over Europe and nuclear disarmament are now things of the past. Today, platform defeats are more likely to focus on public services, and be brushed aside by the front bench. In the Conservative Party, conference resolutions have never been anything more than advisory. They are also usually shorter and more general.

Increasingly, therefore, the conference plenary sessions are used more as rallies, with guaranteed television coverage, than as policy-making vehicles (Stanyer, 2001). Broadcast and political journalists flock to the conference and media coverage is extensive. The governing party will always issue over 1000 press passes. The main opposition party is unlikely to be far behind, though interest does vary, partly with expectations about the party's prospects in upcoming elections. Foreign embassies are heavily represented, especially at the conferences of the government and official opposition parties.

Though plenary sessions remain largely policy-free, the conference fringe is lively with debate. A wide range of pressure groups and NGOs organise their own fringe meetings, as do internal party ginger groups such as the Fabian Society (Labour) and the Bow Group (Conservative). There are panel discussions, set-piece speeches by frontbenchers (often those who failed to make the cut for the main conference) and opportunities for activists to question and debate. Since most of the fringe meetings take place at lunchtime or in the evening, there are considerable opportunities for

party conferences

155

commercial sponsorship, usually by paying for refreshments and making a donation to the voluntary group organising the meeting.

Commercial organisations sometimes organise their own events, but sponsoring an event by activists is usually more fruitful. Just a few thousand pounds is usually sufficient to ensure a minister or opposition spokesman and a lively audience of activists, if the subject matter is interesting enough. The ginger groups that organise meetings are usually associated with a position on the political spectrum within the party, or with interest in a particular cause (for example, Socialist Environment and Resources Association or Tory Green Initiative). Outside organisations also buy space in the exhibition associated with the conference. Key party leaders are usually escorted around to shake hands with the exhibitors.

FURTHER READING

Stanyer, J. (2001) *The Creation of Political News: Television and British Party Political Conferences.* Brighton: Sussex Academic Press.

QL

key concepts in
public relations

Perception Management

A term used to describe what the **public relations** industry does – manage the perceptions of the stakeholders on whom organisation rely on for survival. In the UK in the mid-1990s there was an attempt by a number of prominent agencies to rebrand themselves as perception management consultancies instead of PR consultancies. The agencies could see that the term PR was limiting and did not describe the services they provided. The consultancies felt that their role for their **clients** was to assess and alter stakeholder perception of the client organisation, trying to create a two-way **communication** process, where understanding could lead to acceptance.

The irony of this is that the agencies suggesting the change were ahead of their time and clients and prospective clients could not really understand the new 'perception management' offer. The terms 'PR' and 'Marketing Communications' were understood by clients and prospects. There are signs that in the more sophisticated and knowledgeable business environment of today, however, that the term 'perception manager' is again being used to describe the specialist nature of public relations and differentiate it from other marketing communications services.

FURTHER READING

Borden, N. H. (1964) 'The concept of the marketing mix,' *Journal of Advertising Research*, 4: 2–7
Haywood, R. (1994) *Manage your Reputation*. Kogan Page: London.

EP

Persuasion

Early pioneers of **public relations** in America, such as Ivy Lee and Edward Bernays, were heavily influenced by theories from social psychology and Freudian psychoanalysis concerning influence over the behaviour and attitude of the 'masses'. Stuart Ewen's historical account cites Lee as suggesting that 'Publicity is essentially a matter of mass psychology' (1996: 132), and these early practitioners had no ethical or practical issues in deliberately employing traditional tools of **propaganda** in their PR work. Bernays talked of the processes of 'engineering consent' in the populace using such techniques (see **manufacturing consent**).

Historically such explicit links with overt propaganda became unpalatable after the fascist and communist experiences of the mid-20th century, but whether PR practice can be differentiated from propaganda, deceit and manipulation continues to be a matter of debate among scholars and practitioners alike.

However, one of the classic definers of pure **propaganda** is the idea of the 'big lie', stemming from the proclamations of Hitler and Goebbels

persuasion

157

that if a lie is sufficiently 'big' (that is, too outrageous to be false) and repeated consistently and often, the public will come to believe it, or simply refuse not to believe it. Credibility is a fundamental aspect of any PR or **communications** campaign, particularly in a pluralistic era where so many contradictory or supporting sources of evidence are available. Whether or not 'truth' constitutes an abstract or concrete concept is way beyond the realms of this volume, and whether or not 'telling the truth, but not the whole truth' also equates to deliberate deception is a similarly thorny problem. There can be no doubt however, that once a communications **campaign** is discovered to be consciously lying then the message and the practitioner are absolutely discredited.

Some debates around the differences between propaganda, coercion and persuasion argue that these concepts can be seen as existing on a continuum rather than as distinct, or indeed indistinguishable, phenomena. These ideas may also include an element of the role of the audience as an active and selective consumer of messages (including issues of free will), rather than as a passive receiver.

Part of this also makes reference to theories of *cognitive dissonance* (Festinger, 1957), which suggest that individuals feel psychologically uncomfortable if something they experience or are told contradicts their beliefs or attitudes, and seek to reduce this discomfort by either changing their attitudes or beliefs, or by ignoring the dissonant information. Expressed broadly, people tend to believe what they want to believe.

All of these elements are combined in suggestions that PR has arguably moved away from direct propaganda and more into the realms of persuasion, in which the target audience is aware and complicit, a move that is conceptually encapsulated in the communications model of Grunig and Hunt (1984).

Part of the definition of PR by the UK Chartered Institute of Public Relations (CIPR) suggests that 'It is the planned and sustained effort to establish and maintain goodwill and mutual understanding between an organisation and its publics.'

Proponents of the propaganda definition of public relations may seize upon the 'planned' elements of this definition. However, the Grunig and Hunt model focuses more on the 'mutual' elements of this definition. While two-way asymmetrical communication essentially sums up persuasion, Grunig's subsequent work would suggest that open, mutually beneficial and adaptive dialogue is the epitome of *excellent* PR (Grunig, 1992, 2002).

Most PR practices use persuasive techniques to some extent, whether this is in the use of eloquent and powerful rhetoric, or the creation of notions of social desirability in a target public. Nonetheless, a combination of the recognition and rejection of **spin**, an increasingly media savvy public, and the importance and necessity of **ethics** in an area of communications which seeks to gain professional status and public respect would, some might say optimistically, suggest that the presentation of convincing and persuasive information is more desirable and ultimately more effective than lies, manipulation and propaganda.

FURTHER READING

Brock, T. and Green, M.C. (2005) *Persuasion: Psychological Insights and Perspectives.* Thousand Oaks, CA: Sage.

Ewen, S. (1996) *PR! A Social History of Spin.* New York: Basic Books.

Fawkes, J. (2006) 'Public relations, propaganda and the psychology of persuasion', in R. Tench and L. Yeomans (eds), *Exploring Public Relations.* Harlow: Prentice Hall. pp. 266–87.

Grunig, J.E. and Hunt, T. (1984) *Managing Public Relations.* New York: Holt, Rinehart and Winstone.

L'Etang, J. (1996) 'Public relations and rhetoric', in J. L'Etang and M. Pieczka (eds), *Critical Perspectives in Public Relations.* London: Thomson International Business Press. pp. 106–23.

Moloney, K. (2006) *Rethinking Public Relations.* London: Routledge.

NM

Photo Opportunity

A photo opportunity is what Daniel Boorstin characterised as a 'pseudo event'; something appears to happen so it is reported. One of the founding fathers of modern PR, Edward Bernays, nephew of Sigmund Freud, argues that the profession was very much about 'creating events as **news**' even before the electronic era, providing the media with an event helped to engineer coverage.

Bernays was hired by US President Calvin Coolidge, a man universally regarded as dull, to make him appear more interesting to a cynical electorate. Bernays organised a tea party at the White House for the stars of Hollywood to meet the President. Cross-America coverage the next day showed a very different face of the President; he was chatting with stars and was at ease. As one paper laconically reported: 'The President smiled; almost.' Whether he was dull or not is not the issue; an event was created as news. The White House and Number 10 have learned the lesson well.

Bernays was also hired by a tobacco firm to promote the idea that smoking was chic. At the time in the 1920s, American women did not smoke in public. Bernays organised an Easter Day parade down Broadway in New York of glamorous, designer-clad models conspicuously smoking. Smoking for women in public became chic overnight. In the age of 24/7 **rolling news** the techniques have been perfected.

Such is the appetite of the media for visual images that PR campaigns regularly feature the 'photo opp'. Politicians have always kissed babies; now they visit schools and play football with disadvantaged children. Chief executives don hard hats and visit factories. **NGOs** collect oiled birds for the cameras after a tanker spill. The image of the photo opportunity is all pervading; it is also increasingly evident to an intelligent public, so its use needs to be carefully considered.

FURTHER READING

Jones, N. (2002) *The Control Freaks.* London: Politicos.
Tye, L. (1998) *The Father of Spin.* New York: Henry Holt.

MH

Pitch/Pitching

Pitching is a core skill of the **public relations** practitioner. It is the process of presenting a **communications** programme to an **audience**. The process includes taking a brief, which is the summary of the **communications** issues an organisation faces. The brief will outline the background to the issue, the business and marketing objectives with specific communications objectives. The pitching team then carries out extensive market research, including audience analysis, media analysis and message formation to respond to the brief. The culmination of this process is then a pitch where the research, strategy, programme, ideas and budget are presented. This is commonly known in PR consultancy as a beauty parade, where a number of agencies are pitching for the same work and responding to the same brief. These pitching teams have been chosen specifically to meet the needs of the brief based on expertise and understanding of the market.

In practical terms pitches take place one after another and, in the private sector, there are usually no more than four consultancies pitching for a piece of work. The public sector is slightly different to the commercial sector. Public tenders are offered and any agency may pitch. It is not uncommon for 20 agencies to be pitching for one piece of business. Usually there is a two-tiered process. The first part is a submission of a document outlining specific skills, team composition, budgets and a programme. This will then be refined with the leading contenders selected to pitch for the business. By its very nature pitching is the process of selling an idea or a range of creative programmes to meet specific communications objectives. Therefore the PR practitioner needs to be a strong presenter and have persuasive communications skills.

Pitch documents comprise core elements, these include: business objectives, communications objectives, research and planning, strategic themes, tactics, timetable of activity, team management, evaluation and budgets.

In order to understand the bigger picture, any communications programme needs to reflect the dynamic nature of the business environment in which the client operates. This business environment, coupled with an understanding of business objectives, enables the consultant to develop a communication strategy and plan that is consonant with the business mission of the organisation they represent.

The communications objectives outline specific targets for each campaign and are developed out of the research and planning phase. Here, the practitioner identifies target audiences, key stakeholders, key messages and key media in order to shape strategy and tactics. The strategy outlines the specific direction of the programme while the tactics bring the strategy to life. In any pitch document it is also essential to develop a timetable of activity so all involved know what is happening at any one point in the communications campaign, an outline of the team members to be working on the campaign.

Finally, two very important elements in any pitch are **evaluation** and budgets. Evaluation outlines how the results are going to be measured, while the budget outlines how much delivery will cost and is usually expressed in terms of fees and costs. Fees are the time it takes the team to deliver the campaign and costs any associated third party costs such as printing, mobile phone costs, copying, hotel and food costs etc.

FURTHER READING

Austin, E.W. and Pinkleton, B.E. (2001) Strategic Public Relations Management: Planning and Managing Effective Communication Programs. Mahwah, NJ: Lawrence Erlbaum.

Haywood, R. (1994) Manage Your Reputation. London: Kogan Page.

Kitchen, P.J. (1997) Public Relations: Principles and Practice. London: Thomson Business Press.

Weissman, J. (2003) Presenting to Win: The Art of Telling Your Story. London: FT/Prentice Hall.

EP

PReditorial (practical concept)

A term used to describe the third age of modern **public relations**. The first stage of PR is characterised by the substantial and clear cut divide between editorial content and the PR industry. The second stage reflects the growth of **advertorial**, a **communications** technique which involves a PR agency buying media space in a selected media title and developing a **news** or feature story to communicate particular organisational messages. The advertorial would be designed to look like the editorial in the other parts of the publication, thereby disposing the reader to read an article believing it to be written by a **journalist**, not a PR practitioner. This process describes to coming together of the editorial process with the PR industry.

The third age of PR can be described as the PReditorial age where the PR industry is providing editorial content or **information subsidies** for a range of media. This reflects the fact that there are fewer journalists being asked to provide more content as media moves in to an entertainment-based format. The PR industry is providing that editorial material not only by issuing press releases to highlight a news story on behalf of an organisation which is then re-purposed by a journalist for editorial coverage, but by writing the copy themselves for inclusion, without change, in editorial pages. This movement or trend symbolises the coming together of the **journalism** and public relations industries in a way never before seen.

FURTHER READING

Lewis, J., Williams, A. and Franklin, B. (2008a) 'Four rumours and an explanation: a political economic account of journalists' changing newsgathering and reporting activities', *Journalism Practice*, 2 (1): 27–45.

EP

Press Conferences

Press conferences are losing favour with some **public relations** professionals. It is argued that gathering many **journalists** together in one place to feed a story to them is very much a blunt instrument. Traditionally, the press conference was used to launch, explain or defend an issue but the constraints on journalists' time, which ties them much more to their offices, along with the growing availability of the web, has meant it is no longer the main method of information distribution. Of course, it will always have a place in specialist areas such as **financial public relations** where company results are typically announced at a press conference. The structure of the conference is relatively straightforward; a presentation of around 30 minutes followed by the same time for **Qs and As**. Problems can arise with the electronic media seeking one-to-one interviews with the principal participants before the conference starts, much to the annoyance of their print colleagues. Increasingly personal briefing of selected journalists or telephone hook-ups are finding much more favour with the media and the PR industry, relegating the set-piece press conference to a supporting role.

FURTHER READING

Harrison, S. (1995) *Public Relations: An Introduction*. London: Routledge.
Moss, D. (1991) *Public Relations in Practice*. New York: Routledge.

MH

Press Packs

Press packs have two manifestations. Most usually, the term refers to the 'kit' given to the media as part of a **media briefing** or **press conference**. In the trade, it is often referred to as the 'takeaway' or 'leave behind' and will typically include scripts from a presentation, copies of presentation slides, a **press release** and some frequently asked **Qs and As.**

The other version is what has become known as the 'feeding frenzy'. Generally this refers to the tactics of the tabloid press who indulge in the practice of 'doorstepping' where on occasions their target is effectively ambushed. It is seen regularly in **celebrity** pages of the press with soap stars or footballers leaving nightclubs a bit the worse for drink being prime candidates for a picture and a few quotes. It is also used by investigative **journalists**, especially in television, who literally turn up on the doorstep of someone who has denied them an interview in the normal way, sometimes producing a very effective sequence. Critics argue it amounts to trial by television.

Another major part of the pack's professional life revolves around the Royal Family and this is one of the few areas of the media where there will be some co-operation between journalists, who are otherwise highly competitive. Quotes will be checked and shared and **photo opportunities** will be pooled. The latter follows the introduction of the 'pool system'. The system arose from the Royal Family's need of security and ensures a relative degree of privacy: nominated journalists and photographers cover events on behalf of the whole media.

FURTHER READING

Sabato, L. (2000) *Feeding Frenzy: Attack Journalism and American Politics.* New York: Lanahan Pub.

MH

Press Releases

Press releases can be one of the most misunderstood parts of the PR toolkit. In simplistic terms, they are an invitation to trade, providing basic information about the story, a useable quote and, crucially, 24-hour contact details. However, their use needs careful consideration.

A press release might be the best way to communicate your story provided it is targeted at stakeholders and covers the **key messages.** However, it is a blunt instrument and you might want to consider alternatives such as one-to-one briefings, either **on or off the record.** Many practitioners mistake the press release for something akin to a one-stop shop. It is rarely that.

Much has been written about release construction but what is important is the so-called 'time to view' – how long before your carefully crafted words are consigned to circular file 13 (see **NIBs).** Key elements in a successful release include: a targeted, researched audience; length (no more than one side of A4); the news angle/story line in the first paragraph; a useable quote from a senior executive in the organisation; 24/7 contact numbers; and the setting up of telephone response team to field calls. If you have any doubts, do not issue the release.

Research studies reveal that press releases can be extremely effective in generating subsequent media coverage in the print and broadcast media (Lewis et al., 2008b).

press releases

FURTHER READING

Franklin, B. and Van Slyke Turk, J. (1988) 'Information subsidies: agenda setting traditions', *Public Relations Review,* Spring: 29–41.

Lewis, J., Williams, A. and Franklin, B. (2008b) 'A compromised fourth estate: UK news journalism, public relations and news sources', Journalism Studies, 9 (1): 1–20.

MH

Privacy

There is no general law of privacy in the UK. Prior to the Human Rights Act 1998 the only route to establishing privacy rights in the UK was to take out an action under breach of confidence. However this had obvious limitations, even though the courts were inclined to err on the side of a generous interpretation of the terms involved.

The European Convention on Human Rights does define a right of respect for private life, and though this does not (unlike an EU Regulation) override UK law, the courts are now obliged to have a regard to the Convention and rulings of the Court of Human Rights. Where a court finds an incompatibility between primary legislation and a Convention right it may make a declaration that such an incompatibility exists, but cannot strike down the legislation. It remains a matter for the UK Parliament to decide how, and indeed whether, such an incompatibility should be resolved.

Duncan Bloy (pers.comm.) Believes that if Parliament does not create a specific right to privacy, the courts are likely to create one, much as they created the tort of negligence in the case *Donoghue* v. *Stevenson*. There is now a considerable body of case law under the Convention on which such a right of privacy could be based. In one of the most notable cases – *von Hannover* v. *Germany* – Princess Caroline of Monaco successfully challenged a ruling in the German courts that as a public figure she had no reasonable expectation of privacy.

The question of whether a reasonable expectation exists is critical in any understanding of case law under the Convention and in England and Wales. The media work under the assumption that a person has no reasonable expectation of privacy on the streets, but may have while on private property.

key concepts in
public relations

The print media are signed up to the Code of Practice of the Press Complaints Commission (PCC), which includes similar wording to the Convention on respect for private life, so rulings of the PCC are instructive. In a case involving the actress Julie Goodyear, the Commission ruled that she had a reasonable expectation of privacy when in her back garden, even though she could be seen, and photographed, from a public path. Elizabeth Jagger and Calum Best were thought by the courts to have a reasonable expectation of privacy while having sex in the foyer of a nightclub at 4 a.m. Jagger was able to get an injunction preventing the footage from a CCTV camera being shown on the Internet, purportedly to protect her modelling career. She subsequently made the material available online herself on a pay-per-view site.

FURTHER READING

Hellenic Resources Network: http://www.hri.org/docs/ECHR50.html
Office of Public Sector Information: http://www.opsi.gov.uk/ACTS/acts1998/19980042.htm
Press Complains Commission: http://www.pcc.org.uk/cop/practice.html

QL

Pro Bono

See **Campaign**.

Promotion (1)

Promotion, as in career advancement, has different features in **consultancy** and **in-house** environments. In consultancies, promotion may come more quickly, and there is usually, except in the case of small consultancies, a clear path, progressing from graduate trainee, through account executive, account manager and account director to main board director.

In the early stages of a career promotion will depend principally on account handling skills. Keeping clients happy is key to the success of the business. However, even the best of consultancies experience client 'churn'. **Clients** move on for many reasons, which may be unconnected with account handling skills of the agency. Generating new business (newbiz) is therefore essential.

Rapid promotion to account director level is unlikely without a record in new business, and the main board may be restricted to people with a strong record of business generation. Generating new business often earns commission, and some consultancies have specialist business development teams, which are extremely well remunerated.

In in-house environments such considerations do not apply. However, in both, moving upwards will probably reduce the focus on day-to-day **public relations** skills and involve increasing use of management skills. The choice of in-house or consultancy paths is not, of course, for life. A great many practitioners move between the two and the different skills acquired in one environment can be advantageous in the other.

As a general rule it is probably true to say that promotion in-house requires more generalisation. At the very top level of a public company a PR or corporate affairs director may oversee teams dedicated to each of Haywood's six **publics** (see **public relations**), though the practitioner's internal career path may not have taken in all these teams. By contrast, in consultancy graduate trainees and account executives usually do not specialise, taking on such work as is available, whereas the most senior consultants can often be extremely specialised.

QL

Promotion (2)

Product promotion is one of the core objectives of most PR strategies. While PR, at its best, involves an organisation's full range of publics, including non-marketing publics (see **public relations**), generating product sales is a clear and obvious benefit that **clients** will always respect. Product promotion incorporates a wide range of PR skills and activities including media relations, conferences and exhibitions, point of sale literature and advertising.

In media relations, entry level jobs often involve managing the process of generating product reviews, which may involve managing a loan pool of products for journalists or giving the product to **journalists** (depending both on the product's intrinsic value, and on whether or not it can be reused). It should be noted that this task is one that requires careful handling in terms of ethics. It would not be considered ethical to make a gift to a journalist in exchange for a positive review. In some countries this would even be illegal. Conversely, a journalist cannot be expected to review a product without having access to it, and few PR practitioners would ask for a product to be returned if the journalist is continuing to write reviews.

FURTHER READING

Kitchen, P. (1997) *Public Relations: Principles and Practice.* London: Thomson.

QL

Propaganda

Propaganda is a word derived from the activities of the Catholic Church in the 1600s when it set up the Congregation for the Propagation of the Faith. This body was intended to evangelise or 'sell' Catholicism at a time of increasing encroachment by Protestantism.

During the First World War, America's Committee on Public Information used propaganda to help the recruitment drive. It has been described as the first full service propaganda agency using placed articles, billboards, radio advertisements and what became known as the Minute Men. These were prominent members of local communities who took four minutes before the start, say, of a cinema showing or theatre play and outlined the need for more recruits to fight the war in Europe. They proved to be very successful.

Edward Bernays, regarded as the father of modern **public relations**, was a great proponent of propaganda as he described the process of **manufacturing consent** or getting people to do what you wanted them to. He and his supporters saw propaganda being used as a tool for social control. In short, propaganda aims to shape an outcome to suit the person delivering the message.

In **model** terms, it is one way symmetric without the need for feedback. The view of propaganda remained broadly neutral despite some misgivings until the rise of the Nazi Party. This changed fundamentally people's attitudes towards it. The expertise of Reichminister Josef Goebbels and film-maker Leni Reifenstal in orchestrating the Nuremberg rallies as symbols of Nazi power opened the eyes of many to the dangers inherent in propaganda as a **communication** technique.

Since the Second World War, there has been much scholarly debate as to whether there is such a thing as 'good' or 'bad' propaganda. As its avowed intention is simply **persuasion** it could be argued that the only view to take of propaganda is whether it works or not. Government information campaigns are, typically, propaganda: Stop Smoking. Drive Carefully. Use a Condom. Judgement here should be only about effectiveness; in other circumstances less concerned with public health, it could be argued that the ethics of the issue should come under scrutiny as well. (See **Models in Public Relations** for a review of press agentry and publicity.)

FURTHER READING

Herman, E. and Chomsky, N. (1988) Manufacturing Consent: The Political Economy of the Mass Media. New York: Pantheon.
Tye, L. (1998) The Father of Spin. New York: Henry Holt.

MH

Public Affairs

Public affairs is one of the key disciplines in public relations, alongside **media relations**, **financial public relations** and **public relations** (**internal**). Public affairs is concerned with addressing the political publics defined as one of the six key **publics** by Haywood (alongside customers, investors, neighbours, business partners and staff). Neighbours and local communities are also often classified as being a core target for public affairs.

Organisations in heavily regulated sectors sometimes regard public affairs as being a more critical than **marketing**. For regulated monopolies (such as some utilities) **regulation** is the key factor affecting profitability and public affairs would focus heavily on influencing the policies of regulators. In mergers and acquisitions – an important, and very profitable, area of activity in **financial public relations** – regulation can also be key, as any merger might be subject to regulation by competition authorities. In the UK such regulation could be at the British or European level. Key targets for public affairs **campaigns** are politicians and officials.

Often the most effective public affairs campaigns influence officials below the radar of politicians. For example, when the objective is to influence legislation it is often too late to achieve very much by the time the legislation is announced in Parliament. Aside from high-profile campaigns to influence legislation – by changing its content, blocking it or pushing it through – other areas of public policy could easily be the target of a public affairs campaign. Public procurement policies, for example, are of enormous significance to many organisations. In most European countries the government spending makes up more than 40 per cent of all expenditure in that country. The figure is slightly lower in the USA, but when state and local governments are included, it is nonetheless very high. In some markets governments are near-monopoly buyers – arms manufacture and some branches of pharmaceuticals, for example.

At the level of local government the most significant power that British local authorities exercise is planning and development control. Tesco, for example, has a very substantial department devoted solely to lobbying local authorities with regard to planning permission, as do other supermarkets and developers for both residential and commercial purposes. There is also a large and growing sector of specialist PR consultancies that focus on lobbying local authorities.

Most legislation affecting businesses in EU countries is initiated at the European rather than the nation-state level, though member states often have some flexibility in how the legislation is implemented. There is thus a major branch of the public affairs industry located in Brussels and dedicated to influencing public policy at that level. This is on a much smaller scale than in Washington DC. In part that is probably because member states in the EU – unlike states in the USA – exercise a role in creating European legislation. All laws, whether Regulations (which take effect directly) or Directives (which create an obligation on member states to legislate) need to be approved by the Council of Ministers on which member states are represented. Most economic legislation, however, does not require unanimity in the Council, so an organisation that seeks to exercise influence by persuading only its own government may well fail. Waiting until legislation is proposed in the member states is very dangerous. It is likely that it will be much too late to change any matters of principle. Even the European level is sometimes the second stage of negotiation. In some areas of environmental and trade policy, matters of principle are settled at the United Nations (UN) or World Trade Organization (WTO), potentially several years in advance of legislation being discussed in Brussels. Commercial organisations are some way behind NGOs in seeking to influence discussion at the UN, usually operating through the International Chamber of Commerce rather than lobbying directly in the way that groups such as Greenpeace operate. Global level lobbying is likely to be a growing area over the next few years.

Within the UK there is a developed public affairs industry in Edinburgh to lobby the Scottish Parliament and Executive. Even before devolution, legislation was normally separately implemented in Scotland and sometimes differed significantly. In Wales, by contrast, the much more limited legislative powers of the Welsh Assembly have not yet triggered the development of a substantial lobbying sector. With additional powers now in place, that might change.

FURTHER READING

Budge, I., Crewe, I. and McKay, D. (2007) *The New British Politics*. Harlow: Pearson Longman.

Haywood, R. (1991) *All About Public Relations: How to Build Business Success on Good Communications*. London: McGraw-Hill.

Miller, C. (2000) *Politico's Guide to Political Lobbying*. London: Politico.

key concepts in
public relations

QL

Public Inquiry

A public inquiry is an inquiry commissioned by the government to investigate a particular issue. It may be to explore what has gone wrong in a particular set of circumstances – for example, how Dr Harold Shipman was able to commit so many murders undetected – or to consider policies for the future. Long-term inquiries with wide ranging briefs are often constituted as Royal Commissions.

The key defining factor of a public, as opposed to an internal, inquiry, is that it takes its evidence in public. The fact that evidence is given in public, and can be given on oath, has both strengths and weaknesses. Oppositions normally favour public inquiries, as it is harder for the government to cover up its own mistakes or malfeasance. Conversely, it will normally be impossible to pursue criminal charges against anyone as a result of a public inquiry, because both the inquiry and the attendant media coverage will be prejudicial.

Sceptics have suggested that public inquiries are sometimes used to postpone a controversial decision, perhaps until the politician commissioning it has moved on to another office, or to lay the groundwork for a predetermined decision. A politician will be able to argue that a decision made on the basis of a public inquiry's recommendations is self-evidently correct, or even that his hands are tied. The politician who commissions the inquiry will normally select its members (though sometimes the Opposition will nominate one or more members) and this power can be used to determine the outcome. The government will also write the terms of reference for the inquiry.

Public inquiries are normally chaired by well-known and respected individuals external to the party political debate, such as judges, retired civil servants or academics, and are often known by the name of the chair, e.g. the Phillis Committee, or Hutton Inquiry. In 2005, the Inquiries Act clarified the legal status of public inquiries.

FURTHER READING

Office of Public Sector Information: http://www.opsi.gov.uk/acts/en2005/2005en12.htm

The opinion of particular publics, and arguably the creation or manipulation of this opinion, is central to the practice of public relations. Edward Bernays, one of the earliest practitioners of the modern profession, wrote *Crystallizing Public Opinion* in 1923. Others have continued to talk about manufacturing and creating consent among the public, specifically with reference to participatory democracy and the theories of the public sphere (Habermas, 1989), or indeed the lack of such public opportunity for debate.

Definitions of what constitutes public opinion vary according to the weight that they place on the importance of individual views, and their access to the forums in which issues are debated (Pieczka, 1996). Some theorists would argue that the concept constitutes a collective view of the attitudes and beliefs of a population, while others point out that not all opinions or individuals are equal and that minority opinion can be overshadowed, particularly in a political system based on general expression of opinion.

One facet of the history of public opinion research is that it can be measured using **quantitative methods**. The use of large-scale surveys is a key feature of both commercial and political polling organisations – perhaps the most famous being Gallup (see also MORI and YouGov in the UK).

Another important aspect of any consideration of public opinion is the effect of mass media, and associated concepts of **gatekeeping** and **agenda setting**. There can be no doubt that the media has some effect on public opinion, but the direct impact of this has moved away from an assumption of a passive, unthinking audience (a theory that became known as the *hypodermic needle*) to one of a more active and discerning public that is able to select and filter messages. Thus, public opinion is as likely to have an impact on the media agenda in turn. This has led to a widening of the research methods used to attempt to gauge the opinion of the public, now including techniques such as **focus groups** and **content analysis**, and also in the importance placed on public opinion by practitioners. Polls purporting to measure the public's opinion on a particular topic will often be commissioned by particular interested parties with the aim of placing this issue on the media agenda.

In public relations terms, the influence of particular individuals, and the consensus reached through informed debate, is important to Grunig and Hunt's (1984) model where the identification of *specific* publics, and engaging in dialogue with them, is an integral part of the **communications** process.

FURTHER READING

Cutlip, S.M., Allen, H. and Broom, G. (2000) *Effective Public Relations.* London: Prentice Hall.

Ewen, S. (1996) *PR! A Social History of Spin.* New York: Basic Books.

Gallup Polls: http://www.galluppoll.com/

Lewis, J. (2001) *Constructing Public Opinion: How Political Elites Do What They Like and Why We Seem to Go Along with It.* New York: Columbia University Press.

MORI Polls: http://www.ipsos-mori.com/

Pieczka, M. (1996) 'Public opinion and public relations', in J. L'Etang and M. Pieczka (eds), *Critical Perspectives in Public Relations.* London: Thomson International Business Press. pp. 54–64.

YouGov Polls: http://www.yougov.com/

NM

Public Relations

According to the Chartered Institute of Public Relations (CIPR): 'Public relations is about reputation – the result of what you do, what you say and what others say about you.' It is also 'the planned and sustained effort to establish and maintain goodwill and mutual understanding between an organisation and its publics.' (http://www.cipr.co.uk)

Central to understanding this definition is the concept of the word 'publics' as plural. All organisations have a series of publics, or stakeholders, on whom their success depends. These publics are divided in many different ways, but Haywood's division into six categories is widely accepted. These are: customers (past, present and future); staff (past, present and future), investors (past, present and future); politicians and regulators; neighbours, and business partners (distributors, suppliers, etc.).

Not all organisations have all publics: charities, for example, do not have shareholders. Some commentators, especially those with a marketing background, regard PR as being a sub-discipline of marketing. This view tends to prevail in business schools. In this analysis, there are four elements to the 'marketing mix': product, price, placement and publicity. PR is usually classified as the fifth element of publicity, after mass media, direct promotion, personal selling and sales promotion.

However, if PR is viewed as reputation management, the marketeers' view is plainly flawed. Managing an organisation's reputation with its marketing publics is certainly fundamental, but this is only one of Haywood's six publics. If the CIPR definition (and Haywood's) is accepted, then marketing is a sub-discipline of PR. The balance in importance between the six categories of public will vary widely from one organisation to another. Most commercial organisations regard recruiting and retaining customers as being fundamental to continued success. They are the main income drivers. Yet regulated utility businesses, such as water companies, often operate with regional monopolies. There are no new customers to recruit and existing customers have nowhere else to go. It is the interplay of the political publics – politicians and regulators – that determines profitability. Equally many public sector organisations have little or no interest in finding new customers. This will often increase costs without having any direct bearing on income.

The activity usually most strongly associated with PR is media relations. Building relationships with the media is certainly a core channel of communication with all publics, but there is a very wide range of other activities that PR practitioners are involved with. These often include marketing, sponsorship, exhibitions and events, crisis and issues management, media and presentation training, research and evaluation, and a range of online PR activities. Many practitioners specialise, either in a particular type of PR – investor relations, public affairs, marketing communications, and so on. Others specialise by the type of organisation they work for – consumer, corporate, public sector or charities. Still others specialise by particular markets such as **healthcare public relations**, IT or **financial public relations**.

Also important to understanding the CIPR definition is the emphasis on the word 'planned'. According to this definition, if your PR is not planned, it is not PR. This is not to say there is no place for spontaneity or flexibility. But it is a recognition that *all* organisations have relationships with their core publics. As Haywood puts it, 'PR is not optional'. The difference is between those who professionally manage these relationships, and those who allow them to develop in an unplanned and haphazard manner.

FURTHER READING

Edwards, L. (2006) 'Public relations origins: definitions and history' in R. Tench and L. Yeomans (eds), *Exploring Public Relations*. London: Prentice Hall. pp. 2–17.

Haywood, R. (1991) *All About Public Relations: How to Build Business Success on Good Communications*. London: McGraw-Hill.

Kitchen, P. (1997) *Public Relations: Principles and Practice*. London: Thomson.

Richards, P. (1998) *Be Your Own Spin Doctor*. London: Take That Ltd.

QL

Public Relations Democracy

Public relations democracy is the phrase deployed by Aeron Davis to describe the growing influence of an expansive **public relations** industry on the media of **mass communication** and thereby the production of news – especially political news – in Western liberal democracies. Davis' argument is that *public relations* democracy marks a departure from *liberal democracy* with its emphasis on pluralism and equal access to media by all groups via a competitive market.

The emergence of PR democracy reflects the rapid growth of the public relations industry (11-fold in 20 years, Davis, 2002: ch. 2) alongside an increasingly competitive market for **news** which, in an age of declining newspaper circulations and advertising revenues, has kept **journalists'** salaries and jobs to a minimum. PR has rushed in to fill the consequent 'news vacuum' by providing ever greater **information subsidies** to resource-starved news organisations thereby creating a greater media dependence on the PR industry for news. Franklin has developed a similar

public relations democracy

177

argument in the context of UK local news media (Franklin, 2006). In Davis' words:

> Public relations has therefore increased its influence, not as a result of powerful '**spin doctor**' pressure, or media-source conspiracy, but because working news journalists have become increasingly stretched as a result of rising competition. Public relations professionals, with their rapidly increased resources have thus been ideally placed to make good the shortfall in news-producing industries. (2002: 17)

Davis lists a wide range of organisations including large financial corporations as well as pressure groups, charities, churches and trades unions, which have been successful in using PR to influence media reporting and change the role of media in democratic polities. Davis identifies the 'elite' corporate PR sector, along with the state, as the source which is most successful in helping to shape media agendas and contents (2002: chs 3–5). But Davis' analysis of the extent to which 'outsider' and 'resource poor' groups can influence news media, contests earlier suggestions of the powerlessness of such groups. Davis argues, for example, that even trades unions which typically enjoy poor press coverage, can use professional **communication** techniques to improve media coverage for their activities, to spin elite decision makers and 'occasionally force significant change' (2002: 18).

FURTHER READING

Davis, A. (2002) *Public Relations Democracy: Public Relations, Politics and the Mass Media in Britain*. London: Sage.
Franklin, B. (2006) *Local Journalism and Local Media: Making the Local News*. London: Routledge.

key concepts in public relations

Public Relations Education and Training

For years, the primary route into **public relations** was to work first as a **journalist** and then move into PR in mid-career. One exception was in investor relations, where many practitioners were former investment bankers. In both cases, PR was rarely the career that someone chose when starting out, but something one shifted to, in the case of journalists, normally to make more money.

While some organisations do still recruit people straight from **journalism**, even at very senior levels, this is much rarer than it was. It is also no longer the case that a journalist moving into PR can necessarily expect to earn more money. Education and training are key priorities for the CIPR, and indeed for the other professional institutes affiliated to the Global Alliance for Public Relations and Communication Management.

CIPR sets out several routes for qualification. Much more common than before are the routes which people undertake at the beginning of their careers, including studying for first degrees or post-graduate qualifications in PR, or a related discipline such as political **communications** or corporate communications. Undergraduate degrees are available at a number of UK institutions, but have not become popular at the older and more prestigious universities. Of institutions with university status prior to 1992 (when polytechnics and colleges of higher education were granted such status) only Cardiff and Stirling offer PR courses, but both do so only at postgraduate level. Cardiff is the only university teaching PR that is a member of the Russell Group of 19 research-led universities.

Postgraduate university courses fall into two main categories: diplomas and masters degrees (usually MAs, but sometimes MScs). Broadly, diplomas will be more practically oriented and more likely to offer placement opportunities. MAs will have a stronger academic underpinning. Most courses last 9–12 months.

A variety of in-work training schemes also exist. CIPR itself offers a diploma, which is aimed at practitioners with several years' experience wishing to take on more strategic and managerial functions. There is also a CIPR Advanced Certificate aimed at more junior practitioners. The CAM Foundation (Communications, Advertising and Marketing, part of the Chartered Institute of Marketing) offers a qualification that includes a PR module, but this is a basic introduction to PR offered to people who may not be pursuing PR as a career. These courses are usually offered as evening classes or day release for people in work. CIPR and a variety of commercial suppliers also offer shorter courses or workshops (usually half, one or two days) for practitioners seeking to learn specific skills. CIPR members are required to undertake **Continuous Professional Development** (CPD), which includes, courses, private study, involvement with professional organisations and work experience.

FURTHER READING

CAM Foundation: http://www.camfoundation.com/cam/index.cfm
CIPR: http://www.cipr.co.uk/Training/training.htm and http://www.cipr.co.uk/direct/quals.asp?v1=qualshome

QL

Public Relations (Internal)

Internal PR or internal communications form a core PR discipline. The internal audience is one of the six core publics identified by Haywood (see public relations). It should be self-evident that the success of an organisation depends to no small degree on its ability to generate internal support for its policies. Nonetheless, many organisations see internal public relations as an afterthought.

Haywood identifies several key mistakes that organisations make in planning their internal PR, including abdicating communication channels to unions, communicating *at* rather than *with* employees and failing to realise that information will spread through an organisation whether or not managers so prefer.

While less common in the UK than it was in the 1970s, using unions as the main or sole channel of communication with employees is still common in some countries. It should be obvious that the interests of the unions and the organisation will not always be identical, so alternative channels are essential. This is not, of course, to say that unions, where they exist, should be excluded from employee communications altogether. This is neither desirable, nor even possible. But unions form one part of the internal public, not the whole of it.

Communicating *at* employees without creating feedback channels and training managers to listen as well as talk can also be extremely damaging. In good times, the weaknesses of this approach may not be apparent, but systems using this model are likely to be brittle.

As in many areas of PR, Internet technologies have revolutionised methods of communication, while leaving purposes untouched. While online technologies create first-class channels which *can* be used for two-way communication, they also make it easier and cheaper to broadcast vast quantities of information indiscriminately. It is extremely easy for managers to simply forward emails from head office to their teams, and such practices tend to assume a role as passive recipients for employees. Managers can hide behind email and us it as a substitute for talking and listening. Accountancy firm Ernst & Young has responded to this danger by employing a regional communications manager whose responsibilities include training managers to engage in two-way communication. Corporate videos and intranets need to supplement, not replace, actual communication.

FURTHER READING

Haywood, R. (1991) All About Public Relations: How to Build Business Success on Good Communications. London, McGraw-Hill.

Kitchen, P. (1997) Public Relations: Principles and Practice. London: Thomson Business Press.

Smith, L. and Mounter, P. (2005) Effective Internal Communication. London: CIPR.

Yeomans, L. (2006) 'Internal Communications', in R. Tench and L. Yeomans (eds), Exploring Public Relations. Upper Saddle River, NJ: Prentice Hall. pp. 33253.

public relations (internal)

181

Public Relations Planning

Public relations planning is critical to **public relations**. If the CIPR definition of PR is accepted, planning is essential: PR 'is the planned and sustained effort to establish and maintain goodwill and mutual understanding between an organisation and its **publics**' (http://www.cipr.co.uk). It follows that if your efforts are not planned they are not, in the meaning of the CIPR definition, PR at all.

PR planning involves several distinct phases. These can be categorised as: aims; objectives; definition of target audiences; research; definition of messages; methods; implementation; and evaluation. This is not a strictly chronological approach. Objectives, for example, may well shift somewhat as a result of the research phase. Aims are distinct from objectives in that they are more general. A business may seek, for example, to be more profitable. An objective would refine that aim further by, for example, looking at increasing sales, reducing costs, increasing unit prices, or a combination of any of those. Objectives need to be **SMART objectives**.

A definition of target **audiences** is, naturally, critical to any definition of messages. Without the initial understanding of what the target audiences are, definition of messages is likely to be flawed. PR campaigns can come to grief because the participants had differing understandings of who the target audiences were.

Research is necessary because it is impossible to manage changes in attitudes, beliefs and behaviour if you do not know what they are at your starting point. Evaluation of your end point is also, of course, pointless, if you do not know what your start point was.

FURTHER READING

Gregory, A. (2000) Planning and Managing a Public Relations Campaign – a Step-by-Step Guide. London: CIPR.

Gregory, A. (2006) 'Public relations as planned communication', in R. Tench and L. Yeomans (eds), Exploring Public Relations. London: Prentice Hall. pp. 182–207.

key concepts in public relations

Haywood, R. (1991) All About Public Relations: How to Build Business Success on Good Communications. London: McGraw-Hill.

Kitchen, P. (1997) Public Relations: Principles and Practice. London: Thomson Business Press.

Marketing Teacher: http://www.marketingteacher.com/Lessons/lesson_objectives.htm

QL

Publics

Publics are stakeholders who have taken an collective, aggressive standpoint against an organisation and its actions. Grunig and Pepper have argued that stakeholders are passive; they just happen to be there as workers or residents. Once they convert to being active they become publics. At this juncture, the publics question some aspect of the way an organisation is behaving and set about to promote change.

A classic case study here is Shell UK's decision in 1995 to sink the redundant oil storage platform Brent Spar in the North Sea. In the event this proved to be the correct engineering and environmental solution but Shell had failed to undertake proper **stakeholder analysis** and so was unable to engage with them at any meaningful level. In such circumstances several publics were formed, particularly from the **NGO** community, led by Greenpeace, and a vigorous campaign against the sinking was mounted. Directly following on from this initiative by the publics, Shell revised the whole way in which it deals with its stakeholders through the Societies Changing Expectations programme.

In practical terms it is vital to ensure that there is sufficient knowledge of where in the cycle the various publics are positioned; are they moving from latent to aware to active and if so to what effect? Critical to this is PR's role in **boundary spanning** and horizon scanning; without adequate intelligence gathering it is difficult, if not impossible, to know the character of the public you are meant to be dealing with.

publics

183

FURTHER READING

Grunig, J.E. and Pepper, F.C. (1992) *Excellence in Public relations and Communication Management*. Mahwah, NJ: Lawrence Erlbawm.

MH

Public Service Broadcasting

Public service broadcasting (PSB) embodies the idea that broadcasting should be organised as a public service, rather than a market driven activity. This idea has been highly influential in shaping the development of radio and television broadcasting in the UK during the 20th century; and across both public and private sectors.

The essence of PSB is captured in John Reith's (the first Director General of the BBC) often quoted phrase, which suggested that the fundamental purposes of broadcasting were to 'educate, inform and entertain': and in that order! For Reith, broadcasting had a 'responsibility' to 'improve the audience', to 'carry into the greatest number of homes everything that is best in every department of human knowledge, endeavour and achievement' (Reith, 1924: 34): a responsibility that has frequently triggered the criticism that PSB was – and is – inherently paternalistic (Murdoch, 1989). The changing character of PSB across the intervening 70 years is evident in Dawn Airey's more prosaic ambitions for the newly launched Channel 5 in 1997; namely, a focus on the '3 Fs: Football, films and fucking' (Brown, 2003: 6).

In 1985, the Broadcasting Research Unit (BRU) identified eight 'main principles' of PSB: (1) geographic universality – viewers should be able to access the same programmes wherever they live; (2) universality of appeal – programmes should cater for all tastes; (3) minorities (ethnic or cultural) should enjoy particular programming provision; (4) broadcasters should nurture a sense of national identity and community; (5) broadcasting should be protected from vested interests whether economic and political to ensure impartiality and balance; (6) costs should be shared equally by everyone through the mechanism of the licence fee; (7) broadcasting should be structured to encourage competition between broadcasters resulting in higher quality programming and (8) public guidelines for broadcasting should liberate not restrict programme makers (BRU, 1985: 25–32).

In the 1980s, Thatcherite commitments to market economics and media deregulation, in tandem with developments in cable and satellite delivery systems, generated a multichannel broadcasting system which challenged basic assumptions of public service broadcasting (Franklin, 2001: 1–12). But PSB has proved resilient. The 2000 white paper on broadcasting suggested that PSB should play 'a key role' in television's digital future because (1) 'it ensures that the interests of all viewers are taken into account'; (2) 'it provides 'a counter balance to fears about concentration of ownership and the absence of diversity of views'; and (3) 'there are strong cultural justifications for public service broadcasting ... it allows our community to talk to itself' (DTI and DCMS, 2000: paras 5.3.9–12).

The process of policy change continues. In autumn 2003, Ofcom launched a three-phase review of PSB that made three key recommendations. First, a new public service broadcaster should be established to ensure 'plurality' in public service broadcasting. Second, the BBC should remain fully funded by the licence fee for the duration of the next charter period (beginning 2007) but would subsequently be partially funded by subscription. Finally, Ofcom recommended reducing the public service commitments of Channels 3 and 5 after the analogue 'switch-off' (www.ofcom.org.uk/codes_guidelines/broadcasting/tv/psb_review/reports).

The White Paper on BBC Charter renewal published in March 2006, however, offered support to the licence fee until 2017, suggested replacing the BBC Board of Governors with a trust and a separate executive board and challenged the corporation to remodel its founding principles of 'informing, educating and entertaining' for the digital era. The BBC must address six new goals including the need to deliver programmes and websites of high quality with challenging, innovative, original and engaging contents. Reith's mission to entertain and educate must merge in the digital age. The then Culture Secretary Tessa Jowell argued, 'The BBC should continue to take fun seriously, engraining entertainment into its services' and 'put entertainment at the heart of its mission' but avoid copycat programming and expensive foreign imports (cited in Gibson, 2006: 6).

FURTHER READING

Broadcasting Research Unit (BRU) (1985) *The Public Service Idea in British Broadcasting: Main Principles*. Luton: John Libbey.

DTI and DCMS (2000) *A New Future for Communications*. London: HMSO.

Franklin, B. (2001) *British Television Policy: A Reader*. London: Routledge.

Gibson, O. (2006) 'BBC must take fun seriously as licence fee secured', *Guardian* 15 March.

Murdoch, R. (1989) 'Freedom in broadcasting' the James MacTaggart Memorial Lecture reprinted in B. Franklin (ed.), *Television Policy: The MacTaggart Lectures*. Edinburgh: Edinburgh University Press. pp. 131–8.

Ofcome: http://www.ofcom.org.uk/codes_guidelines/broadcasting/tv/psb_review/reports

BF

Qs and As

Questions and answers (Qs and As), are a vital element in any stakeholder engagement plan. Put simply, they are the answers to the most frequently asked questions or FAQs. The **excellence theory** of **public relations** demands effective **communication** and as Qs and As provide a template for this they will, typically, be generated by **media relations** or corporate advice specialists, with input from the lawyers where necessary. Essentially, they provide an agreed guide for anyone whose role includes stakeholder engagement, giving them a consistent and robust set of statements. For example, public affairs practitioners will need specific Qs and As to deal with government or **NGOs**, while **financial public relations** will want their FAQs aimed at the City and financial **journalists**. It is also vital for **internal communications,** often driven by human resources, to have the same template so the messages remain the same both inside and outside the organisation. An organisations' employees are the best, and worst, ambassadors.

MH

Quantitative and Qualitative Methods

Research methods fall broadly into one of two categories, each with their own advantages and disadvantages. The choice of method is principally determined by the research question and often researchers will use a combination of techniques (the so-called *mixed method* approach, or *triangulation*) to complete the picture.

Qualitative methods are usually in-depth and detailed explorations of attitudes, reasoning and conversational phenomena, such as **focus groups** or **key figure interviews**. They are often exploratory and produce rich and detailed data that can provide essential insight into areas where there is little existing knowledge. For this reason they are often utilised in *inductive* research designs (see **methodology**). The data they produce are however subject to the idiosyncrasies of the particular researcher, since they are closely involved in the research process and their own behaviour, appearance and attitudes can, consciously or subconsciously, affect the ways in which the data is gathered and interpreted. They can also be time-consuming in preparation, conduct and analysis, and, partly as a practical result of these restraints, can rarely be said to be truly representative.

Quantitative methods generally involve counting instances or occurrences, and as such, can produce vast quantities of complex data that can be generalised to a wider population (with appropriate **sampling** considerations) and presented in a very compelling manner with the use of statistics, graphs and tables. Common quantitative research methods include questionnaires and surveys, widely used in **public opinion** polls and **content analysis**. The data produced is generally wide and representative, but provides less opportunity for in-depth exploration of the reasons behind the findings. As such, quantitative methods tend to be descriptive rather than explanatory.

FURTHER READING

Davies, M.M. and Mosdell, N. (2006) *Practical Research Methods for Media and Cultural Studies: Making People Count.* Edinburgh: Edinburgh University Press.

Deacon, D., Pickering, M., Golding, P. and Murdock, G. (1999) *Researching Communications: A Practical Guide to Methods in Media and Cultural Analysis.* London: Arnold.

Denscombe, M. (2003) *The Good Research Guide*. Maidenhead: Open University Press.

Gunter, B. (2000) *Media Research Methods: Measuring Audience Reactions and Impact*. London: Sage.

Wimmer, R.D. and Dominick, J.R. (2006) Mass *Media Research: An Introduction*. Belmont, CA: Wadsworth.

NM

Rebuttals

Rebuttals are the more aggressive form of the **response statement**. They rely on the concept that the best form of defence is attack and need the back-up of sophisticated media monitoring systems to ensure delivery. Rebuttals have enjoyed considerable growth in political PR and **government public relations**. The core idea is that any statement made to the media is checked for accuracy and tone and if it is found wanting a rebuttal will be issued. This takes place on a 24/7 basis to meet the demands of the media. Government and opposition parties are accomplished users of the technique and it covers the whole gamut of responses from the simple Letter to the **Editor** of the paper where the offending article was published to phoning the *Today* radio programme while it is still live on air with a complaint or appearing in a television studio to debate the issues – a technique famously used by Alistair Campbell when Prime Minister Tony Blair's Director of Communications.

FURTHER READING

Fritz, B. (2004) *All The President's Spin*. New York: Touchstone.

Jones, N. (1996) *The Control Freaks*. London: Politicos.

key concepts in public relations

MH

Regulation (Internet)

The **Internet** is largely unregulated and entirely free of central content regulation. Its technological development from DARPANET has ensured this. This is not to say that governments are utterly unable to regulate content. The Chinese government has invested heavily in the so-called 'great firewall of China' which is designed to keep undesirable (by Communist lights) material out. Popular chat spaces in China have a series of banned words and phrases, such as 'Tibet independence' and 'Tiananmen Square'. But the mostly younger people who use these chat spaces are very aware of this and have ways round the restrictions. A common one is to introduce a deliberate spelling error: 'Tiibet independence', for example.

Major Internet suppliers such as **Google** have succumbed to pressure from the Chinese government to disable searches for certain phrases. Google has been strongly criticised for this, especially in the light of its famous CSR statement 'Don't be evil'. But Google responds that even a restricted Internet is better than no Internet at all in terms of engaging China's youth with the world. Given the number of ways around the Communist restrictions, there is much to be said for Google's point of view.

China is far from the only country to impose restrictions on the Internet. In France, it is illegal to buy or sell Nazi memorabilia, and Yahoo! France has agreed to ban such material for sale. This does not prevent French citizens from logging onto the international sites of Yahoo! or eBay and buying the material there. Technologically, there seems to be no way this could be done.

The UN initiated a conference in 2005 with the aim of transferring 'regulation' of the Internet from the USA to the UN. But this ignores the fact that, in terms of content regulation, there is nothing to transfer. ICANN (Internet Corporation for Assigned Names and Numbers), the American registered company which administers the architecture of the Internet, exercises no oversight whatsoever as to content. This is, itself, a controversial position, as some argue that some offensive material, such as child pornography, does need to be excluded. However the human rights record of the countries which initiated the call for UN control of the Internet – including China,

Saudi Arabia, Iran, Zimbabwe and Cuba – leaves much room for scepticism as to their motives. ICANN remains a US registered company, and without the consent of the US there seems to be no avenue for the UN to exercise any control, even of its purely technical functions, let alone to introduce the type of content regulation sought by some countries.

The Internet is not above the national laws of the countries where it operates. Much of the problem in pursuing clandestine activities (such as child pornography and drug smuggling) has been the purely practical one of locating the people who operate the sites and any associated assets. The law of **defamation** continues to apply, and online publishing allows defamed individuals to seek redress in several jurisdictions – at least where it is possible to identify the publisher.

A bill to 'save the Internet' – that is to introduce obligations of impartiality and to control prices charged by service providers – was heavily defeated in the US House of Representatives in June 2006. While supporters argued that it was essential to put Internet publishing on a par with broadcasting, critics responded that broadcasting was regulated at a time when there was only a very limited choice of suppliers. The Internet, by contrast, has minimal barriers to entry. Research by Adamic and Glance (see **blogging**) has in any case suggested that the political balance of **blogs** on the Internet much more closely reflects the balance among voters as a whole than newspapers do.

FURTHER READING

Postrel, V. (1999) The Future and its Enemies: The Growing Conflict Over Creativity, Enterprise and Progress. New York: Touchstone.
Starr, P. (2004) The Creation of the Media: Political Origins of Modern Communications. New York: Basic Books.

QL

key concepts in public relations

Regulation
(Press – Ownership
and Contents)

The claim that the UK press is a free press is certainly true if UK newspapers are compared to their sister papers in Russia or Zimbabwe. But it is equally certain that such a claim requires considerable qualification! In 1992, a government white paper *Open Government* (Cmnd 2290) listed 251 statutory instruments restricting newspapers' ability to report government actions, along with 46 legislative restrictions arising from the various Official Secrets Acts, Prevention of Terrorism Acts and **censorship** (Article 19, 1989).

Regulation of the press can be statutory (that is, mandatory and imposed by government statue) or voluntary and self-regulatory (that is, imposed by a non-governmental body, including newspapers themselves). In both cases one of the key ambitions for regulation of content is to provide an accommodation between protecting the privacy of individuals from unwarranted press intrusion with securing the public's right to know.

In the UK, **journalists** and **editors** oppose statutory regulation with six arguments: (1) it is wrong in principle and constitutes censorship; (2) it is impractical and unworkable; (3) there are already too many statutory controls of the press; (4) there is no evidence that it works; (5) self-regulation is more flexible; and (6) voluntary regulate offers the most effective sanction against offenders – peer review and criticism (Franklin and Pilling, 1998).

During the 1990s, a number of high profile cases of press invasion of privacy, including the publication by *Mirror* newspapers of photographs of the then Princess of Wales exercising in a gym and taken with a hidden camera, prompted calls from MPs and the public to establish statutory regulation. The Calcutt inquiry recommended a statutory press commission with powers to fine newspapers, but the Select Committee *Report on Media Privacy and Intrusion* argued for the closure of the existing Press Council and a new self regulatory body – the Press Complaints Commission (PCC); the PCC came into being on 1 January 1991 (Calcutt, 1990). The PCC, funded by newspapers and with a membership of editors and lay members, developed a code of practice which it uses to adjudicate the complaints it receives from readers. All journalists, and editors, contracts require their compliance with the various clauses of the code which deal with privacy, fairness, and other matters; any breach of the code can result in sacking. But the PCC is regarded as a toothless 'tiger' incapable of restraining the worst excesses of tabloid behaviour in the highly competitive UK market for readers and advertisers. In a review of the first 10 years of its operation, Frost discovered that not a single one of the many hundreds of readers' complaints alleging racist reporting has been upheld (Frost, 2004: 101–14).

Some observers believe that it will not prove possible to regulate the content of UK newspapers until their ownership is more closely regulated (O'Malley and Solely, 2000). There is, of course, no limit on who may own a newspaper or how many, but the regulatory concern here has been to control cross-media ownership: that is, the ownership of papers by large cross-national, corporate monopolies which also own interests in radio, television and online. But across the last 20 years, both Conservative and Labour governments have followed a policy of deregulation. In 1995, the white paper *Media Ownership; The Government's Proposals* (Cmnd 2872) proposed relaxation of controls on cross-media ownership which came to fruition in the Broadcasting Act 1996: The Communications Act 2003 further deregulated ownership of broadcast media but the prohibition against any organisation with a 20 per cent share in a national newspaper from owning an ITV company remains intact.

FURTHER READING

Article 19 (1989) *No Comment: Censorship, Secrecy and the Irish Troubles.* London: The Internatioal Centre on Censorship.

Calcutt, D. (1990) *Report of the Committee on Privacy and Related Matters.* Cmnd 1102. London: HMSO.

Franklin, B. and Pilling, R. (1998) 'Taming the tabloids: markets, moguls and media regulation', in M. Kieran (ed.), *Media Ethics.* London: Routledge. pp. 111–23.

Frost, C. (2004) 'The Press Complaints Commission: a study of ten years of adjudications on press', *Journalism Studies,* 5 (1): 101–14.

O'Malley, T. and Solely, C. (2000) *Regulating the Press.* London: Pluto Press.

BF

Regulation (Radio)

As with television, individual countries have a variety of legislation and industry standards that deal with the content and ownership of radio broadcasting.

The increasing trend is for all **communications** activities to fall under the aegis of a regulatory body.

In the UK, this body is Ofcom which, in consultation with the UK Parliament, is required to advise on the granting and use of the frequency spectrum, in addition to regulatory duties concerning ownership, content and availability that are briefly outlined in **regulation – television**. Similarly, in the USA, the regulation of radio falls under the remit of the Federal Communications Commission (FCC). With a wider available spectrum, local radio stations are prolific in the USA, particularly since the reduction in license regulation in the 1980s and 1990s. There are still the age-old concerns about content however, such as the relatively recent phenomena of the 'shock jock' – deliberately controversial or offensive radio personalities (for example, the infamous Howard Stern), who use such tactics to carve out an audience share in a fiercely competitive environment.

Historically, radio regulation has been principally concerned with spectrum clutter and communications interference. The history of radio is also slightly different to that of television in that it is relatively cheap to set up and transmit to a local area (hence the proliferation of stations), but also to transmit to a wider area – hence the use of radio as a public service and information medium, particularly in less technologically developed countries in the world.

Once again, the rise of digital and Internet radio – such as Shoutcast and Live365 that offer hundreds of different stations from a variety of countries – means that radio regulation is also likely to be influenced by the debates concerning the Internet, particularly those of commercial royalty payments, and debates over acceptable content.

regulation (radio)

193

FURTHER READING

Federal Communications Commission: http://www.fcc.gov/
Feintuck, M. and Varney, M. (2006) *Media Regulation, Public Interest and the Law.* Edinburgh: Edinburgh University Press.

Hendy, D. (2000) *Radio in the Global Age*. Cambridge: Polity Press/Blackwell Publishers.

Hitchens, L. (2006) *Broadcasting Pluralism and Diversity: A Comparative Study of Policy and Regulation*. Portland, OR: Hart Publishing.

Ofcom: http://www.ofcom.org.uk/

NM

Regulation (Television)

The regulation of television generally consists of a mix of legal and industry standards that range from transmission frequencies to specific conditions on the type of programming content and **advertising** conditions, and the ownership of broadcasting networks.

In the UK, the overarching body is Ofcom (Office of Communications), formed with statutory duties and regulatory principles following the Communications Act 2003, and overseeing the regulation of all UK communications activities, including television and radio. It replaced the Radio Authority (RA) and the Independent Television Commission (ITC).

The body is accountable to the UK Parliament on a range of statutory issues, and also has a mandate to act as a public watchdog, often on the standards of programme content. The Broadcasting Code (2005) covers a wide range of issues such as fairness and privacy, programme sponsorship, advertising, as well as content likely to offend.

Members of the public are invited to complain to Ofcom under the various sections of this code and the adjudications are published in a monthly bulletin. Ofcom also deals with consumer issues such as licensing, cost and availability of access to communications services. In the UK, such regulation is traditionally 'light touch', allowing market forces to determine ownership to some extent (the BBC and public service broadcasting are more legislatively overseen, though still under this regulatory body).

Similar bodies exist across Europe under a variety of European Union directives and fundamental principles, although these are administered and regulated individually within countries.

In the USA the Federal Communications Commission acts as an independent regulatory body for all communications activities that reports directly to Congress. Here, the potential for regulation of particular types of content is continually debated within the context of freedom of speech.

Increasing **globalisation** of media content and ownership provides one of the biggest challenges for any form of regulation of television. In the UK, the recent furore over the withdrawal of some services from Rupert Murdoch's *BSkyB* satellite broadcaster for the competing *Virgin Media* cable provider is calling market-driven regulation into question. In Europe, one of the most familiar issues is the influence of political parties and prominent individuals over Italy's broadcast networks (as well as other media platforms), for example the nature of the competition between the state-owned RAI network and Mediaset, principally influenced by former Italian Prime Minister Silvio Berlusconi.

Increasing potential availability of Western broadcast content in China has moved the State Administration of Radio, Film and Television to make a variety of proclamations on content and foreign investment opportunities.

Perhaps one of the greatest challenges for the future is the rise of Internet broadcasting, where user-generated content, the breakdown of geographical boundaries, and recent high-profile cases such as the possibilities of copyright action over entertainment and sports clips on the YouTube site bring both television and radio programming, to a greater extent, into the realms of Internet regulation.

FURTHER READING

Federal Communications Commission: http://www.fcc.gov/

Feintuck, M. and Varney, M. (2006) *Media Regulation, Public Interest and the Law*. Edinburgh: Edinburgh University Press.

Hitchens, L. (2006) *Broadcasting Pluralism and Diversity: A Comparative Study of Policy and Regulation*. Portland, OR: Hart Publishing.

Ofcom: http://www.ofcom.org.uk/

regulation (television)

NM

Reputation Management

A good reputation matters because it is a key source of distinctiveness that produces support for the company and differentiates it from its rivals, says Fombrun and Van Riel (2004). PR practitioners shape company reputation and build effective relationships with key stakeholders. Relationship building is the preferred perspective of mainstream **public relations** scholars as opposed to reputation management.

Hutton (2001) claim reputation is a concept far more relevant to people who have no direct ties to an organisation, whereas relationships are far more relevant to people who are direct stakeholders of the organisation such as employees, customers, stockholders and others who are usually the organisation's most important publics. Consequently, Hutton maintains reputation is generally something an organisation has with strangers but a relationship is generally something an organisation has with friends and associates. And while it is hard to build, it is easily lost. The late Lord Forte (Haywood, 1994: 9), suggested: 'Reputation and respect can only be built on foundations of honesty and trust. Honesty can conceivably get you into trouble but it remains the best policy. Anything less can destroy in a day what may have taken years to achieve.'

A good reputation helps reduce costs, increase profits, and secure a more stable corporate future. The concept of actually managing corporate reputation is a relatively new one. For many years most corporations made little attempt to manage how they were regarded; some ignored criticisms altogether, while others made random, and not always successful, attempts to manage the views of stakeholders. What has changed clearly is the increasing pressure from stakeholders for the corporations to take a broader view of their responsibilities beyond the profit and loss account. They are also required to be more transparent. This has led, inter alia, to the development of programmes supporting **corporate social responsibility** and to auditors increasingly making use of the **triple bottom line** approach to financial reporting. What is clear is that the drive to actively manage reputation continues to gather momentum and provide increasing opportunities for PR professionals.

As the term PR becomes ever more closely connected to negative terms such as **spin doctor** and publicists, moreover, practitioners have differentiated themselves to signify a more strategic approach to communications management and management of reputation. Indeed, Countrywide Communications, a very successful UK consultancy which is now owned by Porter Novelli, used the **advertising** strapline: 'The management of reputation' to describe the character of the public relations consultancy. Research on behalf of the Corporate Communications Institute in 2004 looked at the primary roles of communications practitioners in the Fortune 1000. The highest figure (18.4 per cent), said managing company reputation was their primary role.

FURTHER READING

Fombrun, C.J. and Van Riel, C.B.M. (2004) *Fame and Fortune: How Successful Companies Build Winning Reputations*. Upper Saddle River, NJ: Pearson Education.
Gregory, A. (2002) *Planning and Managing PR Campaigns* London: Kogan Page/CIPR.
Haywood, R. (2002) *Managing Your Reputation*, 2nd ed. London: Kogan Page.
Hutton, J.G. (2001) 'Defining the relationship between public relations and marketing: public relations' most important challenge', in R.L. Heath (ed.), *Handbook of Public Relations*. Thousand Oaks, CA: Sage. pp. 7–15.
Jolly, A. (2001) *Managing Corporate Reputation*. London: Kogan Page.
Kitchen, P. and Schultz, D. (eds) (2001) *Raising the Corporate Umbrella*. London: Macmillan.
L'Etang, J. (1996) *Critical Perspectives in Public Relations*. London: International Thomson Publishing.
Tench, R. and Yeomans, L. (2006) *Exploring Public Relations*. Harlow: Prentice Hall.

MH & EP

Research (Communication)

Communication research is an essential part of a full **public relations** programme. It is, plainly, impossible to manage changes in reputation and public attitude if you do not know how your organisation is currently regarded.

Research can take many forms from engaging professional advisors and fieldworkers to desk-based research. A fairly simple format for desk-based research is to speak to a handful of journalists and comparatively review a series of websites. Commissioning basic professional research for the wider public can these days be done fairly economically by adding questions onto a web-based survey by a company like YouGov in the UK or Zogby in the USA.

More specialised target markets, however, will be more expensive to survey. Detailed research into the opinions, attitudes and behaviour of your core publics is a strong foundation for a PR programme and provides a benchmark against which you can measure the success of your programme as it continues.

PR **evaluation** is conducted in a vacuum if it is not built on solid preliminary research. Intelligent PR **planning** and **SMART objectives** also, of necessity, require an understanding of what your starting position is. PR academics and institutes generally advocate the view that practitioners should make greater use of research and that money spent on research, provided it is proportional to the overall budget, is rarely wasted.

Research can also be used to generate information for use in your PR campaign. Intelligently mining your research data for potential news stories is an excellent way of driving media relations campaigns or other communications campaigns. The advertising slogan 'eight out of ten owners said their cats preferred it' ran for decades, even if regulatory pressure led to the proviso that it was eight out of 10 owners who expressed a preference.

Sometimes the newsworthy research is pursued purely for the purposes of being newsworthy. For example, the research company Globescan and the University of Maryland conducted research in 35 countries to see whether they preferred George W. Bush over John Kerry to win the then upcoming 2004 election. They knew that the results would be newsworthy worldwide especially as there was lopsided support for the challenger, with 30 countries preferring Kerry, something the researchers may have suspected in advance.

The PR company Brands2Life produced some research for a client which seemed to show that Lara Croft was one of the most important role models for young women, which generated considerable coverage around the launch of a new version of the computer game Tomb Raider.

FURTHER READING

Globescan: http://www.globescan.com/news_archives/GlobeScan-PIPA_Release. pdf

Haywood, R. (1991) *All About Public Relations: How to Build Business Success on Good Communications.* London: McGraw-Hill.

Kitchen, P. (1997) *Public Relations: Principles and Practice.* London: Thomson Business Press.

Theilmann, R. and Szondi, G. (2006) 'Public relations research and evaluation', in R. Tench and L. Yeomans (eds), *Exploring Public Relations.* Harlow: Prentice Hall. pp. 208–33.

QL

Research (Sponsored)

There are many reasons why an organisation may wish to sponsor research. **Think tanks** are always seeking sponsorship or other financial support for their work, as are universities. Broadly, reasons for sponsoring research can be categorised under three headings, though in many cases more than one reason will apply:

1. As part of a mission to support good causes. (See **corporate social responsibility**.)
2. To generate positive associations with a good cause, in this case, education. Similar reasons apply to sponsoring sports and the arts. (See **sponsorship**.)
3. To encourage the product of the research in the belief that it will somehow advance the interests of organisation.

Since the principles in the first two cases are little different from supporting other good causes or high-profile events which are covered elsewhere, this article will focus on the third case. This is a sensitive area ethically. Despite wild charges by rival academics and **campaign** groups it would be very unusual for think tank, university or individual academics to accept grant money on the specific understanding that findings favourable to the cause of the sponsoring organisation will be guaranteed. This, nonetheless, is the implication of campaigners, including the Royal Society, in criticising ExxonMobil for making grants to scientists critical of the theory of anthropogenically enhanced global warming.

In general, organisations are more likely to sponsor research by academics whose own predilections they already know in the belief that this will advance a view they favour in an active political debate. It would be unethical for an organisation to offer, or an academic to accept, sponsorship if the strings attached expressly compromised the integrity of the academic inquiry. Nonetheless, critics continue to allege that there implied conditions in such grants which undermine the credibility of the research.

QL

Response Statement

A response statement is always the opening salvo in **crisis public relations**. As its name implies, it is issued in reply to an event or set of circumstances and crucial attributes include brevity, accuracy and speed of delivery. In broad terms it is a positioning device designed to set out the parameters governing how an organisation will deal with an incident. One paragraph is the normal length, ideally transmitted within one hour of the event to which it refers.

Content is obviously driven by circumstance but in the case, for example, of a fatal air crash it will include the following characteristics: sympathy for the relatives; a promise of a quick yet thorough investigation;

and a commitment to publish the results. It must include 24/7 contact numbers and an indication of the forward strategy. For example, will there be a press conference within a set timeframe?

The response statement must always be seen as part of a **media relations** strategy so the issuing of it would always be backed up by **Qs and As**. The growth of the rolling news bulletin makes the professional use of the RS even more central.

MH

Risk Management

Risk management is the business technique of anticipating, minimising and preventing accidental loss through taking precautionary measures. Along with reputation management, risk management is becoming important to business leaders in the UK as it focuses on the development of strong relationships between the organisation and the stakeholders on whom the organisation relies for survival.

Risk, according to the Institute of Risk Management in the UK, can be defined as the combination of the probability of an event and its consequences. It is central to any organisation's strategic management and it is the process where by organisations address the risks attached to their activities. Therefore, the focus of good risk management is the identification and treatment of these risks.

Not only is risk management and **communications** important to business leaders but also to government leaders who need to communicate effectively and responsibly in the midst of a media haze which could potentially cloud public perception on the hazards of modern life and how they affect them. It is vital that governments and officials shape risk messages that are accurate, clear and not misleading. This can often be difficult when fighting against media agendas. UK examples would be the communication of immigration and vaccination issues, stem cell research and cloning.

Dr Peter Sandman, considered to be the guru of risk management and a former environmental protestor turned risk management consultant, maintains that risk equals hazard plus outrage and firms need to adopt outrage management techniques in order to manage public perception.

FURTHER READING

Ball, K., Bostrom, A. and Evans G. (1997) *Risk Communication and Vaccination*. Washington, DC: National Academy Press.

Murray, K. and White, J. (2004) CEO *Views on Reputation Management: A Report on the Value of Public Relations as Perceived by Organisational Leaders*. London: Chime PLC.

Sandman, P. (1993) *Responding to Community Outrage: Strategies for Effective Risk Communication*. Fairfax, VA: American Industrial Hygiene Association.

Seeger, M., Sellnow, T. and Ulmer, R. (2003) *Communications and Organizational Crisis*. Westport, CT: Praeger/Greenwood.

Tench, R. and Yeomans, L. (2006) *Exploring Public Relations*. Harlow: Prentice Hall.

EP

Rogue Sites

A rogue site exists to criticise or mock a, usually well-known, person or organisation. Rogue sites have been established for financial gain (see **cybersquatting**), for political reasons and by campaigning **NGOs**.

One of the most well-known and effective rogue sites was established by Greenpeace in the period immediately before the Sydney Olympics, targeting Coca-Cola®, one of the principal sponsors of the Games. The site was a key part of Greenpeace's campaign against the use of hydrofluorocarbons (HFCs), a refrigerant implicated in global warming, of which Coca-Cola® was one of the world's largest users. Campaigners were seeking a commitment from Coca-Cola® to phase out the use of HFCs in favour of more benign refrigerants. Coca-Cola® initially refused to enter discussions with Greenpeace. The site was an effective pastiche on

Coke's then advertising campaign, which involved the use of polar bears.

The Greenpeace site showed a short film of polar bears trying to exist on a rapidly shrinking icecap. The Greenpeace campaign was launched seven weeks before the Sydney Olympics and had as its target persuading Coca-Cola® to make the announcement that it would phase out HFCs before the Games began. The campaign generated considerable media coverage and an extremely high hit rate on the website, and was successful, in that Coca-Cola® did indeed announce its intention to abandon HFCs before the opening ceremony. Another high-profile campaign was the McLibel site, supporting the defendants in a libel action brought by McDonalds.

Many of the most high-profile political rogue sites such as gwbush.com and bushsucks.com have been removed over the past few years, with the content mostly transferring to less contentious domain names. A rogue site targeting the World Trade Organization (formerly GATT) maintains some legacy rogue sites, including gwbush.com and sites attacking Shell and McDonalds on its site. There is an alternative definition of rogue sites. This refers to websites that will automatically install software, including spyware or viruses, on the computer of anyone who visits them.

FURTHER READING

GATT: http://www.gatt.org/homewto.html

QL

Rolling News

Rolling news or 24/7 was ushered in by the growth of satellite television in the 1980s, particularly Cable Network News (CNN) and British

Satellite Broadcasting (BSB), latterly BskyB, delivering for the first time bulletins without the normal timeframe of the *9 O'Clock News*, or *News at Ten*. Supporters of CNN argue it came of age at Tiananmen Square and was certainly developed further by 9/11.

Whatever the origins, terrestrial broadcasters now routinely provide the same service, for example BBC World. The characteristics across the channels show many common features. For example, news headlines will feature every 15 minutes with an extended bulletin on the hour. In the interim, sport, finance, lifestyle and weather will jockey for position. The pattern is repeated on radio. Throughout the hour, breaking news will be revealed on a streamer across the lower third of the screen, carrying a brief summary of events and pointing to the next full bulletin.

This development is a mixed blessing for **public relations** practitioners. On the one hand, its enormous appetite for material, especially on the business satellite channels such as CNBC and Bloomberg, means many more opportunities for **video news releases** and CEO interviews. The downside is what has become known as the 'CNN factor', after the pioneering work of Cable News Network founded by Ted Turner in Atlanta, Georgia. Literally, there is no longer a corporate hiding place, according to some practitioners. If an organisation has a problem in one country – an oil spill, a product recall – the news will go global very quickly. **NGOs** have become very adept at using this facility as Shell found to its cost when Greenpeace took the company on over the sinking of the Brent Spar oil storage platform. (See Shell.com.)

FURTHER READING

Hawkins, V. (2002) 'The other side of the CNN Factor: the media and conflict', *Journalism Studies*, 3 (2): 225–41.

Lewis, J., Cushion, S. and Thomas, J. (2005) 'Immediacy, convenience or engagement? An analysis of 24-hour news channels in the UK', *Journalism Studies*, 6 (4): 461–79.

Robinson, P. (2000) 'The CNN effect: can the news media drive foreign policy', *Journal of Peace Research*, 37 (5): 301–9.

MH

Rolling News Deadlines

CNN pioneered the concept of 24/7 news with bulletins throughout the day and night. Coverage of the demonstrations in Tiananmen Square did more than anything to establish its reputation as the news provider of immediate record if not considered analysis. The field is now wide open with major players including BBC News 24, Sky News, Al Jazheera and a myriad of dedicated business channels. Radio has been quick to capitalise on the benefits of its lower cost base and lack of reliance on visuals and so provides more and more access to transmission.

Rolling news deadlines (RND) have proved a mixed blessing. The huge appetite for 24/7 coverage drives a constant need for stories, which in turn has helped spawn the growth in 'citizen journalism' with all the validity problems that entails – witness the early coverage of the July bombings in London.

For the **public relations** practitioner there are now many more channels through which to reach a dedicated, self-selecting audience, particularly in the corporate sphere. Bloomberg and CNBC regularly feature lengthy interviews with senior executives. The coverage, by nature, also tends to be positive rather than hostile. There is, too, a burgeoning market for **video news releases** and the radio equivalent. The greatest attribute of RND from the PR profession's point of view is that there is always a channel through which to send your message and it will probably have a global footprint.

FURTHER READING

Lewis, J., Cushion, S. and Thomas, J. (2005) 'Immediacy, convenience or engagement? An analysis of 24-hour news channels in the UK', *Journalism Studies*, 6 (4): 461–79.

MH

rolling news
deadlines

Sampling

Given the practical limitations of any research project, time and money being the most obvious, it is not usually possible to investigate every instance of the issue under study – the *population*. The population could be all the citizens in a particular country, or all the PR professionals working in healthcare, or all newspaper articles concerning an election.

Researchers will therefore try carefully to construct a *sample* of the population to investigate. The basic principle is that this sample will be *representative* of the whole, and therefore any results gained from an investigation of this sample are likely to be generalisable to the entire population. That is to say, if a high proportion of healthcare PR professionals answered a survey in a certain way, the researcher would hope that a similar proportion of the entire profession would answer in this way, given the time and money to conduct the survey with every single one.

Sampling applies to both **quantitative** and **qualitative** research methods, and is very much dependant on your hypothesis or research question (see **methodology**). It will also require some background research about the general characteristics of your population.

Random (non-purposive) sampling is one of the most common forms in **public opinion** research, and often used in large-scale surveys. As the name suggests, members of the population are selected entirely by chance, and each individual unit has the same likelihood of being selected as the next. Individual citizens may be selected from a large database, for instance an electoral register, often by *systematic* random sampling, in which the sampling procedure starts at a random point in the list and then picks every 100th person from there on.

In some research there is a need to compare a balanced sample of particular demographics (for example, age groups, income levels or gender). In this case, the random sample may first be *stratified*, to determine the relevant proportions of these demographic groups that are desired. Similarly, market researchers will often use *quota* sampling, where the researcher has a given number of particular demographic characteristics that they are required to stop in the street. As a tip, saying that you are involved in journalism, PR or advertising can often politely excuse you from completing a tedious street survey about new product packaging on a rainy Saturday afternoon in town.

Non-random (non-purposive) sampling is often used in qualitative research, and here the members of the sample are deliberately selected according to certain criteria. *Purposive* samples may be constructed for small-scale research projects, for example, all articles over a two-week period of election coverage in one newspaper, where any claims are only relevant to that particular newspaper and that particular election, rather than election coverage in all newspapers as a whole.

Volunteer samples and *convenience* samples (for example, where those people most easily available are surveyed) are often employed for techniques such as **focus groups** or **key figure interviews**, where any findings, however useful, can be used only as a snapshot of potentially more widely held views and make no claims to be truly representative.

In **content analysis** other specific features will affect the ways in which issues or key messages are portrayed, whether in print, broadcast or advertising media. Some of these are analogous to demographic considerations when human participants are the focus of the research. For example, the editorial stance of the text; the ownership of the outlet (particularly differences between government-owned, public service and commercial publications or broadcast platforms); circulation or reach (in press terms, the differences between the pressures on journalists to produce stories daily, weekly or at longer intervals; in broadcast terms, the differences between terrestrial, satellite/cable channels, and subscription-only services; in new media terms, the accessibility of the site to the population); target audience – whether this is intended for mass consumption or for a specific type of consumer (for example, the differences between a television news bulletin aimed at a mass peak-time audience and an in-depth, analytical programme aimed at a more actively news-seeking viewer).

Considerations of the characteristics of the entire, carefully defined, population, whether people or texts, will be important in determining an appropriate sample and in the validity of any claims made on the basis of the research findings.

There is no 'magic number' that will give the answer to the question 'how many do I need?'. As in all research, a balance must be struck between what the researcher can defend as a reasonably representative sample, and what is achievable given logistical restraints.

FURTHER READING

Davies, M.M. and Mosdell, N. (2006) *Practical Research Methods for Media and Cultural Studies: Making People Count*. Edinburgh: Edinburgh University Press.

sampling

Deacon, D., Pickering, M., Golding, P. and Murdock, G. (1999) *Researching Communications: A Practical Guide to Methods in Media and Cultural Analysis*. London: Arnold.

Wimmer, R.D. and Dominick, J.R. (2006) Mass *Media Research: An Introduction*. Belmont, CA: Wadsworth.

NM

Sell-in

Sell-in is a key skill of the **public relations** practitioner. The sell-in is the process of selling or pitching your idea to a journalist in order to get coverage of a **client** issue, product, service or goods. Once a story has been developed and **key messages** built into the material, the PR practitioner then 'sells-in' the story to a **journalist** to see if they are interested in the piece and if they want to cover the issue.

The key is being able to present your story in a way the journalist can relate to. The journalist needs to understand why the story would be of interest to his or her readers, listeners or viewers. You have around 20 seconds to make your case so there needs to be a pre-planned structure and hook to the sell-in process.

The **press release** usually forms the basis for discussion and the journalist may just ask you to send them the copy via email, however, many successful sell-ins do not rely on press releases. They are the result of explorative editorial conversations with journalists with whom the practitioner has built up a strong working relationship over time. This is why many journalists make great PR practitioners as they understand the way a journalist needs a story to be packaged. Journalists who move into the PR industry are described as 'poachers turned gamekeepers'.

The art of the sell-in is in even more demand in today's hyper competitive media and public relations landscape. Journalists are bombarded on a daily basis by PR practitioners shaping communications **campaigns** on behalf of clients and trying to get what the industry terms, 'share of voice', to enable key messages to be communicated to target audiences.

Many journalists and media organisations are happy to take this material as there is a huge gap between the media content which needs to be developed on a daily basis and the number of journalists producing that content. In simple terms, there are too few journalists to develop enough copy and there is a very real reliance on the PR industry to provide a constant stream of **news** stories in order to fill this content gap.

FURTHER READING

Bland, M., Theaker A. and Wragg D. (2007) Effective Media Relations – How to Get Results, 3rd ed. London: Kogan Page.
Burton, C. and Drake A (2004) Hitting the Headlines in Europe – a Country by Country Guide to Effective Media Relations. London: Kogan Page.

EP

Situation Analysis

Situation analysis is the first stage in any PR **campaign** and is used to paint a picture of the real **communications** issues with which an organisation is faced. The role of situation analysis in strategic development on communications programmes is to ensure the study of the communications issue is objective rather than subjective. Situation analysis ensures the PR practitioner considers each element of research before developing strategic themes and focuses on a clear understanding of the issues facing the organisation and the **key stakeholders** with whom the organisation needs to communicate with in order to shape communication agendas.

Two tools of analysis assist in the development of situation analysis. SWOT and PESTLE analysis. SWOT stands for strengths, weaknesses, opportunities and threats. The practitioner assesses the communication problem by looking at first the internal measures of strengths and weaknesses inherent within an organisation before turning to an examination of the external measures of opportunities and threats in relation to the external environment of an organisation.

PESTL stands for political, economic, social and technological. These are external factors that affect the environment in which an organisation operates. By analysing and assessing each area, the PR practitioner can get a bird's eye view of the problem and only then can they begin to develop strategic communication themes.

FURTHER READING

Mintzberg, H. and Quinn J.B. (1991) *The Strategy Process, Concepts, Contexts, Cases,* 2nd edn. Upper Saddle River, NJ: Prentice-Hall.
Tench, R. and Yeomans, L. (2006) *Exploring Public Relations.* Upper Saddle River, NJ: Prentice Hall.

EP

SMART Objectives

In defining objectives for a **public relations** (or other) plan, most commentators will advocate the use of SMART objectives. This means they should be Specific Measurable Achievable Relevant and Time-based. Some sources use 'realistic' instead of 'relevant', but this would seem to be redundant after 'achievable'. Other sources use 'agreed' instead of 'achievable'. Objectives are usually seen as being at the heart of the planning process.

Objectives:

• provide the organisation with some measure of control;
• motivate individuals and teams;
• provide focus on agreed aims.

The requirement that the objectives be specific is important in order to provide precision. Objectives need to be measurable, especially if bonuses are to be related to achieving them. It can only create difficulties if there is disagreement about whether or not the objectives have been achieved.

Objectives can be motivating only if they are achievable (or realistic). Relevant refers to the overall aims of the organisation. It is easy to imagine objectives which are both specific and measurable – such as *x* column cm per month – but which do not necessarily communicate the **key messages**. Time-based simply means that there is a deadline by which the objective needs to be achieved.

FURTHER READING

Learn Marketing: http://www.learnmarketing.net/smart.htm
The Practice of Leadership: http://www.thepracticeofleadership.net/2006/03/11/setting-smart-objectives/

QL

Social Marketing

Social marketing is based on the principle that people are more likely to trust their peers than authority figures such as the government, media, business or 'experts'. In part it makes use of **social media**, but it is much older than the use of digital technologies.

The first recorded use of social marketing in any systematic way was by Bernays on behalf of the Wilson administration during the First World War, though it could be argued that the tradition of religious evangelism is a kind of social marketing. Bernays organised a group of 'minute men', all respected figures in their local communities such as religious ministers, factory managers, teachers and publicans, who were charged to speak for one minute on the reasons why America should participate in the European war. Bernays was relying on the fact that the minute men were well known individuals and that a message delivered by them would be especially persuasive. Gladwell writes in *The Tipping Point* of the kind of people who are critical to creating social epidemics. He divides them into 'connectors', 'mavens' and 'salesmen'. The connector is the person with the large personal network, who knows whom to contact to spread a message. The maven is someone who collects information. The salesman is the highly persuasive individual. Gladwell argues that such people are behind unpredictable trends such as fashion. Social marketing is a strategy to make use of such social epidemics in a planned way.

FURTHER READING

Gladwell, M. (2002) *The Tipping Point*. NewYork: Little, Brown and Company.
Postrel, V. (1999) *The Future and Its Enemies: The Growing Conflict Over Creativity, Enterprise and Progress*. New York: Touchstone.
Surowiecki, J. (2005) *The Wisdom of Crowds*. London: Abacus.

QL

Social Media

Social media is a broad term incorporating blogs, wikis, Internet communities and online discussions. Community sites such as Facebook and Myspace are immensely popular with young people and business-oriented alternatives such as LinkedIn and ecademy are widely used in networking. Other sites such as YouTube, where users upload their own videos, or Twitter, used for sending brief messages to other users, can also be considered social media.

For some markets, especially for products aimed at young people, social media are extremely important. The defining feature of social media is that content is created, at least in part, by users. In PR terms, social media provide additional channels for communicating with target **publics**. As non-mediated channels they might be thought to carry less weight than traditional media, but the uncontrolled nature of social media means they have great credibility with some markets. Podcasting and vlogging (video blogging) can also be considered social media and are increasingly used to communicate all types of message.

The boundaries between social media and the mainstream media are becoming increasingly blurred. The *Daily Telegraph* shifted in 2007 to a tri-media newsroom in which journalists must produce all stories in text, audio and video formats. Mainstream media are also major centres for blogging, with journalists producing blogs exclusively for web publication and users being encouraged to add their comments.

FURTHER READING

Gladwell, M. (2002) *The Tipping Point*. New York: Little, Brown and Company.
Postrel, V. (1999) *The Future and Its Enemies: The Growing Conflict Over Creativity, Enterprise and Progress*. New York: Touchstone.
Surowiecki, J. (2005) *The Wisdom of Crowds*. London, Abacus.

QL

Soundbites

Soundbites dominate the world of political PR. Their origin is disputed; some favour Bill Clinton's last Presidential election campaign as defining the product; others point to Winston Churchill's Battle of Britain speech about the 'Few'. Whatever the history, soundbites are now part of the political landscape. In essence, they reduce argument on policy to around 30 seconds of television time or one paragraph of newspaper space. The aim is to produce the memorable quote – 'tough on crime, tough on the causes of crime' – in a format which fits, particularly, television news.

Political speeches routinely carry the soundbites highlighted so the reporter in a hurry is in no doubt about what is important. In an era of being **on message** soundbites have a vital role to play in ensuring consistency but critics argue that the technique emasculates debate by attempting to reduce political complexity to easily absorbed pieces of information and not allowing for a fuller exposure of the issues. Many argued the decision to allow the televising of parliament following a series of experiments in the mid-1980s actually promoted the soundbite giving what one MP, parodying Andy Warhol's famous phrase, called 30

soundbites

213

seconds of fame. Research carried out in elections does indicate the soundbite is getting shorter and 30 seconds is at the top end of the range.

There is little doubt that **rolling news** and 24/7 has increased the appetite for the soundbite; politicians and broadcasters show no inclination for wanting to change this. Many political interviews now conclude with the presenter saying; 'Minister, very briefly, would you care to comment.' And the Minister usually does.

FURTHER READING

Jones, N. (1996) *Soundbites and Spin Doctors*. London: Politicos.
Oborne, P. (2005) *The Rise of Political Lying*. London: The Free Press.
Tye, L. (1998) *The Father of Spin*. New York: Henry Holt.

MH

Sources (Relationships with Journalists)

Gans (1980) famously deployed a dance metaphor to characterise relationships between journalists and sources and their respective roles in the **news** gathering and reporting process: 'It takes two to tango', he suggested 'but sources invariably lead' (Gans, 1980: 116). **Journalists** have typically rejected the implicit collusion of such a formulation: if relationships become 'too cosy' and journalists become 'too close to their sources' they risk losing their journalistic integrity and editorial independence. Journalists perceive the relationship as essentially conflictual – and with journalists as the dominant partner. *Daily Mail* columnist Richard Littlejohn's commitment to this conflictual model is evident. 'The job of someone like me', he argues, 'is to sit at the back and throw bottles. Politicians are among my favourite targets. They employ an entire industry, often using public money, to present themselves as favourably as possible and I certainly don't see it as my job to inflate the egos of little men' (*Guardian*, 22 February 1993). More recently, retiring Prime Minister Tony Blair revealed his perception of the press as highly adversarial when in a valedictory lecture he denounced journalists as 'feral beasts' (Blair, 2007).

But the relationship between journalists and PRs has recently been recast as a 'trading' or 'exchange' relationship in which PR sources trade insider information in return for access to **audiences** via journalists' columns/programmes (Ericson et al., 1989; Franklin, 2006; Jones, 2006). Media theorists Jay Blumler and Michael Gurevitch (1981) offer the classic formulation of this 'exchange' relationship. They suggest that while the relationship between journalists and sources has the potential to become conflictual, on a day-to-day basis they work in a more harmonious, complementary if not collusive way. This occurs because journalists and politicians have ambitions, interests and needs which can be achieved most readily when they can win the co-operation of the other group. There is a 'mutuality of interests' between journalists and sources which has drawn them ever closer together until they have become 'inextricably linked' (Blumler and Gurevitch, 1981: 473).

Journalists, for example, offer sources the opportunity to achieve a public airing for their messages, access to target audiences, opportunities to set news agendas, to inform public opinion, to provide information and to guage public opinion. In return, sources originate many of the stories which journalists publish and they may appear on screen as 'performers' providing on-the-record quotes, or as specialists and 'guests' to be interviewed for broadcast, print or online outlets. Each partner has much to gain from this working relationship which might be characterised as a 'marriage of convenience' which may nonetheless be plagued by temporary separations. But if the relationship begins to break down (because a journalist breaks the unwritten rules which govern the relationship by citing an off-the-record comment or breaking an embargoed story, or a source leaks a major story to another journalist) both sides have a vested interest in re-establishing effective working relations – a process which Blumler and Gurevitch call 'mutual adaptation'.

Metaphors to describe the relationship abound. Political journalist Simon Hoggart (2006) describes the relationship as the '"politics media snake pit" in which we slither all over each other, hissing with hatred, but hopelessly knotted together'. Bernard Ingham (1990) said the relationship is 'essentially cannibalistic in which both both sides feed off each other but

sources

no one knows who is next on the menu'. Each metaphor signals conflict and hostility but constrained within a framework of mutual dependance and reliance. Julia Hobsbawm has recently established an organisation called Editorial Intelligence(EI) intended to acknowledge the complementary intended working relationships between PR practitioners and journalists by facilitating networking between them (Hobsbawm, 2006; White and Hobsbawm, 2007).

FURTHER READING

Blair, T. (2007) Speech to the Reuters Oxford International Institute of Journalism. Available at: http://news.bbc.co.uk/1/hi/uk_politics/6744581.stm

Blumler, J.G. and Gurevitch, M. (1981) 'Politicians and the press: an essay on role relationships', in D. Nimmo and K. Saunders (eds), *Handbook of Political Communication*. London: Sage. pp. 467–97.

Ericson, R.V., Baranek, P. and Chan, J. (1989) *Negotiating Control: A Study of News Sources*. Milton Keynes: Open University Press.

Gans, H. (1980) *Deciding What's News*. London: Constable.

Hobsbawm, J. (2006) *Where the Truth Lies: Trust and Morality in PR and Journalism*. London: Atlantic Books.

Jones, N. (2006) *Trading Information: Lies, Leaks and Tip Offs*. London: Politicos.

White, J. and Hobsbawm, J. (2007) 'Public relations and journalism: the unquiet relationship – a view from the United Kingdom', *Journalism Practice*, 1 (2): 283–93.

BF

Sources (Influence on Editorial)

The suggestion that the activities of **public relations** professionals may help to shape **news** content in national and local news media is increasingly commonplace among **journalists**, academics and PRs (Fletcher, 2006; Hobsbawm, 2006; Jones, 2006). The emergence of Editorial Intelligence, an organisation headed by Julia Hobsbawm, with an ambition to bring journalists and PRs closer together, underscores this new assessment (Plunkett, 2006). *Financial Times* journalist John Lloyd argues that:

> journalists' traditional and adversarial (see above) perceptions of their relationships with sources 'is grossly self serving ... and ... glosses over, ignores or even denies the fact that much of current journalism both broadcast and press is public relations in the sense that stories, ideas, features and interviews are either suggested, or in the extreme actually written by public relations people. Until that becomes open and debated between PR people and journalists, we will continue to have this artificially wide gulf where journalists pose as fearless seekers of truth and PRs are slimy creatures trying to put one over on us. It is not remotely like that. (*Guardian*, 10 April 2006: 3)

A study conducted at Cardiff University (2006) confirmed a good deal of Lloyd's claims. The analysis of the news contents of two separate weeks of national quality newspapers (2027 news stories), along with a sample of radio and television news programmes across the same two weeks (402 news stories), concluded that 30 per cent of print stories were wholly or mainly derived from PR sources with a further 24 per cent of stories revealing some PR influence; for broadcast journalism, results suggested 31 per cent of broadcast items were wholly or substantively sourced from PR with a further 27 per cent displaying some evidence of reliance on PR materials. This is perhaps not surprising given that a decade ago the editor of *PR Week* made similar claims. 'At least 50 per cent of all sections of the broadsheet press' he claims derives from PR sources while 'in the local press and the mid market and tabloid nationals the figure would undoubtedly be higher ... the relationship [between journalists and sources] is utterly interdependent. PRs provide fodder but the clever high-powered ones do a lot of journalists' thinking for them' (cited in the *Guardian*, 13 May 1996: 10)

However, the Cardiff study offers the first independent verification of such speculations and casts doubts upon the independent character of much 'quality' UK journalism. Direct textual comparison of the contents of press releases, the text of Press Association (and other wire copy sources) stories and items published or broadcast in the UK news media, for example, revealed both the extent of journalists' reliance on PR and **news agency** copy, as well as the very modest editorial revisions (if any) which journalists made to such materials before presenting it in the pages of the national press. Franklin's (1986) earlier study of local and regional newspapers' reliance on PR materials, distributed by local government PR departments, suggested an even greater success for these sources in influencing and shaping local news agendas: again, the 'transformation' was minimal with many stories repeating verbatim the contents of **press releases** sourced from the local town hall, (Franklin, 1986; Harrison, 2006).

The Cardiff researchers' analysis of newspaper companies' annual reports across two decades, revealed that while news output (measured by increased pagination and the proliferation of online editions) has expanded substantially, the number of journalists employed had remained largely static. This growing reliance on PR and agency sources of copy has therefore occurred in the context of this relative decline in journalistic resource – and is almost certainly explained by it. Telephone interviews with journalists revealed their perception that the number of stories they were obliged to write during each shift had increased threefold across the last 20 years. In such circumstances, it might be anticipated that the impact of PR activities on editorial contents will continue to increase and hence journalists' editorial independence will inevitably decline.

FURTHER READING

Franklin, B. (1986) 'Public relations, the local press and the coverage of local government', *Local Government Studies*, July/August: 25–33.

Franklin, B., Lewis, J. and Williams, A. (2006) *Interim Report of Findings on the Independence of the British Press.* Cardiff: Cardiff University.

Harrison, S. (2006) 'Local government public relations and the press', in B. Franklin (ed.), *Local Journalism and Local Media: Making the Local News.* London: Routledge. pp. 175–88.

Hobsbawm, J. (2006) *Where the Truth Lies: Trust and Morality in PR and Journalism.* London: Atlantic Books.

Jones, N. (2006) *Trading Information: Leaks, Lies and Tip-Offs.* London: Politicos.

BF

Spin

Spin has for many assumed a central role in public relations theory yet some scholars argue its importance is overstated and its role exaggerated by practitioners. Frequently, spin is associated with an individual identified as a **Spin Doctor**. In the context of PR, the origin of the word spin is disputed (Andrews, 2005). Most likely it derived from the American game of baseball where the pitcher or thrower puts a spin or turn on the ball as it leaves his hand to effect a change of direction while it is in flight and so confuse the batsman.

In PR-speak, spin refers to attempts to twist a story to the advantage of the originator; to put the best possible gloss on what is written or broadcast. (See **Friday Night Drop**.)

As a political technique, spin first came to prominence during the Clinton Presidency. He gathered around him a cadre of young and highly intelligent people whose role was to ensure the media really understand what was being said. For example, following a speech these staffers would, quite literally, descend on the media in order to reinforce the **key messages** of the President in a manner which would leave the journalists in no doubt as to what was important. (See also **On Message**.)

In the UK, Alistair Campbell, Communications Director in the Blair government, will be forever associated with attempting to influence the way the media reported politics (Franklin, 2004; Jones, 1996), although he frequently alleged that it was journalists who were the 'real spinners' and downplayed his role in news management in his recently published Diaries (Campbell, 2007). Accounts of the commitment and effectiveness of the No. 10 Press Office to spinning the news, however, have been more commonplace (Price, 2005).

FURTHER READING

Andrews, L. (2005) 'Spin: from tactic to tabloid', *Journal of Public Affairs*, 5: 1–16.
Ewen, S. (1996) *PR! A Social History of Spin*. New York: Basic Books.
Jones, N. (1995) *Soundbites and Spin Doctors*. London: Politicos.
Miller, D. (2004) *Tell Me Lies*. London: Pluto.

MH

Spin Doctor

The term spin doctor is now commonly used as a mildly pejorative term for a political aid who tries to use the media for the benefit of the party.

Essentially the task of the spin doctor is to produce a story which will shed the best light on the party, by accentuating the positive aspects of the issue or diverting attention away if this is not possible. In practice, this could include: sending specially marked up copies of ministerial speeches to the media in advance to secure more and better coverage; arranging a **photo opportunity** to publicise a policy announcement, or providing a cabinet member for interview to specially selected outlets. In extremis, it would include supplying a diversionary story in the hope of taking the headlines away (Gaber, 2001).

Critics of the role of the spin doctor claim it devalues politics by substituting style for substance; that the presentation assumes greater importance than the policy (Franklin, 2004). In the political sphere, two 'spin doctors' have published detailed but divergent accounts of their activities in presenting and promoting news and information about the Labour government (Campbell, 2007; Price, 2005).

Spin doctors can also be found increasingly outside the political sphere as multi-national corporations increasingly have to explain their actions to a growing number of **Stakeholders**, including **NGOs**.

FURTHER READING

Campbell, A. (2007) *The Blair Years.* London: Hutchinson.
Gaber, I. (2001) 'Government by spin: an analysis of the process', *Media, Culture and Society*, 22 (4): 507–18.
Price, L. (2005) *The Spin Doctor's Diary: Inside No 10 with New Labour.* London: Hodder and Stoughton.

MH

Spoiler

A spoiler is a story or event designed principally to distract attention from another event. Examples include Associated Newspapers relaunching the *Evening News* in competition with its own *Evening Standard* the same week Robert Maxwell launched his own evening paper, the *London Post*. The *Post* failed and the *News* closed soon afterwards, leaving the *Standard* unchallenged, as it had been before.

Lance Price in his book *The Spin Doctor's Diary* tells of No. 10 launching a hurried drugs initiative, with the Home Secretary and Drugs Czar briefed only minutes in advance, purely to deflect questions on the ongoing disagreements between Tony Blair and Gordon Brown.

When Rebekah Wade, **Editor** of the *Sun*, was arrested for an assault on her partner (she was later freed without charge) it seemed likely that this would be a huge story. The *Sun* had been running a campaign against domestic violence and her partner was the notorious TV hardman Ross Kemp. In fact, the alleged hypocrisy of Ms Wade was entirely lost when Steve McFadden, who plays Kemp's onscreen brother in the BBC show *EastEnders*, was also apparently assaulted, this time by an ex-girlfriend, on the same evening. Some media commentators suggested that the assault on McFadden might have been arranged by the *Sun*, as a spoiler to divert attention from Wade's role in the events of the evening. Certainly, the principle of a spoiler story was on display here. A good story – editor ignores own campaign – was largely dropped for a better one – two 'brothers' beaten up by women on the same night. While raising obvious questions, the mere fact that a story was bumped for a better one, cannot be said to demonstrate that the *Sun* employed spoiler tactics.

There is no doubt that an otherwise embarrassing pair of stories in the 2001 election campaign – Blair's confrontation with the partner of a cancer patient and Jack Straw's hostile reception by police officers – were swept aside by John Prescott punching a hunting supporter in North Wales. It has not been widely suggested that Prescott did this with any Machiavellian thoughts in mind.

FURTHER READING

Price, L. (2005) *The Spin Doctor's Diary*. London: Hodder and Stoughton.

QL

Sponsorship

Sponsorship is used as a promotional vehicle in **public relations**. The word sponsor derives from the Latin word for guarantor. To sponsor something is to support an event, activity, person, or organisation financially or through the provision of products or services. Sponsorship is typically done for promotional purposes, to generate publicity, or to obtain access to a wider audience. Kitchen (1997) says sponsorship seems to be a Cinderella subject in academic literature but it is certainly not a Cinderella in the allocation of corporate and marketing PR budgets, with vast sums being spent by organisations on sports sponsorship and a lesser extent on arts sponsorship. He cites work of Goldberg (1983), which highlights the main objectives for sponsoring companies. These included enhancing community relations, promoting corporate image, promote **brand** awareness, gain media exposure, entertain **clients** and increase sales.

There is no doubt that sponsorship has significantly grown as a marketing tool and is also used to create opportunities for name exposure, image association, generating goodwill and building relationships with clients and potential clients.

Sponsorship may be an arrangement to exchange **advertising** for the responsibility of funding a popular event or entity. For example, a corporate entity may provide equipment for a famous athlete or sports team in exchange for brand recognition. The sponsor earns popularity this way while the sponsored can save a lot of money. This type of sponsorship is prominent in sport, the arts, media and the charity sector. It is also becoming increasingly important in education. Many companies want their logo on sponsored equipment in return.

Although a company's motives may be altruistic, sponsorship is more commonly used to derive benefit from the association created for a company's brand or image as a result of the sponsorship. Sponsorship is used heavily in sport, music, art and television and forms a core element of a **marketing** strategy. This can be seen with global events such as the Olympics Games, football and rugby world cups and World Athletic Championships where the brand seeks to link its product to an audience in a positive way. In music, one of the Rolling Stones' world tours was sponsored by Volkswagen cars.

FURTHER READING

Allen, J., Bowdin, G.A.J., O'Toole, W., Harris, R. and McDonnel, I. (2006) *Events Management*. Oxford: Elsevier.

Kitchen, P.J. (1997) *Public Relations, Principles and Practice*. London: International Thomson Business Press.

Goldberg, H. (1983) *Sponsorship and the Performing Arts*: London: Goldberg.

Stakeholder Analysis

Stakeholder analysis underpins the concept of a **communications strategy** and forms an integral part of **horizon scanning**. It is a vital element in the PR practitioner's toolkit looking at the impact of an organisation's behaviour on its surroundings. In so doing it can help interpret for the organisation any feedback received. For example, an extractive industry such as an oil company seeking to expand would need to know the views of the local people: how disruptive could the new pipeline be and would its building lead to costly demonstrations? What are the concerns of government over health and safety and the environment? And what about your own employees, your best and worst ambassadors, are they fully informed about the project?

The idea of stakeholders developed from the narrower definition of shareholders, the ultimate owners of the company. Now a broader church is involved including the media, **NGOs** and academe. Stakeholder analysis leads to a mapping of their concerns and the influence they might wield, for better or worse.

This technique allows the organisation to weight the importance of a particular stakeholder group and then predict their likely impact, measured against their actual power and level of real concern. Stakeholders wielding a lot of power and being very interested in an organisation means they have to be taken very seriously. At the other end of the spectrum stakeholders with much interest but little power pose less of an issue. Knowing where the groups sit within the spectrum and then being able to act accordingly is what mapping and analysis is all about.

FURTHER READING

Gregory, A. (1997) *Planning and Managing a Public Relations Campaign: a Step by Step Guide*. London: Kogan Page.

Harrison, S. (1995) *Public Relations: An Introduction*. London: Routledge.

MH

Strategy

A term that comes from the Greek word *strategos* and means a general. Strategy is a military term used to develop ways of overcoming enemies on the battlefield. In business, the term strategy has been used to describe the way an organisation adapts itself to its external environment. Prominent writers include Henry Mintzberg, Brian Quinn and Michael Porter.

There are two levels of strategy within an organisation: corporate level and competitive level. Corporate level strategy is set by the board of directors of the organisation and this strategy outlines the markets in which the organisation is to compete. At the competitive level, strategy is where senior managers decide how they will compete in their chosen markets.

Danny Moss maintains that **public relations** in its strategic role within an organisation acts in a **boundary spanning** capacity where the practitioner assists at a corporate strategy level by highlighting stakeholder issues to senior managers in order for the organisation to adapt to any changes in its external environment. At the competitive level the PR practitioner assists by building programmes of communication with **key stakeholders** in order to develop strong two-way relationships and mutual understanding. In this sense you could argue that the PR practitioner is at the heart of the battle for the reputation of an organisation.

FURTHER READING

Mintzberg, H. and Quinn J.B. (1991) *The Strategy Process, Concepts, Contexts, Cases*, 2nd edn. Upper Saddle River, NJ: Prentice-Hall.
Tench, R. and Yeomans, L. (2006) *Exploring Public Relations*. Upper Saddle River, NJ: Prentice Hall.

EP

Syndicated Radio Tapes

Syndicated radio tapes (SRTs) are the sound version of the **video news release**. They come in two main forms; a taped interview with a company chairman, a celebrity or other newsmaker, which is distributed free to radio stations for transmission; or a syndicated live interview where the subject goes to a central studio and is interviewed in turn 'down the line' by a series of radio stations around the UK. SRTs are a highly cost effective way of getting **key messages** circulated to end users who frequently lack the resources to produce such interviews themselves. The technique is particularly valuable when a national story has regional implications; this way the interview can be tailored to fit a number of locations and outlets. Increasingly PR agencies are making SRTs available as part of a webstream so stations can pick up as required.

SRTs are also known as 'fillers' or 'COIs', terms used to describe the pre-recorded tapes produced by the Central Office of Information (COI) as part of its various publicity, information and news management campaigns. Distributed free to local radio and regional television journalists, they constitute publicly funded **information subsidies**. In the UK, the COI use of fillers has grown considerably, although they were used extensively during the Conservative government's campaign to promote the poll tax which targeted local news media (Golding, 1989: 6). Take-up rates tend to reflect the station's journalistic resources and the COI acknowledges that 'commercial stations [i.e. less well staffed news outlets] are more adventurous and less likely to dismiss our output as establishment material' (Gardner, 1986: 12). But one independent station conceded that up to 70 per cent of the tapes it received were broadcast (Cobb, 1989: 12).

With local radio stations obliged to operate in increasingly competitive markets, these 'fillers' have enjoyed expansive air time (Franklin, 1997: 129–30). In 1985, the COI distributed more than 400 tapes to local radio stations (Gardner, 1986) but by 2006 the COI annual report claimed, 'over the past year they [fillers] have been transmitted 708,000 times. That's 11,800 hours of donated airtime – the same as 151 years of episodes of *EastEnders*' (COI, 2006: 13).

FURTHER READING

Central Office of Information (2006) *Annual Reports and Accounts 1946–2006*, HC1471. London: HMSO.

Cobb, R. (1989) 'PR has radio taped', *PR Week*, 20 April: 12–13.

Gardner, C. (1986) 'How They Buy the Bulletins', *Guardian*, 17 September.

Golding, P. (1989) 'Limits to leviathan: the local press and the poll tax', paper presented to the Political Studies Association Annual Conference, University of Warwick, 6 April.

BF & MH

A talking head is a media commentator whom the media (especially broadcast) recognise as being able to speak intelligently on a specific subject or range of subjects. Organisations provide talking heads mostly to advocate their own **key messages**, but also to position their brand as being associated with particular expertise and sometimes simply to raise their profile.

Much the most ubiquitous talking head in the UK today – and for more than a decade – is Justin Urquhart Stewart, of Seven Investment Management and formerly of Barclays Capital. Urquhart Stewart comments fluently and informatively on almost any financial story, and can frequently be seen in the media commenting on a wide range of different and highly complex stories in a single day. He is used by almost all broadcasters because they all know that he is reliably able to pitch his commentary to the right level for their audience and that he remains calm and fluent at all times. He is not a broker, financial analyst or investment advisor, and appears to have no job other than commenting in the media. His move from Barclays to Seven did not interrupt his media career at all, and has very effectively raised Seven's profile, since Urquhart Stewart is constantly appearing on business and financial news programmes.

The advantage for broadcasters in using talking heads is not merely to explain complex issues that journalists may not know about. The interrogation procedure for presenting information is inherently superior to simply presenting information, which often appears patronising to the viewer or listener. By having the **journalist** ask the basic-level questions the expert can present the information clearly, without making the viewer feel stupid, since it is the journalist who is playing dumb for the purposes of the interview.

QL

Target Audience

In practical terms this refers to the key audience or audiences an organisation is trying to communicate with as part of the PR **campaign**. Understanding who are the target audiences and how they behave allows the sender of the message to shape **communications** in order to make it relevant. In doing so, there is an increased likelihood that the audience will respond in a positive way to organisational messages.

Target audiences are defined in the situation analysis part of the programme research and planning phase and practitioners develop bespoke stakeholder universe charts to map out who needs to be communicated with as part of a PR campaign.

Generic audience profiles have been developed by the National Readership Survey, which is a non-profit organisation supported by the UK Institute of Practitioners in Advertising. Audiences are put into social grades depending on their occupation and social status. There are six grades, A to E. A comprises the upper middle classes and they are defined as professional and in senior managerial positions. B comprises the middle class and they are defined as professional but mid-managers. C1 comprises the lower middle class comprising junior managers. C2 describes the skilled working class. These are semi- and unskilled workers. E is the group with the lowest level of subsistence such as state pensioners and the lowest grade of unskilled workers.

In defining the target audience in terms of social status, the PR practitioner then sets about understanding how those audiences consume media and messages. In the planning phase of the programme, practitioners will match media, be it, print, broadcast or new media, with the selected target audience in a bid to shape audience perceptions. For example in the UK, if a company wanted to launch a new product aimed at the C2 audience, then the PR practitioner would sell in media coverage to the *Sun* newspaper, the UK's largest circulation daily tabloid newspaper as it is mainly targets the C2 audience. If a PR practitioner wanted to target the upper middle class or social class A then they would try to gain coverage in the broadsheet (both current and recently resized) titles such as the *Daily Telegraph*, *The Times*, *Independent* or *Guardian* as these are news products aimed at the A, B and C1 social groups.

Alasuutari, P. (ed.) (1999) *Rethinking The Media Audience, the New Agenda*. London: Sage.

Brooker, W. and Jermyn, D. (ed.) (2002) *The Audience Studies Reader*. London: Routledge.

Gunter, B. (2000) *Media Research Methods*. London: Sage.

Tench, R. and Yeomans, L. (2006) *Exploring Public Relations*. Upper Saddle River, NJ: Prentice Hall.

EP

Think Tanks

Think tanks are critical players in public affairs. They are normally educational charities, which means they have to remain outside party politics. Notable exceptions to this are the Fabian Society, which is affiliated to the Labour Party, and the Bow Group, which is affiliated to the Conservative Party.

Think tanks are research institutes, which aim to influence public policy by developing and advocating policy ideas. Despite being non-(party) political, and usually without taking a corporate view, each think tank is usually associated with a particular ideological bent, and often therefore with a particular position on the political spectrum. This does mean their fortunes are likely to wax and wane along with the electoral success of the political parties which share their outlook.

In Washington, where there are large numbers of appointed positions available in government, think tanks are where policy wonks go when their party is not in power, and it is to think tanks that incoming presidents look when seeking to staff the senior levels of the federal government.

The influence of think tanks should not be underrated. In praising Anthony Fisher, the poultry farmer who endowed the Institute of Economic Affairs and a series of IEA clones around the world, Oliver Letwin once said: 'Without Fisher, no IEA; without the IEA and its clones, no Thatcher, and possibly no Reagan; without Reagan no star wars; without star wars, no economic collapse of the Soviet Union. Quite a chain of consequences for a chicken farmer!' (*The Times*, 26

key concepts in
public relations

May 1994). Globally, the largest, richest and most influential think tank is the Heritage Foundation in Washington DC.

Think tanks need to raise considerable quantities of money to fund their activities. Public affairs opportunities can be found in companies sponsoring research or other think tank activities as a way of influencing the public policy agenda.

The following table lists some notable think tanks in both the USA and UK.

Table 1. Think tanks

	Right	Left
USA	American Enterprise Institute	Brookings Institute
	Cato	Center for American Progress
	Competitive Enterprise Institute	Center for Budget & Policy Priorities (CBPP)
	Heritage	
	Hoover Institute	Demos
	Hudson Institute	Economic Policy Institute
	Manhattan Institute	New America Foundation
	National Center for Policy Analysis (NCPA)	
	Pacific Research Institute (PRI)	
UK	Adam Smith Institute	Demos
		Fabian Society
	Civitas	Institute for Public Policy Research (IPPR)
	Institute of Economic Affairs (IEA)	
	Social Affairs Unit	

think tanks

229

FURTHER READING

Blundell, J. (2001) *Waging the War of Ideas.* London: Institute of Economic Affairs.

Trade Bodies

Trade bodies are organisations devoted principally to public relations activities. The same can, to a lesser extent, be said of their posher cousins, the professional institutes, though the latter also have a role in providing professional training and qualifications.

Trade bodies represent the views and interests of their members. Some are oriented particularly to public affairs and maintain very sophisticated lobbying or monitoring services. Others participate in public debates, seeking to defuse criticism of member companies or more positively to advocate the use of members' products or services.

Trade bodies are used by companies either to spread the cost of a campaign which benefits all the members or so that individual members can be one step removed from a controversial industry. Where there is a campaign against pollution by a particular industry sector, for example, you will often see the trade body responding rather than an individual company, as the company does not want to be associated in the public mind with pollution. (Often, of course, the spokespeople for the trade bodies will be the same people who speak on behalf of member companies. It is principally a matter of how they are described by the media). Spreading the cost of an expensive public affairs campaign is a key benefit of having an active trade body, especially if many of the member companies are small- or medium-sized enterprises (SMEs).

For larger companies, the benefits of belonging to, or helping to establish, a trade body are more mixed. Where a trade body exists, government departments prefer to consult it, rather than individual companies, on cross-industry matters. However, where a trade body does not exist, they will normally consult with the market leader or leaders. Thus, a market leader is likely to have decidedly mixed feelings about a proposal to establish a trade body. On the positive side, in any controversial debate it can hide behind an anonymous organisation, which it may largely control. On the negative side, it may create a rival for the attention of policy makers, giving a voice to competitive interests.

FURTHER READING

Haywood, R. (1991) All About Public Relations: How to Build Business Success on Good Communications. London: McGraw-Hill.

Trade Association Forum: http://www.taforum.org/

QL

Trade Press

The term trade press refers to specialist business and professional publications, normally published weekly or monthly. Many are subscription only, though some of the more popular titles are available in newsagents. Examples include *Accountancy Age*, *PR Week*, *Utility Week*, *Estates Gazette* and many thousands of others.

Such trade publications have often been effective in breaking stories, through their detailed contacts, which subsequently break into the general media. Often journalists from the trade press are then used as expert commentators in the general media. Despite the continued use of the word 'press' trade publications today frequently break news on their websites. One of the biggest changes in the media and PR over the past decade is the end of the weekly deadline as the online offering of these publications increases in importance. Tighter deadlines put a premium on core PR skills such as writing, news sense and contact building.

There are two principal mistakes which PR practitioners make with regard to the trade press: overestimating and underestimating their importance. The relative ease with which a large organisation can generate coverage in trade publications makes it very tempting to use them for major stories. If clients are judging a practitioner by the number of column centimetres achieved in media coverage, trade publications offer a great many easy hits. The problem is that a great many trade publications do not have the heft of the *Financial Times* or the BBC, and simplistic metrics which fail to take account of this rather obvious fact will distort PR achievements and undermine the wider objectives of the organisation. It would be foolish to forget that most of the people reading your trade publications work for your competitors.

Conversely, given the record of trade publications in breaking stories and the tendency of the general media to use specialist **journalists** as expert commentators, it is unwise to ignore the trade press altogether. Not all the readers are your competitors. A significant proportion will be potential customers and suppliers. Even people who currently work for your competitors are potential future stakeholders. In the war for talent it is a clear competitive advantage to be well-regarded in your sector. And never underestimate the impact on your own staff and the feeling of rivalry many will have with competitor organisations. In many industries and professions competitor firms are concentrated in particular locales and staff use the same pubs, restaurants and wine bars. People love to be able to poke rivals in the eye with the fact that their firm got better coverage in the latest edition of *Legal Week* or *Estates Gazette*.

FURTHER READING

Haywood, R. (1991) All About Public Relations: How to Build Business Success on Good Communications. London: McGraw-Hill.

Kelly, D. (2006) 'Business-to-business public relations', in R. Tench and L. Yeomans (eds), Exploring Public Relations. Harlow: Prentice Hall. pp. 432–6.

QL

Triple Bottom Line

Triple bottom line (TBL) refers to an accounting technique in which the health of a company is not judged solely by its financial record, or bottom line profit and loss, but also by how well it discharged its social and environmental responsibilities. It grew out of the drive for more **corporate social responsibility** and a belief that the behaviour of companies had to be interrogated in a way that went beyond the simple return on capital employed.

A number of accountancy firms now offer the service, which is supported by the major extractive industries such as Royal Dutch Shell. Increasingly, financial institutions are joining in TBL reporting, particularly with regard to ethical investment. For example the Co-operative Bank is known to turn away millions of pounds of new business a year if it fails to meet its ethical targets. Many companies, such as Tesco, are routinely using corporate social responsibility and TBL measurements in their annual reports to stakeholders.

However, the question still being asked by many is how far corporate social responsibility and TBL are short-term responses to outside pressure or have they now become an established part of the reporting landscape and a company's **reputation management?**

FURTHER READING

Klein, N. (2001) *No Logo*. New York: Flamingo.
L'Etang, J. (1996) *Critical Perspectives in Public Relations*. London: Thomson Business Press.
Tench, R. and Yeomans, L. (2006) *Exploring Public Relations*. Harlow: Pearson.

MH

Video News Releases

Video news releases (VNRs) are effectively electronic **press releases**. Made almost exclusively by specialist production companies the VNR can be used at company results time; for a product launch or the chairman's trading statement. The VNR typically comes in two sections: the A roll carrying interviews and voice over commentary; and the B roll containing the pictures backed by sound effects only. In this way the broadcaster can assemble and voice a package using the material provided. Both rolls are supplied free to the broadcaster, sometimes by courier but more and more by web streaming, or 'down the line' electronic delivery direct to the studio.

VNRs show their value when footage is difficult or too costly for a broadcaster to shoot individually. Examples include footage of a factory production line, the interior of a nuclear power station, a delicate medical operation or the launch of a new car. Many terrestrial broadcasters initially refused to carry VNRs because of a perceived threat to editorial independence.

The growth of **rolling news** programming with its enormous appetite for moving pictures, plus the cost of obtaining material of transmission quality, has however led to growing acceptance of the VNR.

A recent study of the impact of VNRs on science journalists' reporting of the Max Planck Society, for example, revealed that over a nine-month period, more than one-third of television reports about the Society were based on these freely distributed 'filler' materials and reports typically lasted longer than coverage not derived from VNRs (Mahill, 2006). In 2003, the Society established its own television studio to produce the 'fillers' and serve as a mediator between the interests of the Society and journalists. Andreas Battenberg, director of the television unit, claims the purpose of the fillers is to present the research work of the Max Planck Society in the public domain in an adequate and high-quality manner. 'If I leave the presentation to chance, there is a great risk of it becoming superficial' (cited in Mahill, 2006: 874). Mahill's study also reported a greater usage of this PR-generated material among private rather than public sector news organisations (Mahill, 2006).

FURTHER READING

Mahill, M., Beiler, M. and Schmutz, J. (2006) 'The influence of video-news-releases on the topics reported in science journalism', *Journalism Studies*, 7 (6): 869–88.

BF & MH

Web 2.0

The phrase Web 2.0 refers to so-called 'second generation' web-based platforms such as social networking sites and **wikis**. It does not refer to a change in the technical specifications of web hosting services, so is not really analogous to the update in a software application which would be designated as 2.0 (or 1.1 for a more minor update). In 2004, O'Reilly Media hosted a conference called 'Web 2.0' and the term has been popular, though controversial, ever since. Pundits such as Battelle have used the term, though it has been criticised by the inventor of the web, Tim Berners-Lee. In general, the term refers to greater opportunities for user interaction and the creation of self-governing communities.

Advocates of Web 2.0 would distinguish between communities such as DailyKos and RedState, which – though they have active community members who police accepted practices – have formal editors, from those such as Wikipedia where the rules of the community as a whole prevail.

In addition to wikis, another feature associated with Web 2.0 is the 'folksonomy'. This is a collaborative social 'tagging' venture such as del.icio.us or digg. These are sites where members can associate web pages with particular search terms. The number of times a page is 'tagged' with a particular label affects how often it will turn up on a search for that tag at that site.

As a system of taxonomy, folksonomy is open to all the criticisms associated with wikis, and others as well. Some of the tags are homonyms or synonyms – that is, the same tag can be used with different meanings while multiple tags with the same meaning are also in use. Folksonomies can be seen as an alternative to search engines and their advocates argue they are superior and may eclipse search engines in the future.

FURTHER READING

Wikipedia: http://en.wikipedia.org/wiki/Folksonomy

QL

Western Model (Dominance of)

The development of **public relations** as a profession can be traced to the USA, and perhaps to a lesser extent, the UK and Europe, from the early 20th century. Consequently, many of the models of theory and practice are heavily influenced by Western philosophy, culture and business practices. The modern business and **communications** environment has, however, become increasingly multicultural, multinational and transnational, reflecting the importance of **globalisation** and the revolution in **mass communications**.

As a result, PR practitioners and academics are increasingly interested in the impact of different cultures, philosophies, markets and media systems on established PR techniques. Pioneering work on cultures (e.g. Hofstede, 1980) is now being complemented by authors such as Chen, Culbertson, Sriramesh and Vercic as individual differences in communications environments become recognised as increasingly salient in a global profession.

FURTHER READING

Culbertson, H.M. and Chen, N. (1996) *International Public Relations: A Comparative Analysis*. Hillsdale, NJ: Lawrence Erlbaum.
Ewen, S. (1996) *PR! A Social History of Spin*. New York: Basic Books.
Sriramesh, K., Ananto, E.G., Chen, N. and Flora, C. (2004) *Public Relations in Asia: An Anthology*. Singapore: Thomson Learning.

Van Ruler, B. and Vercic, D. (2004) *Public Relations Communications and Management in Europe: A Nation-by-Nation Introduction to Public Relations Theory and Practice.* Berlin: Walter de Gruyter.

Vercic, D. and Sriramesh, K. (2003) *The Global Public Relations Handbook: Theory, Research and Practice.* Mahwah, NJ: Lawrence Erlbaum.

NM

Wikis

According to *Webster's New Millennium Dictionary of English* a wiki is 'a collaborative Web site set up to allow user editing and adding of content'. Much the most famous is Wikipedia founded by Jimmy Wales and supported by donations.

Wikipedia is deeply controversial in academic circles, many academics insisting that it cannot be a valid reference because anyone can post to it. Just because, the argument goes, a view is popular, it is not, of necessity, correct. It is easy to respond that just because a view is presented by an expert, it is not, of necessity, correct. A reasonable academic basis on which to assess Wikipedia is not whether the theory is flawed, but whether the practice is. Is the information on Wikipedia less accurate than another comparable source? The respected scientific journal *Nature* set out to answer this question. Its answer, of course, is controversial.

Nature compared Wikipedia with Britannica.com. This was the first area of controversy. A search on Britannica.com produces articles not only from the encyclopaedia but also from the Britannica Book of the Year, which Britannica claims is edited to different standards and in which its authors make more contentious statements than would be expected in the encyclopaedia. *Nature* then sent these articles to a selected group of experts for peer review. The experts found more errors in the Wikipedia articles than in those from Britannica, though *Nature* concluded that the difference was small. Britannica disputed this interpretation, and also challenged *Nature's* categorisation of some errors. In Britannica's view its experts are (at least) as good as *Nature's* and if there is a difference of opinion between them it is not necessarily the case that Britannica is in the wrong. *Nature* concedes this point, but argues that there is no reason to suppose it will affect the relative difference between Wikipedia and Britannica.

The argument is still very much alive. Where Wikipedia, of necessity, is at an advantage over offline sources is in its speed. Articles can be updated to take account of breaking news in minutes. Nonetheless, problems with the wiki format continue.

Wikipedia has been victim of vandalism, though an IBM survey suggested that most acts of gross vandalism – deleting of pages for example – are corrected within five minutes. Other, more subtle, vandalism is harder to spot. For some time the biography of John Seigenthaler claimed, quite falsely, that he was at one time suspected of involvement in the assassinations of President Kennedy and his brother Robert and also that for some years Siegenthaler lived in the Soviet Union.

Wikipedia has tightened up its procedures since then and users now register, which makes deliberate acts of vandalism easier to trace. One wiki-sceptic, in an effort to prove the site's lack of merit, posted 13 misleading or fictitious amendments to Wikipedia articles, expecting them to stay in place for months. In fact, all were deleted within three hours and he had received messages asking him to desist from his vandalism.

Some articles, such as that on President George W. Bush, may not be edited by unregistered or newly registered users, because they have been the subject of persistent vandalism. There are other, more subtle forms of abuse. Congressional staffers have been caught editing the biographies of their bosses in accurate, but flattering, ways.

Founder Wales describes Wikipedia as 'a work in progress' and looks forward to a time when some of the more widely debated articles can become settled, and only edited through a more restrictive procedure. A good rule of thumb might be to cite Wikipedia as one would a statement of opinion, thus 'According to Wikipedia, "Bush belongs to one of the most politically influential American families"' and not 'Bush "belongs to one of the most politically influential American families" (Wikipedia)'. Another would be to use it only for very general knowledge which, if suitably rephrased, would not need citing. One would not say that 'according to Wikipedia Bush is the 43rd President of the United States', and indeed, the quote about Bush used above is of a similar character.

FURTHER READING

Nature: http://www.nature.com/nature/britannica/index.html (including links to Britannica's criticism of *Nature*)
Surowiecki, J. (2005) *The Wisdom of Crowds*. London, Abacus.
Telegraph Media Group: http://www.telegraph.co.uk/arts/main.jhtml;jsessionid=U4FFM 4TR3WZFBQFIQMFCFFWAVCBQYIV0?xml=/arts/2006/10/28/ftwiki28.xml

wikis

references

Abimbola, T. (2006) 'Market access for developing economies: branding in Africa', *Place Branding*, 2 (2): 108–17.

Adam, S.G. (1993) *Notes Towards a Definition of Journalism*. St Petersburg, FL: Poynter Institute.

Ainley, B. (1994) *Blacks and Asians in the British Media: An Investigation of Discrimination*. London: London School of Economics.

Akehurst, G. and Alexander, N. (1996) *Retail Marketing*. London: Routledge.

Alasuutari, P. (ed.) (1999) *Rethinking The Media Audience, the New Agenda*. London: Sage.

Allen, J., Bowdin, G.A.J., O'Toole, W., Harris, R. and McDonnel, I. (2006) *Events Management*. Oxford: Elsevier.

Andrews, L. (2005) 'Spin: from tactic to tabloid', *Journal of Public Affairs*, 5: 1–16.

Anholt, S. (2005) *Brand New Justice: The Upside of Global Branding*. Burlington, MA: Elsevier Butterworth-Heinemann.

Anholt, S. (2006) 'The Anholt-GMI City Brands Index. How the world sees the world's cities', *Place Branding*, 2 (1): 18–31.

Aronson, E. (1972) *The Social Animal*. New York: Viking.

Article 19 (1989) *No Comment: Censorship, Secrecy and the Irish Troubles*. London: The Internatioal Centre on Censorship.

Atton, C. (2002) *Alternative Media*. London: Sage.

Atton, C. (2004) *Alternative Internet*. London: Sage

Atton, C. (2006) 'Football fanzines and local news', B. Franklin (ed.) *Local Journalism and Local Media: Making the Local News*. London: Routledge pp. 280–289.

Atton, C. and Wickenden, E. (2005) 'Sourcing routines and representation in alternative journalism: a case study approach', *Journalism Studies*, 6 (3): 347–60.

Austin, E.W. and Pinkleton, B.E. (2001) *Strategic Public Relations Management: Planning and Effective Communication Programs*. Mahwah, NJ: Lawrence Erlbaum.

Bainbridge, J. and Curtis, J. (1998) 'The UK's biggest brands, part 1', *Marketing*, 30 July: 22–5.

Baines, P., Egan, J., Jefkins, F. and Jefkins, F.W. (2003) *Public Relations: Contemporary Issues and Techniques*. London: Butterworth-Heinmann.

Baistow, T. (1985) *Fourth Rate Estate: An Anatomy of Fleet Street*. London: Macmillan.

Baker, S. (2005) 'The alternative press in Northern Ireland and the political process', *Journalism Studies*, 6 (3): 375–86.

Barbour, R.S. and Kitzinger, J. (2001) *Developing Focus Group Research: Politics, Theory and Practice*. London: Sage.

Barker, M. and Petley, J. (1997) *Ill Effects: The Media/Violence Debate*. London: Routledge

Barnett, S. (2005) 'Opportunity or threat?' The BBC, Investigative Journalism and the Hutton Report', S. Allan (ed.), *Journalism: Critical Essays*. Milton Keynes: Open University Press pp. 328–341.

Barnett, S. and Gaber, I. (2001) *Westminster Tales: The Twenty First Century Crisis in Political Journalism*. London: Continuum.

Barnett, S. and Seymour, E. (1999) *A Shrinking Iceberg Slowly Travelling South: Changing trends in British television – A Case Study of Drama and Current Affairs.* London: Campaign for Quality Television.

Baskin, O. and Aronoff, C. (1992) *Public Relations: The Profession and The Practice.* New York: C Brown Ltd.

Battelle, J. (2006) *The Search: How Google and Its Rivals Rewrote the Rules of Business and Transformed Our Culture.* Boston, MA: Nicholas Brealey Publishing.

Beard, M. (2001) *Running a Public Relations Department,* 2nd edn. London: Kogan Page.

Belbin, R. (1997) *Team Roles at Work.* Oxford: Butterworth-Heinmann.

Benson, R. Rainbird, D., Midgley, N., Braddock, K. and Stasler, B. (2005) *Creativeworld: The Fish Can Sing's Guide is the New Creative Economy.* London: The Fish Can Sing Ltd.

Bernays, E.L. (1923) *Crystallizing Public Opinion.* New York: Liveright.

Bevins, T.H. (1993) 'Public relations, professionalism, and the public interest', *Journal of Business Ethics,* 12: 117–26.

Blair, T. (2007) Speech to the Reuters Oxford International Institute of Journalism. Available at: http://news.bbc.co.uk/1/hi/uk_politics/6744581.stm

Bland, M., Theaker A. and Wragg D. (2007) *Effective Media Relations – How to Get Results,* 3rd ed. London: Kogan Page.

Blick, A. (2004) *People Who Live in the Dark: The History of the Special Adviser in British Politics.* London: Politicos.

Blumler, J.G. and Gurevitch, M. (1981) 'Politicians and the press: an essay on role relationships', in D. Nimmo and K. Saunders (eds), *Handbook of Political Communication.* London: Sage. pp. 467–97.

Blumler, J.G. and Katz, E. (1974) *Current Perspectives on Gratifications Research.* Beverley Hills, CA: Sage.

Blundell, J. (2001) *Waging the War of Ideas.* London: Institute of Economic Affairs.

Borden, N. H. (1964) 'The concept of the marketing mix,' *Journal of Advertising Research,* 4: 2–7

Boyce, G. Curran, J. and Wingate, P. (eds) (1978) *Newspaper History from the 17th Century to the Present Day.* London: Constable.

Boyd Barrett, O. (1980) *The International News Agencies.* London: Sage.

Brandenberg, H. (2007) "Security at the source' embedding journalists as a superior strategy to military censorship', *Journalism Studies,* 8 (6): 948–63.

Brassington, F. and Pettitt, S. (2000) *Principles of Marketing.* Harlow: Pearson.

Breitbat, A. and Ebner, M. (2005) *Hollywood Interrupted: Insanity Chi in Babylon. The Case Against Celebrity.* New York: John Willey & Sons.

Broadcasting Research Unit (BRU) (1985) *The Public Service Idea in British Broadcasting: Main Principles.* Luton: John Libbey.

Brock, T. and Green, M.C. (2005) *Persuasion: Psychological Insights and Perspectives.* Thousand Oaks, CA: Sage.

Brooker, W. and Jermyn, D. (ed.) (2002) *The Audience Studies Reader.* London: Routledge.

Broom, G.M. and Dozier, D.M. (1990) *Using Research in Public Relations: Applications to Program Management.* Eaglewood Cliffs, NJ: Prentice Hall.

Brown, M. (2003) 'Now – can Channel 5 maintain momentum', *Guardian,* 14 July: 6–7.

Ball, K., Bostrom, A. and Evans, G. (1997) *Risk Communication and Vaccination.* Washington, DC: National Academy Press.

Buderi, R. and Huang, G.T. (2006) *Guanxi (The Art of Relationships): Microsoft, China, and Bill Gates's Plan to Win the Road Ahead.* New York: Simon and Shuster.

Budge, I., Crewe, I. and McKay, D. (2007) *The New British Politics.* Harlow: Pearson Longman.

Burton, C. and Drake A (2004) *Hitting the Headlines in Europe – a Country by Country Guide to Effective Media Relations.* London: Kogan Page.

Calcutt, D. (1990) *Report of the Committee on Privacy and Related Matters.* Cmnd 1102. London: HMSO.

Cameron, G., Ju-Pak, K. and Kim, B.H. (1996) 'Advertorials in magazines', *Journalism and Mass Communication,* 73: 722–33.

Campbell, A. (2007) *The Blair Years.* London: Hutchinson.

Carey, A. (ed.) (1995) *Taking The Risk Out Of Democracy: Corporate Propaganda Versus Freedom and Liberty.* Sydney: University of South Wales Press.

Carpenter, P. (2000) *eBrands: Building an Internet Business at Breakneck Speed.* Boston, MA: Harvard Business School Press.

Central Office of Information (2001) *Annual Reports and Accounts 2000-1,* HC53. London: HMSO

Central Office of Information (2006) *Annual Reports and Accounts 1946-2006,* HC1471. London: HMSO

Chalip, L. and Costa, C.A. (2005) 'Sport event tourism and the destination brand: towards a general theory', *Sport in Society,* 88 (2): 218–37.

Chen, X. and Chen, C.C. (2004) 'On the intricacies of the Chinese *guanxi*: a process model of *guanxi* development', *Asia Pacific Journal of Management* 21: 305–24.

Clarke, N. (2003) *Shadow of a Nation.* London: Weidenfeld and Nicholson.

Clutterbuck, D. (1992) *Actions Speak Louder: A Management Guide to CSR.* London: Kogan Page

Cobb, R. (1989) 'PR has radio taped', *PR Week,* 20 April: 12–13.

Cockerell, M. Hennessey, P. and Walker, D. (1984) *Sources Close to the Prime Minister: Inside the Hidden World of the News Manipulators.* London: Macmillan.

Cole, P. (2006) 'Educating and training local journalists', in B. Franklin (ed.), *Local Journalism and Local Media: Making the Local News.* London: Routledge. pp. 95–104.

Cooper, D. (2002) 'Searching for the creative edge in public relations', unpublished MA dissertation, School of Journalism, Media and Cultural Studies, Cardiff University.

Costera Meijer, I. (2001) 'The public quality of popular journalism: developing a normative framework', *Journalism Studies,* 2 (2): 189–206.

Cross, R.L., Cross, R. and Parker, A. (2004) *The Hidden Power of Social Networks: Understanding How Work Really Gets Done in Organisations.* Boston, MA: Harvard Business School Press.

Culbertson, H.M. and Chen, N. (1996) *International Public Relations: A Comparative Analysis.* Hillsdale, NJ: Lawrence Erlbaum.

Curran, J. and Seaton, J. (1997) *Power Without Responsibility.* London: Routledge.

Cutlip, S.M. (1994) *The Unseen Power: Public Relations, A History* Hillsdale, NJ: Lawrence Erlbawm

Cutlip, S.M. (2000) *Effective Public Relations*, 8th edn. Upper Saddle River, NJ: Prentice Hall.

Cutlip, S.M., Allen, H. and Broom, G. (2000) *Effective Public Relations*, 8th edn. London: Prentice Hall International.

Davies, M.M. and Mosdell, N. (2006) *Practical Research Methods for Media and Cultural Studies: Making People Count*. Edinburgh: Edinburgh University Press.

Davis, A. (2002) *Public Relations Democracy: Public Relations, Politics and the Mass Media in Britain Today*. London: Sage.

Davis, A. (2003) *Everything You Should Know About Public Relations*. London: Kogan Page.

Davis, A. (2007) *Mastering Public Relations*. New York: Palgrave Macmillan.

Davis, A. (2008) 'Public relations in the news', in B. Franklin (ed.) *Pulling Newspapers Apart: Analysing Print Journalism*. London: Routledge. pp. 272–81.

Deacon, D. (1996) 'The voluntary sector in a changing communication environment', *European Journal of Communication*, 11 (2): 173–99.

Deacon, D. and Golding, P. (1994) *Taxation and Representation: The Media, Political Communication and the Poll Tax*. London: John Libbey.

Deacon, D., Pickering, M., Golding, P. and Murdock, G. (1999) *Researching Communications: A Practical Guide to Methods in Media and Cultural Analysis*. London: Arnold.

Delano, A. (2000) 'No sign of a better job: 100 years of British journalism', *Journalism Studies*, 1 (2): 261–73.

Delano, A. and Henningham, J. (1995) *The News Breed: British Journalists in the 1990s*. London: The London Institute.

Delli Carpini, M. and Williams, B. (2001) 'Let us infotain you: politics in the new media environment', in W. Lance Bennet and R. Entman (eds), *Mediated Politics: Communication in the Future of Democracy*. Cambridge: Cambridge University Press. pp.160–81.

Denscombe, M. (2003) *The Good Research Guide*. Maidenhead: Open University Press.

Department of Trade and Industry and Institute of Public Relations (2003) *Unlocking the Potential of Public Relations: Developing Good Practice*. London: European Centre for Business Excellence.

Dilenschneider, R. (1990) *Power and Influence*. New York: Prentice Hall Press.

Donoghue, G.A. Tichenor, P.J. and Olien, C.N. (1995) 'A guard dog perspective on the role of the media', *Journal of Communication*, 45 (2): 115–32.

Downing, J. (2001) *Radical Media; Rebellious Communication and Social Movements*. Thousand Oaks, CA: Sage.

Dozier, D.M., Grunig, L.A. and Grunig, M.E. (1995) *Manager's Guide to Excellence in Public Relations*. Mahwah, NJ: Lawrence Erlbaum.

DTI and DCMS (2000) *A New Future for Communications*. London: HMSO.

Edwards, L. (2006) 'Public relations origins: definitions and history' in R. Tench and L. Yeomans (eds), *Exploring Public Relations*. Harlow: Prentice Hall. pp. 2–17.

Elkington, J. (1994) 'Towards the sustainable corporation: win-win-win business strategies for sustainable development', *Californian Management Review*, 36 (2).

241

Emmott, B., Crook, C. and Michlethwait, J. (2002) Globalisation: Making Sense of an Integrating World: Reasons, Effects and Challenges. London: Economist.

Engel, M. (1996) *Tickle the Public*. London: Victor Gollancz.

Entman, R. (1990) 'News As Propaganda', *Journal of Communication*, 40: 124–7.

Ericson, R.V., Baranek, P. and Chan,J. (1989) *Negotiating Control: A Study of News Sources*. Milton Keynes: Open University Press.

Evans, H. (1994) *Good Times, Bad Times*. London: Coronet Books.

Evans, H. (1996) 'Speech to the Guild of Editors', reprinted in *Press Gazette*, 1 November: 10.

Evans, H. (2002) 'Attacking the devil', *British Journalism Review*, 13 (4): 6–15.

Ewen, S. (1996) *PR! A Social History of Spin*. New York: Basic Books.

Fairchild, M. (1999) *The Public Relations Research and Evaluation Toolkit: How to Measure the Effectiveness of PR*. London: Institute of Public Relations and Public Relations Consultants Association with PR Week.

Fall, L.T. (2004) 'The increasing role of public relations as a crisis management function: an empirical examination of communication restrategising efforts among destination organisation managers in the wake of 11th September, 2001', *Journal of Vacation Marketing*, 10 (3): 238–53.

Fallows, J. (1996) *Breaking The News: How the Media Undermine American Democracy*. New York: Pantheon Books.

Fawcett, L. (2001) *Political Communications and Development in Northern Ireland*, End of Award Report, ESRC Award no L327253040.

Fawkes, J. (2001) 'What is public relations', A. Theaker (ed.), *The Public Relations Handbook*. London: Routledge pp. 3–12

Fawkes, J. (2006) 'Public relations, propaganda and the psychology of persuasion', in R. Tench and L. Yeomans (eds), *Exploring Public Relations*. Harlow: Prentice Hall. pp. 266–87.

Fedorcio, D., Heaton, P. and Madden, K. (1991) *Public Relations in Local Government*. Harlow: Longman

Feintuck, M. and Varney, M. (2006) *Media Regulation, Public Interest and the Law*. Edinburgh: Edinburgh University Press.

Festinger, L. (1957) *A Theory of Cognitive Dissonance*. Stanford, CA: Stanford University Press.

Fletcher, K. (2006) 'A fine line between journalism and PR', *MediaGuardian*, 31 July: 7.

Fombrun, C.J. and Van Riel, C.B.M. (2004) *Fame and Fortune: How Successful Companies Build Winning Reputations*. Upper Saddle River, NJ: Pearson Education.

Foot, P. (1999) 'The slow death of investigative journalism', in S. Glover (ed.), *Secrets of the Press: Journalists on Journalism*. London: Allen Lane. pp. 79–90.

Franklin, B. (1986) 'Public relations, the local press and the coverage of local government', *Local Government Studies*, July/August: 25–33.

Franklin, B. (1987a) 'The metropolitan counties campaign against abolition', *Local Government Studies*, 13 (4): 11–24.

Franklin, B. (1987b) 'Local government public relations: the changing institutional and environment 1974–1987', *Public Relations*, Winter: 25–30.

Franklin, B. (1988) Public Relations Activity in Local Government. London: Charles Knight.

Franklin, B. (1994) *Packaging Politics: Political Communication in Britain's Media Democracy*. London: Arnold.

Franklin, B. (1997) *Newszak and News Media*. London: Arnold.

Franklin, B. (1998) *Tough on Soundbites, Tough on the Causes of Soundbites: New Labour and News Management*. London: The Catalyst Trust.

Franklin, B. (2001) *British Television Policy: A Reader*. London: Routledge.

Franklin, B. (2004) *Packaging Politics; Political Communication in Britain's Media Democracy*. London: Arnold.

Franklin, B. (2005) 'McJournalism? The McDonaldization thesis, local newspapers and local journalism in the UK', in S. Allan. (ed.), *Journalism Studies: Critical Essays*. Milton Keynes: Open University Press. pp. 110–21.

Franklin, B. (2006a) 'Attacking the devil: local journalists and local newspapers in the UK', in *Local Journalism and Local Media: Making the Local News*. London: Routledge. pp. 3–16.

Franklin, B. (2006b) *Local Journalism and Local Media: Making the Local News*. London: Routledge.

Franklin, B. (2008) *Pulling Newspapers Apart; Analysing Print Journalism*. London: Routledge.

Franklin, B. and Murphy, D. (1991) *What News? The Market, Politics and the Local Press*. London: Routledge.

Franklin, B. and Murphy, D. (1998) 'Changing times: local newspapers, technology and markets', in B. Franklin and D. Murphy (eds), *Making the Local News: Local Journalism in Context*. London: Routledge. pp. 7–23.

Franklin, B. and Pilling, R. (1998) 'Taming the tabloids: markets, moguls and media regulation', in M. Kieran (ed.), *Media Ethics*. London: Routledge. pp. 111–23.

Franklin, B. and Van Slyke Turk, J. (1988) 'Information subsidies: agenda setting traditions', Public Relations Review, Spring: 29–41.

Franklin, B., Court, G. and Cushion, S. (2006) 'Downgrading the 'local' in local reporting of the 2005 UK General Election', in B. Franklin (ed.), *Local Journalism, Local Media Making the Local News*. London: Routledge. pp. 256–70.

Franklin, B., Lewis, J. and Williams, A. (2006) *Interim Report of Findings on the Independence of the British Press*. Cardiff: Cardiff University.

Fritz, B. (2004) *All The President's Spin*. New York: Touchstone.

Frost, C. (2004) 'The Press Complaints Commission: a study of ten years of adjudications on press', *Journalism Studies*, 5 (1): 101–14.

Gaber, I. (2001) 'Government by spin: an analysis of the process', *Media, Culture and Society*, 22 (4): 507–18.

Galtung, J. and Ruge, M. (1965) 'The structure of foreign news: the presentation of the Congo, Cuba and Cyprus crises in four Norwegian newspapers', *Journal of International Peace Research*, 1: 64–91.

Gandy, O. (1982) *Beyond Agenda Setting: Information Subsidies and Public Policy*. New York: Ablex.

Gans, H. (1980) *Deciding What's News*. London: Constable.

Gardner, C. (1986) 'How They Buy the Bulletins', *Guardian*, 17 September.

Garner, B. (2006) 'Hungry media need fast food; the role of the Central Office of Information', B. Franklin (ed.) *Local Journalism and Local Media; Making the Local News*. London: Routledge. 189–99.

Gerbner, G. and Gross, L. (1976) 'Living with television: the violence profile', *Journal of Communication*, 26 (2): 172–94.

Gerbner, G., Gross, L., Signorielli, N., Morgan, M. and Jackson-Beeck, M. (1979) 'The demonstration of power: violence profile no. 10', *Journal of Communication*, 29 (3): 177–96.

Gerbner, G., Holsti, O., Krippendorf, K., Paisley, W. and Stone, P. (1969) *The Analysis of Communication Content*. New York: John Wiley.

Gibson, O. (2006a) 'BBC must take fun seriously as licence fee secured', *Guardian*, 15 March.

Gibson, O. (2006b) 'Internet means end for media barons says Murdoch', *Guardian*, 14 March: 5.

Gladwell, M. (2002) *The Tipping Point*. New York: Little, Brown and Company.

Glasgow Media Group (1976) *Bad News*. London: Routledge and Kegan Paul.

Goldberg, H. (1983) *Sponsorship and the Performing Arts*. London: Goldberg.

Golding, P. (1989) 'Limits to leviathan: the local press and the poll tax', paper presented to the Political Studies Association Annual Conference, University of Warwick, 6 April.

Gower, K. (2003) Legal and Ethical Restraints on Public Relations. PLACE: Waveland Press.

Graen, G.B. (ed.) (2003) *Dealing with Diversity*. Champaign-Urbana,IL: IAP.

Graydon, S. (2003) Made You Look – How Advertising Works and Why You Should Know. Toronto: Annick Press.

Green, A. (1999) *Creativity in Public Relations*. PLACE: Kogan Page.

Gregory, A. (2000) *Planning and Managing Public Relations Campaigns*. London: Kogan Page.

Grunig, J.E. (1992) *Excellence in Public Relations and Communication Management* Hillsdale, NJ: Lawrence Erlbaum Associates.

Grunig, J.E. and Hunt, T. (1984) *Managing Public Relations*. New York: Holt Reinhart and Winston.

Grunig, J.E. and Pepper, F.C. (1992) *Excellence in Public Relations and Communication Management*. Mahwah, NJ: Lawrence Erlbaum.

Grunig, L.A., Grunig, J.E. and Dozier, D.M. (2002) *Excellent Public Relations and Effective Organizations: A Study of Communication Management in Three Countries*. Mahwah, NJ: Lawrence Erlbaum.

Gunter, B. (2000) *Media Research Methods. Measuring Audience Reactions and Impact*. London: Sage.

Haas, T. (2005) 'From "public journalism" to the "public's journalism"? Rhetoric and reality in the discourse on Weblogs', *Journalism Studies*, 6 (3): 387–96.

Habermas, J. (1989) *The Structural Transformation of the Public Sphere*. Cambridge: Polity Press

Hadwin, S. (2006) 'Real readers, real news: the work of a local newspaper editor', B. Franklin (ed.), *Local Journalism and Local Media: Making the Local News*. London: Routledge. pp. 140–9.

Hagerty, B. (2002) 'Announcing the greatest editor of all time', *British Journalism Review*, 13 (4): 6.

Hall, S. (1973) 'The determination of news photographs', in S. Cohen and J. Young (eds), *The Manufacture of News: Deviance, Social Problems and the Mass Media*. London: Constable. pp. 226–243.

Hallin, D. (1994) *We Keep America on Top Of the World*. New York: Routledge.

Hamer, M. (2000) 'The Press Association at work: an examination of a news agency's contribution to the media and public sphere', unpublished MA thesis, Liverpool John Moores Unviersity.

Hamer, M. (2006) 'Trading on trust: news agencies, local journalism and local media', in B. Franklin (ed.), *Local Journalism and Local Media: Making the Local News*. London: Routledge. pp. 210–19.

Hanitzsch, T. (2005) 'Journalists in Indonesia: educated but timid watchdogs', *Journalism Studies*, 6 (4): 493–508.

Hansen, C. (2004) 'The Jayson Blair case and newsroom ethics', *Journalism Studies*, 5 (3): 399–409.

Harcup, T. (1994) *A Northern Star: Leeds Other Paper and the Alternative Press 1974–1994*. Upton: The Campaign for Press and Broadcasting Freedom (North).

Harcup, T. (2004) *Journalism: Principles and Practice*. London: Sage.

Harcup, T. (2005) "I'm doing this to change the world': journalism in alternative and mainstream media', *Journalism Studies*, 6 (3): 361–74.

Harcup, T. and O'Neill, D. (2001) 'What is news? Galtung and Ruge revisited', *Journalism Studies*, 2 (2): 261–80.

Hargreaves, I. and Thomas, J. (2002) *New News, Old News*. London: ITC/BSC.

Harlow, R (1976) 'Building a Public Relations definition' *Public Relations Review* 2, 36

Harrison, S. (1995) *Public Relations: An Introduction*. London: Routledge.

Harrison, S. (2006) 'Local government public relations and the press', in B. Franklin (ed.), *Local Journalism and Local Media: Making the Local News*. London: Routledge. pp. 175–88.

Harvard Business Review (2001) *Managing Diversity*. Boston, MA: Harvard Business School Press.

Hattersley, R. (2001) 'The unholy alliance; the relationship between members of parliament and the press', James Cameron Lecture 1996, in H. Stephenson (ed.), *Media Voices: The James Cameron Memorial Lectures*. London: Polity. pp. 227–45.

Hawkins, V. (2002) 'The other side of the CNN Factor: the media and conflict', *Journalism Studies*, 3 (2): 225–41.

Haywood, R. (1991) All About Public Relations: How to Build Business Success on Good Communications. London: McGraw-Hill.

Haywood, R. (1994) *Manage your Reputation*. London: Kogan Page.

Heath, R.L. (2001) *Handbook of Public Relations*. Thousand Oaks, CA: Sage.

Hendy, D. (2000) *Radio in the Global Age*. Cambridge: Polity Press/Blackwell Publishers.

Herman, E. (2000) 'The propaganda model; a retrospective', *Journalism Studies*, 1 (1): 101–12.

Herman, E. and Chomsky, N. (1988) *Manufacturing Consent: The Political Economy of the Mass Media*. New York: Pantheon.

Herscovitz, H. (2004) 'Brazilian journalists' perceptions of media roles, ethics and foreign influences on Brazilian journalism', *Journalism Studies*, 5 (1): 71–86.

Hetherington, A. (1985) *News, Newspapers and Television*. London: Macmillan.

Hiebert, R. (1966) *Courtier To The Crowd* Ames: Iwoa State University Press

Hingstone, M. (1990) 'A decade of growth', in *The Public Relations Yearbook 1990*. London: Financial Times Business Information, pp. 44–7.

references

245

Hitchens, L. (2006) *Broadcasting Pluralism and Diversity: A Comparative Study of Policy and Regulation*. Portland, OR: Hart Publishing.

Hobsbawm, J. (2006) *Where the Truth Lies: Trust and Morality in PR and Journalism*. London: Atlantic Books.

Hofstede, G. (1991) *Cultures and Organizations: Software of the Mind*. New York: McGraw-Hill.

Hofstede, G. (2001) *Culture's Consequences: International Differences in Work-related Values*. Thousand Oaks, CA: Sage.

Hofstede, G. and Hofstede, G.J. (2005) *Cultures and Organizations: Software of the Mind: Intercultural Cooperation and its Importance for Survival*. New York: McGraw-Hill.

Hoggart, S. (2006) 'The hissing snake pit', *Guardian*, 1 September.

Holmes, S. and Redmond, S. (ed.) (2006) *Framing Celebrity*. London: Routledge.

Horgan, J. (2001) 'Government sources said last night … the development of the parliamentary press lobby in modern Ireland', H. Morgan (ed.), *Information, Media and Power Through the Ages*. Dublin: University College Dublin Press. pp. 259–71.

Hoyer, S. (2003) 'Newspapers without journalists', *Journalism Studies*, 4 (4): 451–65.

Huffington, A. (2006) 'Now the little guy is the true pit bull of journalism', *Guardian*, 14 March: 30.

Humphrys, J. (2005) 'First do no harm', in B. Franklin (ed.) *Television Policy: The MacTaggart Lectures*. Edinburgh: Edinburgh University Press. pp. 265–74.

Hussey, M. (1998), 'Seriously, it's Barbie', *Express*, 26 January: 19.

Hutton, J.G. (2001) 'Defining the relationship between public relations and marketing: public relations' most important challenge', in R.L. Heath (ed.), *Handbook of Public Relations*. Thousand Oaks, CA: Sage. pp. 7–15.

Ingham, B. (1990) 'Government and media: co-existence and tension', unpublished lecture delivered at Trinity and All Saints College, University of Leeds.

Jobber, D. (1995) *Principles and Practice of Marketing*. New York: McGraw-Hill.

Johnson, T. and Kay, B. (2004) 'Wag the blog: how reliance on traditional media and the Internet influence credibility perception of weblogs among blog users', *Journalism and Mass Communication Quarterly*, 81: 622–42.

Jolly, A. (2001) *Managing Corporate Reputation*. London: Kogan Page.

Jones, N. (1999) *Sultans of Spin*. London: Orion Books.

Jones, N. (2003) *The Control Freaks*, 2nd edn. London: Politicos.

Jones, N. (2006) *Trading Information: Lies, Leaks and Tip Offs*. London: Politicos

Jones, N. (2008) 'Politics', in B. Franklin (ed.), *Pulling Newspapers Apart: Analysing Print Journalism*. London: Routledge. pp. 172–80.

Jones, N. (1995) *Soundbites and Spin Doctors*. London: Politicos.

Journalist Training Forum (2002) *Journalists at Work: Their Views on Training, Recruitment and Conditions*. London: The Journalists Training Forum.

Kao, J. (1996) *Jamming*. London: HarperCollins.

Katovsky, B. and Carlson, T. (2003) *Embedded: The Media at War in Iraq: An Oral History*. Guilford, CT: The Lyons Press.

Kellner, P. (1983) 'The lobby, official secrets and good government', *Parliamentary Affairs*, 36 (3): 275–82.

Key Note (2006) Public Relations Industry: Market Assessment 2006, Hampton, Middx: Key Note.

Kim, Y. (2003) 'Professionalism and diversification: the evolution of public relations in South Korea', K. Sriramesh and D. Vercic (eds), *Global Public Relations Handbook: Theory, Research and Practice*. Mahwah, NJ: Lawrence Erlbaum.

Kitchen, P. (1997) *Public Relations: Principles and Practice*. London: Thomson Business Press.

Kitchen, P. and Schultz, D. (eds) (2001) *Raising the Corporate Umbrella*. London: Macmillan.

Klaehn, J. (2005) *Filtering the News: Essays on Herman and Chomsky's Propaganda Model*. New York: Black Rose Books.

Klein, N. (2000) *No Logo*. London: Flamingo.

Knightley, P. (2003) 'The natural history of war reporting', *Guardian*, April.

Konecnik, M. (2004) 'Evaluating Slovenia's image as a tourism destination: a self-analysis process towards building a destination brand', *Journal of Brand Management*, 11 (4): 307–16.

Kotler, P. (2003) *Marketing Insights from A to Z: 80 Concepts Every Manager Needs to Know*. New York: John Wiley & Sons.

L'Etang, J. (1996) 'Public relations and rhetoric', in J. L'Etang and M. Pieczka (eds), *Critical Perspectives in Public Relations*. London: Thomson International Business Press. pp. 106–23.

L'Etang, J. (2004) *Public Relations in Britain: A History of Professional Practice in the Twentieth Century*. Mahwah NJ: Lawrence Erlbawm

L'Etang, J. (2008) *Public Relations, Concepts, Practice and Critique*. London: Sage.

Langer, J. (1998) *Tabloid Television: Popular Journalism and the 'Other News'*. London: Routledge.

Larey, K. (1995) *Public Relations in Health Care, A Guide for Professionals*. New York: Jossey-Bass.

Lattimore, L.L., Baskin, O.W., Heiman, S.T., Toth, E.L. and Van Leuven, J.K (2004) *Public Relations: The Practice and the Profession*. New York: McGraw-Hill.

Lewin, K. (1947) 'Frontiers in group dynamics', *Human Relations*, 1 (2): 143–53.

Lewis, D. and Bridger, D. (2003) *The Soul of the New Consumer*. London: Nicholas Brealey.

Lewis, J. (2001) *Constructing Public Opinion: How Political Elites Do What They Like and Why We Seem to Go Along with It*. New York: Columbia University Press.

Lewis, J., Brookes, R., Mosdell, N. and Threadgold, T. (2006) *Shoot First and Ask Questions Later: Media Coverage of the 2003 Iraq War*. New York: Peter Lang.

Lewis, J., Cushion, S. and Thomas, J. (2005) 'Immediacy, convenience or engagement? An analysis of 24-hour news channels in the UK', *Journalism Studies*, 6 (4): 461–79.

Lewis, J., Williams, A. and Franklin, B. (2006) *Final Report on the Independence of British Journalism*. Cardiff: Cardiff University.

Lewis, J., Williams, A. and Franklin, B. (2008a) 'Four rumours and an explanation: a political economic account of journalists' changing newsgathering and reporting activities', *Journalism Practice*, 2 (1): 27–45.

Lewis, J., Williams, A. and Franklin, B. (2008b) 'A compromised fourth estate: UK news journalism, public relations and news sources', *Journalism Studies*, 9 (1): 1–20.

Lloyd, J. (2004) *What the Media Are Doing to Our Politics*. London: Constable.

Lynn, J. and Jay, A. (eds) (1989) *The Complete Yes Minister: The Diaries of the Right Hon. James Hacker*. London: BBC Books.

Mace, R., Holden, C.J. and Shennan, S. (2005) *The Evolution of Cultural Diversity. A Phylogenetic Approach*. London: Routledge Cavendish.

Machon, A. (2005) *Spies, Lies and Whistleblowers: MI5 and the David Shayler Affair.* London: Pluto.

Macnamara, J.R. (1992) 'Evaluation of public relations: the Achilles' heel of the PR profession', *International Public Relations Review*, 15.

Mahill, M., Beiler, M. and Schmutz, J. (2006) 'The influence of video-news-releases on the topics reported in science journalism', *Journalism Studies*, 7 (6): 869–88.

Mancini, P. (1993) 'Between trust and suspicion: how political journalists solve the dilemma', *European Journal of Communication*, 8 (March): 33–53.

Marconi, J. (2004) *PR: The Complete Guide.* London: Thomson.

Marr, A. (2004) *My Trade: A Short History of British Journalism.* Basingstoke: Macmillan.

McCombs, M. (2005) 'A look at agenda setting: past, present and future', *Journalism Studies*, 6 (4): 543–58.

McCombs, M. and Shaw, D. (1972) 'The agenda setting function of mass media', *Public Opinion Quarterly*, 36: 176–87.

McCombs, M. and Shaw, D. (1976) 'Structuring the unseen environment', *Journal of Communication*, 26 (2): 18–22.

McCombs, M., Shaw, D. and Weaver, D. (1997) *Communications and Democracy: Exploring the Intellectual Frontiers of Agenda Setting.* Mahwah, NJ: Lawrence Erlbaum.

McCusker, G. (2004) *Talespin.* London: Kogan Page.

McLuhan, M. (1964) *Understanding Media: The Extensions of Man.* New York: Signet.

McLuhan, M. (2006) 'The medium is the message', in M.G. Durham and D.M. Kellner, D.M. (eds) *Media and Cultural Studies: Keyworks.* Malden, MA: Blackwell. pp. 107–16.

McNair (1996) 'Performance in Politics and the Politics of Performance: Public Relations, the public Sphere and Democracy' in L'Etang, J and Piecka M (Eds) *Critical Perspectives in Public Relations* London: International Thompson

McNair, B. (1997) *News and Journalism in the UK: A Text Book*, 2nd edn. London: Routledge.

McNair, B. (1999) *News and Journalism in the UK.* London: Routledge.

McNair, B. (2000) *Journalism and Democracy: An Evaluation of the Political Public Sphere.* London: Routledge.

McNair, B. (2005) 'What is journalism?', in H. de Burgh (ed.) *Making Journalists.* London: Routledge. pp. 25–43

McQuail, D. (2000) *Mass Communication Theory*, 7th edn. London: Sage.

McQuail, D. (2005) *Mass Communication Theory.* London: Sage.

Meier, K. (2007) 'Innovations in Central European newsrooms: a case study and overview', *Journalism Practice*, 1 (1): 4–19.

Meyer, O. (2008) 'Contextualising alternative journalism: *Haolem Hazeh* and the birth of critical Israeli Newsmaking', *Journalism Studies*, 9 (3): 374–91.

Michie, D. (1998) *The Invisible Persuaders.* London: Bantam.

Miller, C. (2000) *Politico's Guide to Political Lobbying.* London: Politico.

Miller, D. (1998) 'Public relations and journalism: promotional strategies and media power', in A. Briggs and P. Cobley (ed.), *The Media: An Introduction.* London: Longman. pp. 65–80.

Miller, D. (2004) *Tell Me Lies: Propaganda and Media Distortion in the Attack on Iraq.* London: Pluto Press.

Miller, D. and Dinan, W. (2000) 'The rise of the PR Industry in Britain 1979–98', *European Journal of Communication*, 15 (1): 5–35.

key concepts in
public relations

Mintzberg, H. and Quinn J.B. (1991) *The Strategy Process, Concepts, Contexts, Cases,* 2nd edn. Upper Saddle River, NJ: Prentice-Hall.

Mitchie, D. (1998) *The Invisible Persuaders.* London: Bantam Press.

Moloney, K. (2006) *Rethinking Public Relations.* London: Routledge.

Moncrieff, C. (2001) *Living on a Deadline: A History of the Press Association.* London: Virgin Books.

Morgan, J. (1996) 'Marr hits at broadsheet rivals', *UK Press Gazette,* 18 October: 14.

Morgan, N., Pritchard, A. and Pride, R. (2004) *Destination Branding: Creating the unique destination proposition.* Oxford: Elsevier Butterworth-Heinemann.

MORI (2004) *Annual Corporate Social Responsibility Study.* London: MORI.

Moss, D. (1991) *Public Relations in Practice.* New York: Routledge.

Murdoch, R. (1989) 'Freedom in broadcasting', The James MacTaggart Memorial Lecture reprinted in B. Franklin (ed.), *Television Policy: The MacTaggart Lectures.* Edinburgh: Edinburgh University Press. pp. 131–8.

Murray, K. and White, J. (2004) CEO *Views on Reputation Management: A Report on the Value of Public Relations as Perceived by Organisational Leaders.* London: Chime PLC.

National Conference of Alternative Papers (1984) Editorial and Workshop Reports Conference held in Leeds in Spring 1984.

Neil, A. (1997) *Full Disclosure.* London: Pan Books.

Nerone, J. and Barnhurst, K. (2003) 'US newspaper types, the newsroom and the division of labour 1750–2000', *Journalism Studies,* 4 (4): 435–50.

Nyan, B. (2004) *All the President's Spin.* New York: Touchstone.

O'Malley, T. and Solely, C. (2000) *Regulating the Press.* London: Pluto Press.

Oborne, P. (1999) *Alastair Campbell, New Labour and the Rise of the Media Class.* London: Aurum Press.

Oborne, P. (2005) *The Rise of Political Lying.* London: The Free Press.

Oborne, P. and Walters, S. (2004) *Alastair Campbell.* London: Aurum Press.

Ofcom (2007) *The UK Communications Market 2007.* London: Ofcom.

Patterson, M. and Urbanski, S. (2006) 'What Jayson Blair and Janet Cooke say about the press and the erosion of public trust', *Journalism Studies,* 7 (6): 828–50.

Peters, T. (1996) *A Passion for Excellence.* London: Fontana.

Phillis, R. (2004) *The Government Communications Review.* Available at: http://www.gcreview.gov.uk

Philo, G. and Berry, M. (2004) *Bad News from Israel.* London: Pluto.

Philo, G. and Miller, D. (1999) 'The effective media', in G. Philo (ed.), *Message Received.* London: Longman. pp. 21–33.

Pieczka, M. (1996) 'Public opinion and public relations', in J. L'Etang and M. Pieczka (eds), *Critical Perspectives in Public Relations.* London: Thomson International Business Press. pp. 54–64.

Pilger, J. (1991) *Heroes.* London: Cape.

Pilger J. (1992) *Distant Voices.* London: Vintage.

Plunkett, J. (2006) 'Press and PR partnership – networking or not working?', *Media Guardian,* 10 April: 3.

Plunkett, J. (2008a) 'Record audience figures for Moyles', *Guardian,* 31 January: G2.

Plunkett, J (2008b) 'Pagers have been ditched and it's back to radio diaries to measure listening', *Guardian,* 28 April: Media 8.

Postrel, V. (1999) *The Future and its Enemies: The Growing Conflict Over Creativity, Enterprise and Progress.* New York: Touchstone.

Pottker, H. (2003) 'News and its communicative quality: the inverted pyramid – when and why did it happen?', *Journalism Studies*, 4 (4): 501–12.

Price, L. (2005) *The Spin Doctor's Diary; Inside No. 10 with New Labour.* London: Hodder and Stoughton.

Proctor, R. (1994) *Finance for the Perplexed Executive.* London: Harper Collins.

Randall, D. (1996) *The Universal Journalist.* London: Pluto.

Ray, V. (2003) *The Television News Handbook.* London: Macmillan.

Regester, M. and Larkin, J. (2001) *Risk Issues and Crisis Management.* London: Kogan Page.

Reith, J. (1924) *Broadcasting Over Britain.* London: Hodder and Stoughton.

Richards, P. (1998) *Be Your Own Spin Doctor.* London: Take That Ltd.

Richardson, J.E.R. (2005) 'Circulation', in *Journalism Studies: Key Concepts.* London: Sage. pp. 36–7.

Ries, A. and Ries, L. (2001). *The Fall of Advertising and the Rise of PR.* New York: HarperCollins

Robinson, P. (2000) 'The CNN effect: can the news media drive foreign policy', *Journal of Peace Research*, 37 (5): 301–9.

Romano, C. (1989) 'Slouching Towards Pressology', *Tikkun.*

Rusbridger, A. (2000) 'No more ghostly stories', *Guardian*, 15 July: 20.

Sabato, L. (2000) *Feeding Frenzy: Attack Journalism and American Politics.* New York: Lanahan Pub

Sadler, P. (2001) *National Security and the D Notice System.* Aldershot: Ashgate.

Sampson, A. (1996) 'The crisis at the heart of our media', *British Journalism Review*, 7 (3): 42–56.

Sandman, P. (1993) *Responding to Community Outrage: Strategies for Effective Risk Communication.* Fair, VA: American Industrial Hygiene Association.

Schlesinger, P. (1989) 'From production to propaganda', *Media, Culture and Society*, vol no: 11.

Schlesinger, P. (1990) 'Rethinking the sociology of journalism: source strategies and the limits of media centrism', M. Ferguson (ed.), *Public Communication: The New Imperatives.* Thousand Oaks, CA: Sage.

Schudson, M. (2002) The Sociology of News. London: W.W. Norton & Co. Ltd.

Schwartz, P. (1999) *When Good Companies Do bad Things.* New York: John Wiley & Sons.

Scott, G. (1968) *Reporter Anonymous.* London: Hutchinson and Co.

Seldon, A. (2001) *The Blair Effect.* London: Little Brown.

Semetko, H. and Valkenburg, P. (2000) 'Framing European Politics: content analysis of press and television news', *Journal of Communication*, 50 (2): 93–109.

Seeger, M. and Ulmer, R.R. (2003) *Communications and Organizational Crisis.* Westport, CT: Praeger/Greenwood.

Sellnow, T. and Ursell, G. (2003) 'Creating value and valuing creation in contemporary UK television: or dumbing down the workforce', *Journalism Studies*, 4 (1): 31–46.

Sivulka, J. (1998) *Soap, Sex and Cigarettes: A Cultural History of American Advertising.* Belmont, CA: Wadsworth.

Smallman, A. (1996) 'Telling the editorial from the Adverts', *Press Gazette*, 10 May: 11.

Smith, C. (2006) *Marketing For Dummies.* Chichester: John Wiley & Sons.

Smith, L. and Mounter, P. (2005) *Effective Internal Communication.* London: CIPR.

So, Y.L. and Walker, A. (2005) *Explaining Guanxi: The Chinese Business Network*. Abingdon: Routledge.

Society of County and Regional Public Relations officers (1985) 'The Image of Local government', *County Councils Gazette*, January, p. 310.

Society of Editors (2004) *Diversity in the Newsroom: Employment of Minority Ethnic Journalists in Newspapers*. Cambridge: Society of Editors.

Spiro, H.T. (1996) *Finance for the Non Financial Manager*. New York: John Wiley & Sons.

Sriramesh, K., Ananto, E.G., Chen, N. and Flora, C. (2004) *Public Relations in Asia: An Anthology*. Singapore: Thomson Learning.

Stanyer, J. (2001) *The Creation of Political News: Television and British Party Political Conferences*. Brighton: Sussex Academic Press.

Starr, P. (2004) *The Creation of the Media: Political Origins of Modern Communications*. New York: Basic Books.

Stauber, J. and Rampton, S (1995) Toxic Sludge Is Good for You: Lies, Damn Lies and the PR Industry. Monroe, ME: Common Courage Press.

Stewart, A.S. (1998) *Intellectual Capital: The New Wealth of Organizations*. London: Nicholas Brearley.

Surowiecki, J. (2005) *The Wisdom of Crowds*. London, Abacus.

Szondi, G. (2006) 'International context of public relations', in R. Tench and L. Yeomans (eds), *Exploring Public Relations*. Harlow: Prentice Hall. pp. 112–40.

Tench, R. and Yeomans, L. (2006) *Exploring Public Relations*. Harlow: Prentice Hall.

Theilmann, R. and Szondi, G. (2006) 'Public relations research and evaluation', in R. Tench and L. Yeomans (eds), *Exploring Public Relations*. Harlow: Prentice Hall. pp. 208–33.

Thelen, G. (2003) 'For convergence', *Journalism Studies*, 4 (4): 513–16.

Thussu, D.K. and Freedman, D. (eds) (2003) *War and the Media*. London: Sage.

Tuchman, G. (1972) 'Objectivity as a strategic ritual: an examination of newsmen's notion of objectivity', *American Journal of Sociology*, 77 (4): 660–70.

Tumber, H. and Palmer, J. (2004) *Media at War: The Iraq Crisis*. London: Sage.

Tunstall, J. (1971) *Journalists at Work*. London: Constable.

Tunstall, J. (1983) *The Media in Britain*. London: Constable.

Tye, L. (1998) *The Father of Spin*. New York: Henry Holt.

Van Ruler, B. and Vercic, D. (2004) *Public Relations Communications and Management in Europe: A Nation-by-Nation Introduction to Public Relations Theory and Practice*. Berlin: Walter de Gruyter.

Vasterman P. and Sykes, R. (2001) *Communication in Local government: A Survey of Local Authorities*. London: Local Government Association.

Vercic, D. and Krishnamurthy, S. (ed.) (2003) *The Global Public Relations Handbook: Theory, Research, Practice*. Mahwah, NJ: Lawrence Erlbaum.

Vercic, D. and Sriramesh, K. (2003) *The Global Public Relations Handbook: Theory, Research and Practice*. Mahwah, NJ: Lawrence Erlbaum.

Wall, M. (2006) 'Blogging Gulf War 11', *Journalism Studies*, 7 (1): 111–26.

Weaver, D. (2005) 'Who are journalists?', in H. de Burgh (ed.), *Making Journalists*. London: Routledge. pp. 44–58.

Weaver, D., Graber, D., McCombs, M. and Eyal, C. (1981) *Media Agenda Setting in a Presidential Election; Issues, Images and Interests*. New York: Praeger.

references

Weissman, J. (2003) *Presenting to Win: The Art of Telling Your Story*. London: FT/Prentice Hall.

West, R (1963) *PR The Fifth Estate; An Inquiry into Public Relations in Great Britain Today*. London: Mayflower Books

White, D.M. (1950) 'The "gatekeeper": a case study in the selection of news', *Journalism Quarterly*, 27 (3): 383–90.

White, J. and Dozier, D. (1992) 'Public relations and management decision making', in J.E. Grunig (ed.), *Excellence in Public Relations and Communications Management*. Hillsdale, NJ: Lawrence Erlbaum. pp. 91–108.

White, J. and Hobsbawm, J. (2007) 'Public relations and journalism: the unquiet relationship. A view from the United Kingdom', *Journalism Practice*, 1 (2): 283–92.

Wildy, T. (1985) 'Propaganda and Social Policy in Britain 1945–50: Publicity for the Social legislation of the Labour Government', unpublished PhD thesis, University of Leeds.

Wilke, J. (2003) 'The history and culture of the newsroom in Germany', *Journalism Studies*, 4 (4): 465–78.

Williams, A. and Franklin, B. (2007) *Turning Around the Tanker: Implementing Trinity Mirror's Online Strategy*. Cardiff: Cardiff University.

Williams, G. (2006) 'The Danish cartoon controversy', *Free Press*, 151 (March/April): 2–3.

Wilson, D. and Andrews, L. (1993) *Campaigning: The A–Z of Public Advocacy*. London: Hawksmere.

Wimmer, R.D. and Dominick, J.R. (2006) *Mass Media Research: An Introduction*. Belmont, CA: Wadsworth.

Winston, B. (2001) 'Towards tabloidisation? Glasgow revisited 1975–2001', *Journalism Studies*, 3 (1): 5–20.

Woolmar, C. (1990) *Censorship*. London: Hodder Wayland.

Yeomans, L. (2006) 'Internal communications', R. Tench and L. Yeomans (eds), *Exploring Public Relations*. Harlow: Prentice Hall. pp. 332–53.

Zelizer, B. (2004) *Taking Journalism Seriously: News and the Academy*. London: Sage.

WEBSITES

Association of National Advertisers (ANA): http://www.ana.net/

Advertising Standards Authority (ASA): http://www.asa.org.uk/

BARB Broadcasters' Audience Research Board: http://www.BARB.co.uk

Battelle Media: http://battellemedia.com/

Blair's Reuters Address about Journalism: http://news.bbc.co.uk/1/hi/uk_politics/6744581.stm

CAM Foundation: http://www.camfoundation.com/cam/index.cfm

CIPR Diversity: http://www.cipr.co.uk/diversity

CIPR Membership: http://www.cipr.co.uk/direct/membership.asp?v1=code

CIPR Qualifications: http://www.cipr.co.uk/direct/quals.asp?v1=qualshome

CIPR Code of Conduct: http://www.cipr.co.uk/member_area/cpd/main.asp

CIPR Training: http://www.cipr.co.uk/Training/training.htm

D Notices: http://www.dnotice.org.uk/system.htm

Echo Research: http://www.echoresearch.co.uk

European Advertising Standards Alliance (EASA): http://www.easa-alliance.org

key concepts in public relations

Federal Communications Commission: http://www.fcc.gov/

Gallup Polls: http://www.galluppoll.com/

GATT: http://www.gatt.org/homewto.html

Globe Scan (publicity research): http://www.globescan.com/news_archives/GlobeScan PIPA_Release.pdf

Googlewhack: http://www.googlewhack.com/

The European Convention on Human Rights: http://www.hri.org/docs/ECHR50.html

ICANN (Internet Corporation for Assigned Names and Numbers): http://www. icann. org/udrp/udrp.htm

Info World ('Yahoo! to help measure the value of online ads' December 16 2005): http://www.infoworld.com/article/05/12/16/HNyahoomeasureads_1.html

Intellectual Property Office (definition of Copyright) http://www.ipo.gov.uk/whatis copy.htm

Lexis PR: http://www.Lexispr.com (accessed April 20, 2007)

Marketing Teacher (SMART Objectives): http://www.marketingteacher.com/Lessons/ lesson_objectives.htm

Mediatenor: http://www.mediatenor.com/

MORI Polls : http://www.ipsos-mori.com/

Nature ('Internet encyclopaedias go head to head' 15 December 2005): http://www. nature.com/nature/journal/v438/n7070/full/438900a.html

Newspaper Index (2005): http://blog.newspaperindex.com/2005/12/10/un-to-investigate-jyllands-posten-racism/

Newspaper Society (2006): http://www.newspapersoc.org.uk/Default.aspx?page=951

Number 10 Press Office: http://www.Number-10.gov.UK

Ofcom: http://www.ofcom.org.uk/

Ofcom Guidelines (2005): http://www.ofcom.org.uk/codes_guidelines/broadcasting/tv/psb_ review/reports

The Phillis Committee (Government Communications Review): http://www.gcreview. gov.uk

Press Complaints Commission (PCC): http://www.pcc.org.uk/cop/practice.html

Public Relations Society of America (PRSA) (Code of Conduct): http://prsa.org/_About/ ethics/preamble.asp?ident=eth3

PRSA (National Capital Chapter): http://www.prsa-ncc.org

PRSA Networking: http://www.prsa.org/_Networking/ipa/index.asp?ident=ec1

PRSA Resources: http://www.prsa.org/_Resources/resources/commaudit.asp?ident=rsrc3

Search Engine Watch: http://searchenginewatch.com/

Trade Association Forum: http://www.taforum.org/

The Daily Telegraph ('Wiki's World' 28 October 2006): http://www.telegraph.co.uk/arts/main.jhtml;jsessionid=U4FFM4TR3WZFBQFIQMF CFFWAVCBQYIV0?xml=/arts/2006/10/28/ftwiki28.xml

YouGov: http://www.yougov.com/

CASES

Kasky v *Nike, Inc.*, 27 CFal. 4th 939 (2002).